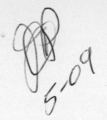

D0195837

PENGUIN
COMPASS

GOD AGAINST THE GODS

Jonathan Kirsch is the author of the bestselling and critically acclaimed *The Harlot by the Side of the Road: Forbidden Tales of the Bible; King David: The Real Life of the Man Who Ruled Israel; Moses: A Life;* and *The Woman Who Laughed at God.* A member of the National Book Critics Circle, PEN Center USA West, and a book columnist for the *Los Angeles Times,* Kirsch writes and lectures widely on biblical, literary, and legal topics. He lives in Los Angeles, California.

GOD AGAINST THE GODS

The History of the War Between

Monotheism and Polytheism

◆

Jonathan Kirsch

PENGUIN COMPASS

PENGUIN BOOKS
Published by the Penguin Group
Penguin Group (USA) Inc., 375 Hudson Street, New York, New York 10014, U.S.A.
Penguin Books Canada, 10 Alcorn Avenue, Toronto,
Ontario, Canada M4V 3B2 (a division of Pearson Penguin Canada Inc.)
Penguin Books Ltd, 80 Strand, London WC2R 0RL, England
Penguin Ireland, 25 St Stephen's Green, Dublin 2, Ireland (a division of Penguin Books Ltd)
Penguin Group (Australia), 250 Camberwell Road, Camberwell,
Victoria 3124, Australia (a division of Pearson Australia Group Pty Ltd)
Penguin Books India Pvt Ltd, 11 Community Centre,
Panchsheel Park, New Delhi – 110 017, India
Penguin Group (NZ), cnr Airborne and Rosedale Roads, Albany,
Auckland 1310, New Zealand (a division of Pearson New Zealand Ltd)
Penguin Books (South Africa) (Pty) Ltd, 24 Sturdee Avenue,
Rosebank, Johannesburg 2196, South Africa

Penguin Books Ltd, Registered Offices:
80 Strand, London WC2R 0RL, England

First published in the United States of America by Viking Compass,
a member of Penguin Group (USA) Inc. 2004
Published in Penguin Books 2005

7   9   10   8   6

Copyright © Jonathan Kirsch, 2004
All rights reserved

Title-page art: Andrea Celesti (1637–1706). *Moses Ordering the Destruction of the Golden Calf.*
Palazzo Ducale, Venice, Italy. Credit: Cameraphoto/Art Resource, NY

LIBRARY OF CONGRESS HAS CATALOGUED THE HARDCOVER EDITION AS FOLLOWS:
Kirsch, Jonathan, 1949–
God against the gods : the history of the war between monotheism
and polytheism /
Jonathan Kirsch.
p.   cm.
Includes bibliographical references (p. 315) and index.
ISBN 0-670-03286-7 (hc.)
ISBN 0 14 21.9633 9 (pbk.)
1. Monotheism—History.   2. Polytheism—History.   I. Title.
BL221.K57 2004
291.1'4—dc21   2003053793

Printed in the United States of America
Set in Minion
Designed by Francesca Belanger
Map by James Sinclair

For
Ann Benjamin Kirsch,
Jennifer Rachel Kirsch,
Adam Benjamin Kirsch and Remy Elizabeth Holzer,
my beloved and gifted family.

And for
Laurie Fox,
my agent, muse, fellow writer and cherished friend.

" *. . . inscribe us in the Book of Life . . .* "

Acknowledgments

My first thought, as always, is for Ann Benjamin Kirsch, my wife and lifelong best friend, and our gifted and accomplished children, Jennifer Rachel Kirsch and Adam Benjamin Kirsch, whose constancy, companionship and love have been essential to the writing of *God Against the Gods* and everything else I do.

This book is dedicated to my family and to someone who has been crucial to my writing life ever since the publication of *The Harlot by the Side of the Road*—Laurie Fox, whom I first met when she worked behind the counter of a bookstore in West Hollywood and soon came to know as a cherished friend. Laurie is my literary agent, and the kind of agent whom every writer dreams about, but that is only one of her gifts—she is also an accomplished artist, poet and novelist, a wise counselor on whom I have relied for her vision, sagacity, good advice.

Janet Goldstein, my editor at Viking, guided me through the conception and writing of both *The Woman Who Laughed at God* and *God Against the Gods*, and I am grateful for her discerning eye, expert editorial hand and lively spirit.

I am deeply grateful, too, to Clare Ferraro at Viking, who has given me so many opportunities over the years, starting with *The Harlot by the Side of the Road* and including the present book.

Among the many people at Viking with whom I worked closely on the present book were Beena Kamlani, Carolyn Coleburn, Cindy Hamel, Melanie Thurston, Rakia Clark, Ann Mah, Francesca Belanger, Greg Mollica, and Trent Duffy and I deeply enjoyed the opportunity to do so.

At Viking, I also appreciated the opportunity to work with Mike Brennan, Nancy Sheppard, Phil Budnick, Fred Huber, and Glenn Timony.

Susan Olinger, a gifted writer who shares my fascination with the ancients, provided expert and imaginative research assistance, and I made good use of research conducted for my earlier books by Adam Kirsch, Andrew Solomon, Leonard Braman and Vera Tobin. Michele Goldman ably assisted in map research and proofing the manuscript and galleys.

I have been supported and encouraged in important ways by family, friends, and colleagues to whom I express my heartfelt appreciation:

Judy Woo and Eui Sook (Angie) Yoon, my cherished friends and colleagues.

Remy Elizabeth Holzer, my daughter-in-law, and her family, Harold, Edith and Meg Holzer.

Candace Barrett Birk and Raye Birk, Maryann Rosenfeld and Shelly Kadish, Pat and Len Solomon.

K. C. Cole, my dear friend and a writer whose work on science has shaped my own work on the history of religion.

Janet Fitch, Diane Leslie, Mary Rakow, Carolyn See and Bernadette Shih, each of whom I admire as a fellow writer and depend on as a dear friend.

Linda Chester and her colleagues at the Linda Chester Agency.

Linda Michaels and Teresa Cavanaugh at Linda Michaels Ltd. International Literary Agents.

Steve Wasserman, Tom Curwen, Nick Owchar, Orli Low, Kristina Lindgren, Sara Lippincott, and Ethel Alexander at the *Los Angeles Times Book Review*.

Doug Brown, Tom Crouch, Lara Furar and Barbara Morrow and at the *Los Angeles Times*.

Jan Nathan and Terry Nathan at the Publishers Marketing Association.

Larry Mantle, Kitty Felde, Aimee Machado, Jackie Oclaray, Linda Othenin-Girard and Polly Sveda at KPCC-FM.

Rob Eshman at *The Jewish Journal.*

Sarah Spitz at KCRW-FM.

Gwen Feldman and Jim Fox at Silman-James Press, and Tony Cohan at Acrobat Books.

Connie Martinson, host of *Connie Martinson Talks Books.*

Doug Dutton, Lise Friedman and Ed Conklin at Dutton's Books in Brentwood; Linda Urban at Vroman's in Pasadena; Stan Madson and Jeanne D'Arcy at the Bodhi Tree in West Hollywood; Lita Weissman and Peggy Jackson at Border's; Michele Yanow at Tree of Life Judaica & Books in Seattle; Abigail Yasgur at the Jewish Community Library in Los Angeles; and Michael Graziano.

Charlie Alexiev, Scott Baker, Lillian Heller Conrad, Jacob Gabay, Inge-Lise DeWolfe, Fred Huffman, Jill Johnson Keeney, Les Klinger, Rae Lewis, Dennis Mitchell and Dolores Sloan.

At various significant points, I have relied on the published work and the generous encouragement of Jack Miles, Donald Harmen Akenson, Karen Armstrong, David Noel Freedman, Leonard Shlain and David Rosenberg, each of whom has inspired my own work in important ways.

Contents

*A map of the Ancient World Under Constantine and Julian
appears on pages xii–xiii.*

GOD AGAINST
THE GODS

BRITAIN

Rhine River

Paris

Trier

GAUL

ITALY

SPAIN

Rome

Carthage

MEDITERRANEAN SE.

AFRICA

N

0   250   500
Scale of Miles

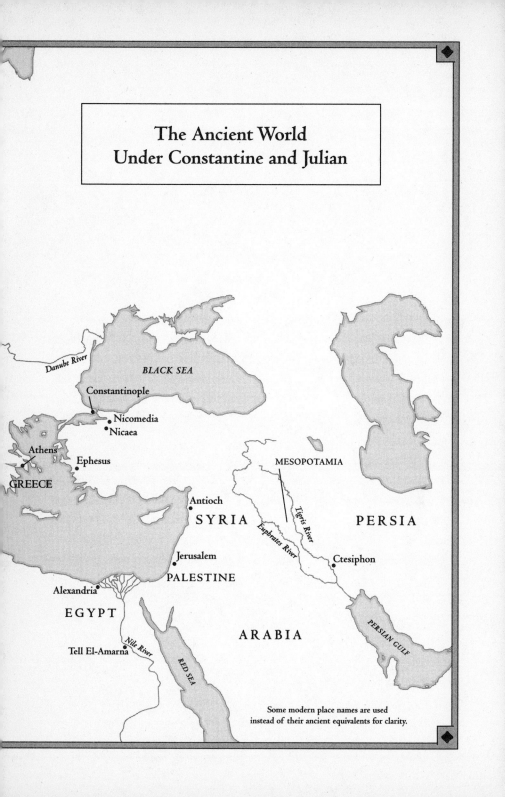

The Ancient World
Under Constantine and Julian

Danube River

BLACK SEA

Constantinople

Nicomedia

Nicaea

Athens

Ephesus

GREECE

MESOPOTAMIA

Antioch

SYRIA

Tigris River

Euphrates River

PERSIA

Jerusalem

Ctesiphon

PALESTINE

Alexandria

EGYPT

Nile River

ARABIA

PERSIAN GULF

Tell El-Amarna

RED SEA

Some modern place names are used
instead of their ancient equivalents for clarity.

THE EVERLASTING FIRE

The Dark Side of Monotheism, the Bright Side of Polytheism

> Religious intolerance was inevitably born
> with the belief in one God.
>
> —Sigmund Freud,
> *Moses and Monotheism*

Something deep in human nature prompts us to imagine the existence of a power greater than ourselves, whether we call it "Yahweh" or "Christ" or "Allah," "Mother Nature" or "the Higher Power" or "the Universe." Religious belief and practice begins with the origin of the human species—the Neanderthals invented rituals for the burial of the dead—and modern medical science proposes that the idea of "god" is literally hard-wired into the anatomy of the brain. Human beings, in fact, can be distinguished from lower orders of animal life not because we use language or make tools or fight wars, but because we are the only creatures who conceive of a higher power and who are inspired to offer worship and sacrifice to that power.

"Indeed, there is a case for arguing that *Homo sapiens* ['Rational man'] is also *Homo religiosus* ['Religious man']," writes Karen Armstrong in *A History of God*. "Men and women started to worship gods as soon as they became recognizably human; they created religions at the same time as they created works of art."[1]

Nothing in human nature, however, suggests the inevitability of the notion that there is only *one* god. On the contrary, men and women in every age and throughout the world have offered worship to literally thousands of gods, goddesses and godlings, male and female alike, and they still do. Only very late in the development of *Homo religiosus* did monotheism—"one-god-ism"—first emerge, and whenever some visionary king or prophet sought to impose the worship of one deity to the exclusion of all others, he would discover that ordinary people so cherished their many beguiling gods and goddesses that the very idea of monotheism was appalling. That is why the very first recorded experiment in monotheism was an abject failure, and polytheism has survived every effort to destroy it.

But, fatefully, monotheism turned out to inspire a ferocity and even a fanaticism that are mostly absent from polytheism. At the heart of polytheism is an open-minded and easygoing approach to religious belief and practice, a willingness to entertain the idea that there are many gods and many ways to worship them. At the heart of monotheism, by contrast, is the sure conviction that only a single god exists, a tendency to regard one's own rituals and practices as the only proper way to worship the one true god. The conflict between these two fundamental values is what I call the war of God against the gods—it is a war that has been fought with heart-shaking cruelty over the last thirty centuries, and it is a war that is still being fought today.

The Roots of Religious Terrorism

On September 11, 2001, we were reminded once again of the real meaning of the 3000-year-old conflict between monotheism and polytheism. The men who hijacked and crashed four civilian airliners were inspired to sacrifice their own lives, and to take the lives of several thousand "infidels," because they had embraced the simple but terrifying logic that lies at the heart of monotheism: if there is only one god, if there is only one right way to worship that god, then there is only one fitting punishment for failing to do so—death. At that moment, we were shown, yet again, the power and the consequences of true belief in monotheism.

Nowadays, the bloodiest acts of violence in the name of God seem to come from the Islamic world, and the hijackers who piloted airplanes into the World Trade Center and the Pentagon are only the most horrific examples. Other recent incidents include the dynamiting of ancient Buddhist statuary in Afghanistan by the Taliban, who condemned the 1600-year-old artifacts as "false idols" and "gods of the infidels,"[2] the sentencing of Nigerian women to stoning for the sin of adultery and Iranian journalists to death for the sin of blasphemy, and suicide bombings by Palestinian adolescents who seek martyrdom in a *jihad* ("holy war") against nonbelievers by blowing themselves up in the streets of Jerusalem and Tel Aviv.

But the roots of religious terrorism are *not* found originally or exclusively in Islamic tradition. Quite the contrary, it begins in the pages of the Bible, and the very first examples of holy war and martyrdom are found in Jewish and Christian history. The opening skirmishes in the war of God against the gods took place in distant biblical antiquity, when Yahweh is shown to decree a holy war against anyone who refuses to acknowledge him as the one and only god worthy of worship. Holy war passes from biblical myth into recorded history during the wars of national liberation fought by the Maccabees against the pagan king of Syria and later by the Zealots against the pagan emperor of Rome, which provide us with the first accounts of men and women who are willing to martyr themselves in the name of God. The banner is taken up by the early Christians in the first century of the Common Era, when they bring the "good news" of Jesus Christ to imperial Rome, where the decisive battle in the war between monotheism and polytheism is fought.

The crucial encounter takes place in Rome during the fourth century, when the Roman emperor Constantine worked a revolution in the name of monotheism and then his nephew, the emperor Julian, sought to work a counterrevolution in the name of polytheism. The years in which these two men reigned, one in living memory of the other, would literally change the history of the world. "For better or worse," remarks Gore Vidal in a novel based on the life of Julian, "we are today very much the result of what they were then."[3] And yet the final victory of God against the gods was not inevitable, and we can see with our own eyes how the Western world teetered between two possible fates during the lifetimes of these two willful, ruthless and charismatic men. Above all, we will glimpse something that is rarely considered in our churches, synagogues and mosques—the dark side of monotheism, and the bright side of polytheism.

Four Kings

Monotheism is classically understood to be a "gift of the Jews," according to Thomas Cahill's felicitous phrase, but the fact is that an eccentric young pharaoh of ancient Egypt was apparently inspired to worship a single god even before "one-god-ism" was embraced by the ancient Israelites. The first recorded experiment in monotheism took place in ancient Egypt in the fourteenth century B.C.E. under the reign of a pharaoh called Akhenaton, and it is likely that the Israelites borrowed the idea from the Egyptians.

Unlike other inventors of new religions, including Moses, Jesus and Mohammed, Akhenaton was not a prophet who preached his gospel to skeptical crowds; rather, he was the absolute ruler of the single most powerful empire in the ancient world. Still, just like those more famous monotheists, Akhenaton discovered that the idea of monotheism is not especially appealing to men and women who are accustomed to worshipping many gods and goddesses. But popularity does not matter when the prophet is also a king—the fiery young pharaoh possessed the power to impose monotheism on an unwilling populace by royal decree.

Akhenaton may have been the first monarch to order his subjects to worship a single god, but he was hardly the last one to do so. Monotheism eventually reached and rooted itself in the land of Israel, but it was rejected by the majority of Israelites as something strange and unappealing. Starting with Moses, all the prophets who scold the Israelites in the pages of the Bible are wholly unsuccessful in persuading them to confine their worship to the God of Israel. Not until the reign of King Josiah in the seventh century B.C.E.—another monarch who was also a fiery religious reformer—was the religion of ancient Israel fully purged of its pagan taint, and only then because Josiah, like Akhenaton, enjoyed the power to make it so.

But Josiah's war on the gods, like Akhenaton's, did not result in a lasting victory. When Josiah died in battle against an Egyptian pharaoh, many of the Jews drifted back to their old and easygoing ways of worship, and the prophets resumed their bitter but fruitless complaints. Later, the land of the Jews came under the seductive but corrosive influence of the pagan culture called Hellenism—to be an educated and civilized man or woman, according to the Hellenistic ideal, required a familiarity with pagan arts and letters and participation in pagan rituals and celebrations. Now and then, the most pious and zealous of the Jews struggled against the temptations of Hellenism, seeking to enforce the worship of the God of Israel at the point of a sword, but monotheism seemed at risk of remaining only an historical curiosity, the tribal practice of a tiny and powerless people who lived in a backwater of the Near East.

Indeed, the final victory in the war of God against the gods was not achieved until a new superpower emerged in the ancient world—the empire of Rome—and the men who ruled it acquired the apparatus of autocracy. The Roman empire of late antiquity has been characterized as the first totalitarian state in history, and the Roman emperors were able to call on the expert services of an imperial bureaucracy that included spies, informers, inquisitors, torturers and executioners. The king who perfected the Roman autocracy was Constantine, a pagan general who intrigued, conspired and battled his way to the imperial throne in the opening years of the fourth century—and then, fatefully, found God.

To Rome came *all* the faiths of the ancient world, not only the familiar gods and goddesses of Hellenism but a fantastic assortment of weird, raucous and highly exotic deities from all over the empire. Among the many competitors for the hearts and minds of the Roman citizenry, in fact, the oddest of all were those who confined their worship to only a single all-powerful god—the Jews, of course, and an obscure sect of Judaism that came to be called Christianity. By then, the Jews had made a separate peace with paganism, and they found a way to carry on the worship of the God of Israel throughout the Diaspora without disturbing (or being disturbed by) their pagan neighbors. But the Christians had taken up the old traditions of zealotry that were written large and plain in the pages of the Bible. They called themselves "Soldiers of Christ," and they were eager to fight and die in the name of God.

Constantine favored Christianity, but he refrained from bringing the full weight of imperial authority to bear in the war that the Soldiers of Christ were fighting against all manner of paganism. And so, after the long reigns of Constantine himself and his three Christian sons, the emperor who next took the throne was able to entertain the remarkable idea of restoring the worship of the old gods and goddesses whom he found so enthralling. His name was Julian, and he is recalled in pious Christian history as "the Apostate"—a term that was coined to condemn anyone who has repudiated the teachings of true belief. But Julian also represented the last, best hope for the preservation of everything that was elevating and ennobling about paganism. Between Constantine and Julian, the world faced a choice between two futures, and so the lives and reigns of these two men present us with one of the great "what ifs" of human history.

A Parade of Horribles

Over the last thirty centuries of religious propaganda, starting in the Bible and continuing through the TV evangelists of our own era, paganism has been painted as a parade of horribles. We are instructed to regard paganism as an "abomination," as the biblical authors so insistently put it, a dark and demonic force compounded of harlotry, idolatry, sorcery and human sacrifice. "The error of polytheism," argues historian Hans Lietzmann, "led the peoples into darkness and moral chaos."[4] The classical paganism of late antiquity—which was, after all, the faith of the high civilization of ancient Greece and Rome—is flatly condemned by one nineteenth-century Christian historian as "the moral disease of the Roman world."[5] Even today, a celebrity cleric like Jerry Falwell insists that the horrors of September 11 can be attributed to the lingering evil of paganism.

The pagan world, to be sure, was hardly a benign place. Common criminals were routinely tortured before they were put to death, and prisoners of wars were sold off as slaves when they were not crucified *en masse*. Women and children in conquered lands were placed in the same category as cattle and chattel—spoils of war that belonged to the victor. But the religious practices and beliefs of paganism were kinder and gentler than we have been taught to believe by our rabbis, priests, ministers and imams. The core value of paganism was religious tolerance—a man or woman in ancient Rome was at liberty to offer worship to whatever god or goddess seemed most likely to grant a prayerful request, with or without the assistance of priests and priestesses, as long as he or she didn't do it in the streets, as a Victorian-era wit once said of women preachers, and scare the horses.

"What does it matter by which wisdom each of us arrives at truth?" muses Symmachus, a pagan prefect of the fourth century. "It is not possible that only one road leads to so sublime a mystery."[6]

By the first century of the Common Era, paganism offered a fabulous array of beliefs and practices from which to choose, ranging from the sedate and stately rituals of worship offered to the gods and goddesses of the traditional Greco-Roman pantheon to the eerie and exotic rites that roused the devotees of such imported deities as Isis, Mithra and the Great Goddess. A few of the pagan cults still engaged in celebrations so spirited that we might characterize them as orgies, but the most common ceremonies of classical paganism—ranging from animal sacrifice to the offering of cakes and libations—were strikingly similar to the rituals that the Hebrew Bible prescribes for the worship of the God of Israel.

Indeed, many of the commonplaces of paganism will strike the modern reader as both familiar and inoffensive. Tossing a coin in a fountain, for example, is a distant echo of the offerings of jewelry or coins that were made to the gods who were thought to reside in lakes, streams and pools. The horoscope in the morning newspaper recalls the daily astrological readings that a cautious pagan would consult before taking a bath or getting a haircut. Tying a ribbon around a tree is our way of honoring a missing child, but the same gesture was used by the ancients to honor an unseen god. And the essential feature of the shrines where oracles were thought to channel the voices of the gods—"the conjunction of an uncanny place and a canny person," as historian J. L. Myers describes them—can be found in *any* place where one might have a "spiritual" experience, whether a single god or many gods or no gods at all are worshipped there.[7]

Nor was sexual adventure quite as common in paganism as we are led to believe by the scenes of orgiastic excess that we find in biblical writings or Hollywood epics. Although we will encounter a few examples of sex, sacred or otherwise, taking place in the precincts of a pagan temple, the fact is that paganism was as capable of prudery and puritanism as the strictest forms of monotheism. The more exotic rites and rituals were regarded as scandalous by the sober senators of pagan Rome, who insisted, for example, that the worshippers of Bacchus, the god of wine, do their drinking off the public streets. Virginity until marriage and fidelity during marriage were as highly praised—if also as rarely practiced—by the worshippers of Jupiter as by the worshippers of Yahweh. Priestly celibacy was enforced in some pagan cults long before it was adopted by the Christian clergy and in fact the Christians may have copied the whole idea from the hated pagans.

Nor did the pagans seek from their many gods and goddesses anything different from what Christians, Jews and Muslims seek from the deity that they regard as the one and only god. Pagans prayed for health and happiness, safety and security, a good life here on earth and some kind of salvation in the afterlife. They embraced the values of justice and mercy, and, by and large, they sought to live decent and moral lives: "Temperance, courage, chastity, obedience to parents and magistrates, [and] reverence for the oath and the law," according to the venerable historian Franz Cumont, were the core values of paganism as it was practiced in ancient Rome.[8]

But one crucial quality distinguished Christianity from classical paganism. Polytheists, as we have seen, were not inclined to dictate to others how and to whom prayer and sacrifice should be offered. They were perfectly willing to mix and match gods and goddesses, rituals and beliefs, and they sought the divine favor of many different deities at once. A conquered people might embrace the gods of their conqueror—and the conqueror might return the favor. Nowhere in the ancient world was the open-mindedness more apparent than in imperial Rome. Indeed, Roman paganism was not a religion in the same sense that we use the word to describe Judaism, Christianity and Islam. Rather, what we call "paganism" was, as historian Ramsay MacMullen puts it, "no more than a spongy mass of tolerance and tradition."[9]

" 'Paganism' to the pagan never existed," explains historian John Holland Smith in *The Death of Classical Paganism*. "It is not far from the truth to say that before Christianity invented it, there was no Roman religion, but only worship, expressed in a hundred-and-one different ways."[10]

The Only True God

Monotheism, by contrast, insists that only a single deity is worthy of worship for the simple reason that only a single deity exists. On this point, Judaism, Christianity and Islam agree, at least in principle: the deity that is variously called "Yahweh" or "Lord" or "Allah" is thought to be one and the same god. Pagans certainly understood and embraced the idea that some gods are more powerful than other gods, and phrases like "Supreme God" and "Highest God" fit comfortably into the language and theology of polytheism. But monotheism insists that the other gods to whom worship is offered are not merely inferior in power or stature; rather, they are false, according to the Hebrew Bible, or even demonic, according to the Christian Bible.

"For though there be gods many and lords many," explains Paul, "but to us there is but one God."[11]

The point is made plain in a phrase that is found in the scriptures of both Christianity and Judaism. The god of monotheism is not only "the living God," not only "the everlasting King," as the prophet Jeremiah puts it, but "the *True God.*"[12] The apostle John is even more plainspoken—the god of monotheism is "the *Only True God.*"[13] By contrast, all of the gods, goddesses and godlings of paganism are "no-gods," in the words of Jeremiah,[14] or even worse, "devils," according to the apostle Paul.[15] To worship the wrong god, according to the value system of biblical monotheism, is not only a sin but a crime, and a crime that is punishable by death.

Monotheism, for example, cruelly punishes the sin of "heresy," but polytheism does not recognize it as a sin at all. Significantly, "heresy" is derived from the Greek word for "choice," and the fundamental theology of polytheism honors the worshipper's freedom to choose among the many gods and goddesses who are believed to exist. Monotheism, by contrast, regards freedom of choice as nothing more than an opportunity for error, and the fundamental theology of monotheism as we find it in the Bible threatens divine punishment for any worshipper who makes the wrong choice. Against the open-mindedness of the pagan Symmachus, who allows that there are many roads to enlightenment and salvation, Bishop Fulgentius (468–533) insists that only a single narrow path leads to the Only True God.

"Of this you can be certain and convinced beyond all doubt," declares Fulgentius, "not only all pagans, but also all Jews, all heretics and schismatics will go into the everlasting fire which has been prepared for the Devil and his angels."[16]

Here is the flash point of the war of God against the gods. The deity who is worshipped in Judaism, Christianity and Islam is described in the Bible as a "jealous" and "wrathful" god, and he is believed to regard the worship of any god other than himself as an "abomination." The deities who populate the crowded pantheon of classical paganism, by contrast, were believed to be capable of thoroughly human emotions, including envy and anger, but they were never shown to deny one another's existence or demand the death of someone who worshipped a rival god or goddess.

"The pagan gods, even the gods of mysteries are not jealous of one another," explains historian and anthropologist Walter Burkert. " 'Envy stands outside the divine chorus,' as the famous saying of Plato's puts it."[17]

The polytheist can live in harmony with the monotheist: "[M]any pagans could still extend to the new worship," writes historian Robin Lane Fox, "a tolerance which its exclusivity refused to extend to them."[18] Pagan Rome offered the ultimate gesture of respect to the Jews and Christians by adding the God of Israel to the pantheon of gods and goddesses, where he was called Iao and offered worship along with Apollo and Zeus, Isis and Mithra. "If the Supreme God was unknowable, who was to say which one of the many cults of different peoples was right or wrong?" explains Fox. "At its heart, therefore, pagan theology could extend a peaceful coexistence to any worship which, in turn, was willing."[19] But the pagans who did so, of course, missed the whole point of monotheism, and the Jews and Christians refused to reciprocate.

Indeed, the monotheists condemned not only the rude and crude deities of the "barbarians" but even the elegant and refined deities of the Greco-Roman pantheon who were so richly embroidered into the fabric of classical civilization and high culture. A sixth-century Christian militant called Martin of Braga, for example, describes the most revered gods and goddesses of Greece and Rome as demons who had been cast out of heaven along with Satan and now tricked the benighted pagans into offering them worship.

"So one said he was Jove, who was a magician and so incestuous in his many adulteries that he had his sister as his wife, who was called Juno [and] corrupted his daughters, Minerva and Venus," insists Martin of Braga. "Another demon called himself Mars, who was a perpetrator of strife and discord. Then another chose to call himself Mercury, who was the wretched inventor of all theft and fraud. Another demon took the name of Saturn, who, basking in cruelty, even devoured his sons at birth. Another demon feigned to be Venus, who was a whore. She did not only whore with innumerable adulterers but even with her father Jove and her brother Mars."[20]

For true believers like Martin of Braga, then, the tales that are told in the pages of Homer are not merely charming myths, and the pagan gods are not merely "no-gods"—rather, they are all the work of the Devil. Indeed, the monotheists of late antiquity were convinced that they lived in a world populated with evil spirits, and they relied on amulets and charms, prayers and exorcisms, to keep the Devil and his minions at bay. A vigilant Christian who passed a pagan shrine in town or country, for example, would hiss out loud and make the sign of the cross to scare off the unseen demons that he or she believed to linger there. "The air between heaven and earth is so crammed with spirits, never quiet or finding rest," writes the Christian sermonizer John Cassian in the fifth century, "that it is fortunate for men that they are not permitted to see them."[21]

Thus the militant monotheist condemns polytheism in general as an "abomination,"[22] in the words of the Hebrew Bible, and pagan Rome in particular as the "mother of harlots and the abominations of the earth,"[23] according to the Christian Bible. Precisely because the monotheist regards the polytheist with such fear and loathing, peaceful coexistence between the two theologies is possible only from the pagan's point of view and never for the true believer in the Only True God.

The Tragic Legacy

The strict and uncompromising attitude of monotheism, approvingly described in the Bible itself as "zeal" for the True God,[24] sometimes manifests itself in a strange phenomenon that historians of religion call *rigorism*—that is, "extreme strictness" in religious belief and practice.[25] The Jewish men and women who were the custodians of the Dead Sea Scrolls, for example, disciplined themselves to refrain from bowel movements on the Sabbath lest they defile the "Lord's holy day of rest." Among the hermit-monks of early Christianity were men who banished themselves to the desert wilderness, spending years atop stone pillars and feeding themselves only on crushed greens. But paganism, too, produced its own rigorists—some of the Romans who worshipped Isis, a deity who was borrowed from the pantheon of ancient Egypt and embraced throughout the Greco-Roman world, were inspired to show the same kind of devotion to their goddess. "Three times, in the depths of winter, the devotee of Isis will dive into the chilly waters of the Tiber, and shivering with cold, will drag herself around the temple upon her bleeding knees," observes the Roman satirist Juvenal (c. 60–40). "[I]f the goddess commands, she will go to the outskirts of Egypt to take water from the Nile and empty it within the sanctuary."[26]

But, tragically, rigorism is not always or only expressed through acts of self-discipline and self-affliction. Extreme strictness in religious observance is possible only when a man or woman is so convinced of the truth of a certain religious teaching that it becomes quite literally a matter of life or death. Turned inward, rigorism may inspire a true believer to punish himself by holding back a bowel movement or feeding himself on raw vegetables. Turned outward, however, rigorism may inspire the same man or woman to punish others who fail to embrace the religious beliefs that he or she finds so compelling. The history of religion reveals that rigorism in one's beliefs and practices can readily turn into the kind of zealotry that expresses itself in unambiguous acts of terrorism. Indeed, the very first use of the word "zeal" in the Bible is used to describe God's approval of an act of murder, one Israelite murdering another Israelite and his Midianite lover.[27]

Examples can be found in every faith, in every place and in every

age, including our own. A Jewish man in Israel, for example, was recently moved by his own religious passions to open fire with a machine
gun on Muslims at prayer in a mosque at the Tomb of the Patriarchs.
A Christian man in America was inspired by *his* religious passions to
pick up a sniper's rifle and shoot down a doctor who performed abor-
tions. Neither of these true believers would be quick to recognize a
kindred spirit in the other, but they both share the same tragic legacy
of rigorism, a legacy that is deeply rooted in monotheism.

Nowadays, of course, religious terrorism is carried out by true believers in one or another variety of monotheism against their fellow
monotheists, and the same has been true ever since the final victory
of monotheism over polytheism in the war of God against the gods.
Ironically, the worst excesses of the Crusades and the Inquisition
were inflicted by Christians on Jews and Muslims, all of whom
claimed to believe in the same god. But the first casualties in the war
of God against the gods were found among those tolerant polytheists
whom we are taught to call "pagans."

Christian Soldiers

"Pagan" is a word invented by early Christians to describe anyone
who refused to recognize the Only True God, and no self-respecting
pagan ever described himself as one. Paganism, in fact, has been so
thoroughly defamed that our language lacks the words and phrases
to describe it in value-neutral terms. "A pagan," according to one of
the dictionary definitions of the word, is "an irreligious or hedonistic
person."[28] All of the synonyms and variants—"heathen" or "idolater"
or "infidel" or "barbarian"—are equally dismissive or derogatory. We
are left with the dry and highly technical terms that distinguish between someone who worships only a single god, a "monotheist," and
someone who worships more than one god, a "polytheist."

One explanation for the root meaning of "pagan" allows us to see
what was at stake in the encounter between monotheism and polytheism in ancient Rome. The word derives from the Latin "*paganus*,"

which originally referred to a "village-dweller" and carried the sense
of a "country bumpkin." But the word was also used in Roman military circles to mean "civilian" and to distinguish one who is ready to
fight in war from someone who stays behind. According to some
scholars, that's precisely the meaning of "pagan" that inspired its first
use by Christians—the Christian rigorists regarded themselves as
soldiers, ready to march forth as crusaders in a holy war, and they
characterized anyone who refused to take up arms in the service of
the Only True God as a civilian, a slacker, a "paganus."

"Pagan" eventually came to mean anyone who worshipped any
god or goddess other than the deity who was recognized as the Only
True God in Jewish, Christian and Islamic tradition. For that reason,
the term encompasses a multitude of supposed sins, ranging from
the elegant rituals of the Roman senator who represented the highest
expression of classical civilization in the ancient world to the cruder
rituals of the Celtic tribesman who painted himself blue and fought
naked against the Roman legions. And Christianity would ultimately
carry the holy war in the name of the Only True God to every corner
of the Roman empire and far beyond—no distinction was made between the patrician and the barbarian, and the religious practices of
each were regarded as equally "abominable" and equally worthy of
persecution.

Now and then, a willful and hateful monarch might abandon the
long tradition of tolerance that characterized the world of classical
polytheism and undertake a war of his own against monotheism—the
persecution of Christians in pagan Rome, of course, is the most famous example. Whether the Roman persecutions were quite as perva-
sive or quite as horrific as depicted in the martyrologies, however, has
been the subject of hot debate for several centuries—Edward Gibbon,
for example, characterized the worst atrocities as "extravagant and indecent fictions" that were invented to inspire the faithful.[29] Indeed, the
spectacle of men and women who went willingly and even ardently to
their deaths—and, long afterward, the memory of these martyrdoms
and the relics of the martyrs themselves—only stirred the fires of true

belief and inspired ever greater acts of zealotry. Sometimes the pagan magistrates literally begged the Christians to make some gesture of compromise in order to save their own lives.

"Unhappy men!" cried one Roman proconsul to the all-too-willing martyrs. "If you are thus weary of your lives, is it so difficult for you to find ropes and precipices?"[30]

What the pagans found most provocative was not the fact that the Christians chose to worship their own deity in their own way, but that they stubbornly refused to drop a pinch of incense on the altar fire or mumble a few words of prayer in honor of the Roman deities. Ironically, the word "atheist" was first used by *pagans* to describe *Christians* because they denied the very existence of the gods and goddesses whom the pagans so revered. What the Christians saw as an act of conscience, the pagan saw as an act of disloyalty and disrespect—all that was required of them was some simple demonstration of their "civic virtue," which is the phrase that was used by one school administrator to justify the recital of the Pledge of Allegiance when a California court recently ruled it unconstitutional because it includes the phrase "under God."

Whether or not the "Great Persecution" of the early fourth century, the tenth and last of the persecutions carried out against Christianity by pagan Rome, would have been successful in extinguishing or at least containing the fires of true belief, we will never know. Remarkably—and, according to Christian tradition, miraculously—the Christians were rescued from their torturers and executioners when Constantine, one of the many pagan contenders for the imperial crown, managed to prevail in battle over all the others and then put himself under the protection of the Christian god. Here is one of the rare moments when the willful act of a single human being can be said to have changed the course of history.

"Behold, the Rivers Are Running Backwards"

We are encouraged to regard monotheism as a self-evident truth that could not fail to win the heart and mind of anyone to whom it was revealed. "But nothing made its final victory inevitable," insists historian Diana Bowder. "[T]he final triumph of Christianity and extinction of paganism [were] still far from certain or obvious."[31] Among the many faiths on offer in ancient Rome, all but Christianity and Judaism were polytheistic in origin—and Christianity, as historian Kenneth Scott Latourette concedes, "seemed to be one of the least of many rivals and with no promise of success against the others."[32] Indeed, even after the famous conversion of the emperor Constantine to Christianity, the outcome could not have been predicted with confidence at any time until the ultimate victory.

"If Christianity had been checked in its growth by some deadly disease, the world would have become Mithraic," speculates the nineteenth-century historian Ernest Renan.[33] "[I]magine how the history we trace in this book would have unfolded," proposes the contemporary historian James Carroll in *Constantine's Sword*, "had the young emperor been converted to Judaism instead."[34]

Indeed, as we shall see, the revolution that Constantine had set in motion was still imperfect and incomplete on his death—the ruling class, the culture and the vast majority of the population of the Roman empire were still pagan. When Julian, no less ambitious and no less visionary than Constantine, ascended to the imperial throne, he promptly revealed his intention to undo everything his uncle had done in the name of the Christian god. "Behold, the rivers are running backwards, as the proverb says!" writes Julian in one of the elegant, highly literate and often bitterly ironic discourses that were his real passion and his only enduring monument. The ancient proverb that Julian quotes was understood to signify that "all is topsy-turvy"—and thus does he acknowledge his own audacity in seeking to undo the revolution that Constantine set into motion and work a revolution of his own.[35]

The Christian emperor and the pagan emperor, in fact, shared much in common. Both of them, like other famous makers of both religions and revolutions, were masters of self-invention. Each was convinced that blessings had been bestowed upon him from on high, although each credited a different god for his curious fate, and both claimed to have seen divine visions and received divine visitations. Yet they were both driven as much by grudges and grievances as by true belief, and intimate family politics mattered as much as the wars and conspiracies in which they were engaged. Both were so enmeshed in scandal, intrigue and betrayal that their life stories resemble something between a soap opera and a Shakespearean tragedy. Each of them was deeply and decisively influenced by the women in his life—mother, sisters, wives and concubines. Above all, each one sought to remake the world over which he reigned, and each one very nearly did so.

Julian, of course, ultimately failed to reverse the flow of the river of history that Constantine had turned in the direction of monotheism. A spear thrust ended his life, and thus ended his pagan counter-revolution, only two years into his reign. He was still a young man when he died in battle, and if he had lived as long as his uncle, the war of God against the gods—a war that has never really ended—might have turned out much differently. Indeed, as we shall see, it is tantalizing to consider how close he came to bringing the spirit of respect and tolerance back into Roman government and thus back into the roots of Western civilization, and even more tantalizing to consider how different our benighted world might have been if he had succeeded.

BOOK ONE

THE GOD THAT FAILED

*You have rejected the Lord who is among you, and
have troubled him with weeping, saying, "Why,
now, came we forth out of Egypt?"*

—Moses, *Numbers* 11:20

◆

CHAPTER ONE

AGAINST ALL THE GODS OF EGYPT

A Young Pharaoh's Experiment in Monotheism
and Why It Failed

God is a latecomer in the history of religion.

—G. van der Leeuw

Only rarely does an archaeological discovery challenge everything we have been taught to believe about the history of religion. But that is what happened when an expedition of so-called biblical archaeologists began to excavate the ruins at Tell el-Amarna, a remote site near the banks of the Nile in southern Egypt, in the late 1880s. Suddenly, all that the Bible tells us about the origin of monotheism was called into question.

By a tradition that is embraced in all three of the monotheisms—Judaism, Christianity and Islam—the first person to recognize and worship the single all-powerful deity variously known as "Yahweh" or "Lord" or "Allah" was Abraham, whose encounter with the God of Israel in the land of Canaan is memorably depicted in the Book of Genesis: "And the Lord appeared unto Abram,[1] and said, 'Unto thy seed will I give this land,' and he built there an altar unto the Lord."[2]* A distant descendant of the first patriarch, the man called Moses—yet another prophet who is honored by Jews, Christians and Muslims alike—is shown in the Book of Exodus to challenge the pharaoh of Egypt on the fundamental theological issue that divides monotheism

*See the Bibliography for notes on biblical sources and usage.

and polytheism, the rivalry between the single all-powerful god who calls himself "Yahweh" in the Hebrew Bible and the countless gods, goddesses and godlings of Egypt.

"Who is Yahweh, that I should obey his voice?" a bemused pharaoh asks Moses. "I know not Yahweh."[3]

"Against all the gods of Egypt, I will execute judgment," promises Yahweh. "I *am* the Lord."[4]

The diggings at Tell el-Amarna, some 180 miles south of modern Cairo, tell a very different tale. The inscriptions on the stones and shards that were scratched out of the ground at el-Amarna show us the remarkable life of a young man who worked a revolution in ancient Egypt by scorning all the old gods and goddesses of the Egyptian pantheon, and worshipping one god alone. The man was not Moses; rather, he was a pharaoh who never met or even heard of a man called Moses. But perhaps the most surprising fact about the world's first monotheist is that his daring new religion died and was buried with him.

Cats and Crocodiles, Leeks and Onions

Some 3500 years ago, a young man ascended to the rule of Egypt under the throne name of Amenhotep IV (died c. 1347 B.C.E.).[5] The name refers to the deity called Amon, the loftiest of the fantastic array of gods and goddesses who were worshipped by the men and women of Egypt. Amon was associated with the sun—the deity was thought to be the most powerful of the many gods, just as the sun is the brightest of the many objects in the sky—but there were plenty of others to whom prayer and sacrifice were offered.

Indeed, the high king may have chosen a name that honored the high god, but his subjects continued to worship the jackal-headed Anubis, who was thought to weigh the hearts of the newly dead and watch over their tombs; the fertility goddess called Isis and her sibling-lover, Osiris, who was believed to reign over the netherworld where pious Egyptians hoped to spend their afterlives; and the troll-like Bes, ugly and misshapen, but cherished as the cheerful god of music and dancing and the good-hearted protector of children. Like everyone else in the ancient world, the Egyptians were ardent and unquestioning polytheists.

The Egyptians, in fact, were famous in the classical world for their sheer inventiveness in matters of faith, which included the worship of deities who were symbolized not only by household pets and wild animals but even by otherwise humble vegetables. "The comic writers and satirists never tired of scoffing at the adorers of the cat, the crocodile, the leek and the onion," reports Franz Cumont, citing as an example the most famous satirical poet of first-century Rome: "Juvenal says ironically: 'O holy people, whose very kitchen-gardens produce gods.'"⁶

The worship of gods and goddesses, however, was not merely a matter of whim or whimsy. Each of the most prominent deities was served by a priestly caste that consisted of men and women who were both proud and protective of the temples where they lived and worked and of the ceremonies over which they presided so solemnly. Like clergy in every place and every age, they courted the favor of the rich and powerful, and the pharaohs of Egypt were flatteringly likened to one or another of the gods. Over the centuries, the polytheism of ancient Egypt rooted itself in the political and economic establishment, and the pharaohs came to be regarded both as gods and kings.

The pharaohs who preceded Amenhotep to the throne of Egypt regarded themselves as the bearers of an old and fixed tradition, and they dutifully consulted the priests of Amon and the other gods and goddesses before embarking upon any enterprise. Nor did they have reason to doubt that the gods favored Egypt above all other nations of the known world—Egypt was what we would today call a superpower, and it dominated the ancient Near East, not only because of its superior military strength but also because it was regarded as the

center of art, commerce and diplomacy. Indeed, museums throughout the modern world are filled with the rich artifacts that attest to
the superb achievement of Egyptian civilization.

But the young pharaoh called Amenhotep was not content with
following the example of the seventeen dynasties that had come before him. He resolved to use the power that he possessed as pharaoh
of Egypt to decide, not only for himself but for his subjects, what
gods and goddesses ought to be worshipped. Here we encounter another new and terrible phenomenon in the history of religion—the
fusing of religion and politics into a single instrument of power
wielded by a single human being. Amenhotep now decided to defy all
of the old traditions and invent some new ones of his own making.

Virgin Soil

Amenhotep was born and raised among the opulent and elegant ceremonies of worship that constituted the state religion of ancient
Egypt. But something inspired him to reject the status quo, to re–
invent himself and revolutionize his spiritual beliefs and practices.
The young pharaoh repudiated all of the gods and goddesses in favor
of the single high god called Aton, a word that means "sun disk," and
he renamed himself in honor of his new and all-powerful deity. Just
as Abram became Abraham when he embarked upon the worship of
the new god called Yahweh, the pharaoh signified his new faith by
changing his throne name from Amenhotep ("Beloved of Amon") to
the one by which he is known and remembered today: Akhenaton,
which is translated as "Splendor of Aton."[7] So named, the restless and
willful young pharaoh was ready to carry out a purge and work a revolution in the kingdom that he ruled.

Aton, just like Amon, was identified with the sun. But Akhenaton
forbade any depiction of Aton that might remind his worshippers of
a living thing, animal or vegetable. By royal decree, Aton was symbolized by an austere circle of gold that was meant to suggest the sun
shining at its brightest in the noon sky. For that reason, no idols were

fashioned in the image of Aton because, remarkably, he was a god whose form could not be imagined.

And, just as remarkably, the pharaoh insisted that Aton, quite unlike Amon, was a jealous god who refused to share the affection or the attention of his worshippers with other gods and goddesses. At Akhenaton's command, the shrines and temples of rival deities were closed, the rituals of worship were suppressed, the statues that symbolized the other divinities were shattered and their names and images were literally chiseled off the stone monuments of ancient Egypt. The high priest of Amon, whose services were no longer needed, was put to work in a stone quarry like a common slave.

To put himself beyond the taint or temptation of the old gods, Akhenaton abandoned the royal capital of Thebes, where generations of pharaohs had reigned and were now buried beneath pyramids and sphinxes, and he built a new capital on virgin soil along the bank of the Nile. Here he established not only a new religion, with temples dedicated to Aton alone, but also a new style of art and architecture, a new royal entourage and a new government. Like other true believers who would follow his example in the centuries to come, Akhenaton convinced himself that the brave new world he had created would replace all that had come before and would last forever.

In the Mansion of the Sun

Like Moses, who is shown in the Bible to condemn the worship of a golden bull and other graven images, Akhenaton rejected all the traditional icons of paganism and chose a simple geometric shape to symbolize the god Aton. Like Solomon, he built a temple to the new god, the so-called Mansion of the Sun-Disk. Like Constantine, who founded the city of Constantinople to replace pagan Rome as capital of the Roman empire, Akhenaton personally participated in the planning and design of the new city dedicated to Aton.

Akhenaton can be compared to these famous monotheists, but— as far as we know—he was the first person to embrace these ideas, and he deserves the credit for inventing something wholly new in human history. New gods and goddesses had already been imagined and embraced throughout human history, no less in ancient Egypt than elsewhere around the world, and that is exactly why the pantheon of polytheism was always so crowded. Nor was there anything unprecedented or even unusual in a god who was understood to be the higher in rank than all other deities—both Amon and Aton were, after all, identified with the sun, the brightest but hardly the only object in the sky above Egypt.

Akhenaton, however, was the inventor of a religion with a crucial and fateful difference. Never before had a deity been understood to demand that all other gods and goddesses be rejected and abandoned. Akhenaton did not regard Aton merely as the one god among many who specially favored him and thus deserved his special attention in prayer and sacrifice. Rather, he regarded Aton as the *one* and *only* god, and he refused to allow anyone else to believe or act otherwise. "The monotheistic revolution of Akhenaton," explains Egyptologist Jan Assmann, "was not only the first but also the most radical and violent eruption of a counter-religion in the history of humankind."[8]

The Forgotten God

What turned the pharaoh of Egypt, inheritor of a rich and accommodating tradition of polytheism, into a revolutionary and a rigorist? At the heart of monotheism, of course, is the notion of the Only True God who reveals himself to ordinary men and women, causes the scales to fall from their eyes and thus turns them from benighted sinners into true believers. Did Akhenaton, too, experience an epiphany like the one that was visited upon Moses when a divine voice addressed him from within "a bush that burned with fire but was not consumed"[9] or the one that manifested as "a light from heaven"[10] and sent Paul to his knees in awe and terror on the road to Damascus?

Such is the common vocabulary of true belief in the history of monotheism. But there are other ways of understanding what happened to the excitable young pharaoh who embraced the solar god with such fervor. One theory, which has been applied to Constantine and Julian as well as Akhenaton, suggests that he was expertly manipulated into undertaking his missionary work by one of the guileful women in his life—a theory that relies on the primeval stereotype of woman as seducer and thus echoes the tale of Eve and her notorious apple. Perhaps Akhenaton, who is described by one scholar as "a sensitive aesthete,"[11] fell under the influence of his mother, who may have been the first member of his family to worship Aton. Or perhaps it was his wife, the celebrated Queen Nefertiti, who prevailed upon the impressionable young king to join the cult of the sun god.

Another theory, which also prefigures the political conflicts that raged in the courts of both Constantine and Julian, proposes that Akhenaton was courted by the rival priesthoods of Amon and Aton, one based in the old royal capital at Thebes and the other in the "Sun-City" of On (Heliopolis), each faction vying against the other for the wealth, power and privilege that were the rewards for winning the favor of the new king. When it came to converting Akhenaton to the cult of the sun god, "[i]t is likely that economic factors," insists historian John Bright, "played as great a part as did religious zeal."[12] The priesthood of Aton, which prevailed over the priests of the old and established cults, provided the pharaoh with a ready supply of the "new men" who now served in the royal court as generals, chamberlains, chroniclers and butlers.

Of one thing, however, we can be sure—Akhenaton failed to win the hearts and minds of the ordinary men and women of ancient Egypt. Living and ruling in his remote capital for nearly seventeen years, he was distrusted and detested by the worshippers of the old gods and goddesses. Promptly upon his death, the monotheistic revolution that he imposed from above on ancient Egypt was wholly undone—the royal capital and the temples of Aton were abandoned, and the newfangled cult was forgotten. Just as Akhenaton had once erased the names of the old gods from the monuments of ancient

Egypt, now it was Akhenaton's name that was chiseled out of the stone inscriptions and stricken from the lists of kings that the Egyptians maintained with such meticulous care.

Akhenaton was succeeded on the throne by his son-in-law, who moved the royal court back to Thebes, reopened the old shrines, changed his name from "Tut-ankh-*aton*," a name that honored the god Aton, to "Tut-ankh-*amon*," thus proclaiming his allegiance to the old and beloved Amon—he is the celebrated King Tut whose magnificent tomb was found in 1922. The royal tomb where Akhe-naton was buried, by contrast, was pillaged. When the tomb was finally uncovered by the archaeologists at work at Tell el-Amarna, the mummified corpse of the founder of monotheism was gone.

The Gift of the Egyptians

But Akhenaton and the religion he invented may have been preserved and passed down through history in intriguing if obscure ways. Indeed, the startling discoveries at el-Amarna have prompted some scholars to wonder whether monotheism was, in fact, a gift of the Egyptians. If so, an argument can be made that Judaism, Christianity and Islam are all daughter religions of the failed experiment that took place in prebiblical antiquity.

One of the pious hymns that Akhenaton himself may have composed—"O Thou only God, there is no other God than Thou"[13]—seems to prefigure the fundamental credo of Judaism: "Hear O Israel, the Lord thy God, the Lord is One."[14] And some scholars propose that the solar imagery that can be found in the Psalms—"You are clothed in glory and majesty, wrapped in a robe of light; You spread the heavens like a tent cloth"[15]—was not merely inspired by the pharaoh's praise-song to Aton but is a Hebrew translation of the original Egyptian text. "Were not the Egyptian 'Aton' and the Hebrew 'Adonai' the same name?" muses Jan Assmann,[16] and Sigmund Freud takes the argument to its furthest reach in *Moses and Monotheism* by suggesting that Moses himself was a priest in the cult of Aton who converted the Israelites to the new faith after the Egyptians repudiated the dead pharaoh. "The man Moses, the liberator and lawgiver of the Jewish people, was not a Jew but an Egyptian," proposes Freud. "Moses conceived the plan of finding a new people, to whom he could give the religion that Egypt disdained."[17]

Such speculation is still capable of provoking anger and outrage among the pious in all three monotheisms. But the simple proposition that the faith of ancient Israel was not something wholly new is now beyond debate—many of the beliefs and practices that are written into the biblical text were borrowed from the peoples among whom the Israelites lived and against whom they fought, sometimes as the victors and more often as the vanquished. And the borrowings were not always based on a belief in the Only True God—the Bible itself is covered with the fingerprints of polytheism, and even the biblical authors find themselves forced to concede that the people of ancient Israel, no less than the people of ancient Egypt, were reluctant monotheists.

The original theology of the Israelites, for example, may have envisioned Yahweh as one god among many. One of the Hebrew words used in the Bible to describe the God of Israel is *Elohim*, a plural noun that means "gods." God sometimes speaks of himself in the plural: "Let us make man in *our* image," he muses out loud in the Book of Genesis, "after *our* likeness."[18] According to one odd and awkward passage in Genesis, described by Bible scholar Ephraim Speiser as "controversial in the extreme,"[19] Elohim appears to have sired a whole brood of godlings—"the sons of the gods," according to a literal translation of the biblical text.[20] "The divine beings saw how beautiful the daughters of men were, and took wives from among those that pleased them," reports the biblical storyteller in the Book of Genesis, using words that seem more appropriate to Greek myth than Jewish scripture. "The divine beings cohabited with the daughters of men, who bore them offspring."[21]

Nor were the Israelites able to resist the undeniable charms and comforts of idolatry. The biblical authors readily concede that the worshippers of Yahweh commonly owned *teraphim*—that is, the house-hold idols that were used for the veneration of various fertility god-desses of the ancient world. The matriarch Rachel, for example, so covets her father's collection of *teraphim* that she purloins his whole cherished collection.[22] Michal, daughter of Saul and wife of David—both men chosen by God to serve as kings of Israel—keeps an idol on hand in the royal household.[23] Moses hands down the famous com-mandment against the making of graven images—"or any likeness of any thing that is in heaven above, or the earth beneath, or the water"[24]—and then appears to violate the commandment by fashion-ing a snake out of bronze and using it as a kind of magic wand for the cure of snakebite.[25]

Moses, in fact, is plainly shown to be something other than a strict monotheist at one unsettling moment in the Bible. After God assists the Israelites in defeating the army of the pharaoh at the Red Sea, Moses leads the worshippers of Yahweh in a praise-song in which he entertains the notion that Yahweh may be the *best* god, at least as far as the Israelites are concerned, but seems to concede that he is not the *only* god: "Who is like you, O Yahweh, among the gods?"[26] The notion may be startling to those who regard the Bible as a manifesto of monotheism, but it was commonplace among the polytheists of the ancient world—including more than a few of the Israelite kings—who acknowledged the existence of many gods and goddesses even if they offered worship only to their own tutelary god.

God and His Asherah

Further evidence of polytheism among the ancient Israelites can be found outside the pages of the Bible. No remnant of the Temple of Solomon has been recovered from the soil of the Holy Land, no trace of the stone tablets on which the Ten Commandments were inscribed by the finger of God, but archaeologists have found literally hundreds of *teraphim*, artfully fashioned out of rare ivory or humble clay, depicting naked women, some touching their breasts or genitals. Until recently, such artifacts could be dismissed as pagan relics that had nothing to do with the monotheism of ancient Israel—but new archaeological discoveries, fully as startling as the ones at Tell el-Amarna, suggest that they were used by worshippers of the God of Israel, too.

Not long ago, at an archaeological site in the wilderness of Sinai called Kuntillat 'Ajrud, archaeologists discovered a large ceramic storage jar that has been dated to the late ninth century B.C.E. At that place and time, the strict and uncompromising code of monotheism as set forth in the Ten Commandments—"Thou shalt have no other gods before me"[27]—had been in effect for four hundred years, or so the Torah suggests. But the jar is inscribed with a prayerful wish that is starkly at odds with the official theology of the Bible.

"I bless thee by Yahweh," goes the inscription, "and by his Asherah."[28]

The goddess called Asherah is conjured up in the Bible, of course, but only as an alien and evil deity who is worshipped by the pagan tribes and nations whom the Israelites vow to exterminate or expel from the land of Canaan. She is symbolized in pagan ritual by a living tree or a carved wooden pole set upright in the ground, and these so-called *asherim* are found in "uncanny places" all over the land of Israel—"upon the high mountains, and upon the hills, and under every leafy tree."[29] At every mention of Asherah in the Bible, she is condemned as something so vile and so detestable that the biblical author is reduced to sputtering rage—the worship of all gods and goddesses is condemned as "that which was evil in the sight of the Lord, after the abominations of the heathens, whom the Lord cast out before the children of Israel."[30]

What is significant about the inscription at Kuntillat 'Ajrud, and others like it, is the confirmation that both the Israelites *and* the native-dwelling pagans of Canaan embraced the goddess Asherah. Putting aside such cracks in the theological wall of the Torah as the one found in the tale of "the sons of the gods," the Hebrew Bible insists that God does not consort with goddesses and does not sire godlings. But the flesh-and-blood men and women of ancient Israel, like polytheists all over the world and in every age, seemed to imagine that deities, too, came in pairs, male and female, king and queen, husband and wife, Yahweh and his Asherah.

The God That Failed

So even the strictest and sternest of the biblical authors were forced to confront the undeniable fact that the Israelites under the rule of their anointed kings, no less than the Egyptians under the pharaoh Akhenaton, refused to put aside "that which was evil in the sight of the Lord." Indeed, the kings of ancient Israel themselves are some of the worst offenders. Solomon, for example, is famously depicted in the Bible as so favored by God that "all the earth sought to hear his wisdom, which God had put in his heart"[31]—and yet it is also frankly reported that King Solomon "loved many strange women," including some seven hundred wives and three hundred concubines, many of whom lured him into the worship of gods and goddesses other than Yahweh.

"When he grew old, his wives turned his heart to follow other gods," the biblical author concedes, "and he did not remain wholly loyal to the Lord his God as his father David had been."[32]

To the biblical authors, the explanation for these "abominations" is simple and straightforward—God offers to bestow his blessings on the Israelites as his chosen people in exchange for compliance with his sacred law, but the Israelites fail to live up to their end of the bargain. "Now then, if you will obey me faithfully and keep my covenant, you shall be my treasured possession among all the peoples," God instructs Moses to tell the Israelites.[33] But they yield so readily to their appetites and curiosities that God loses patience with the Israelites and, more than once, threatens to carry out the mass murder of his own chosen people and start all over again with the children of Moses.

"Now let me be, that my anger may blaze forth against them, and that I may destroy them," God tells Moses after the Israelites defy the commandment against the making of graven images and offer worship to an idol in the form of a golden calf, "and I will make of you a great nation."[34]

Moses manages to talk Yahweh out of killing *all* the Israelites by boldly reminding the God of Israel of how an act of divine genocide would look to all those abominable pagans back in Egypt: "Let not the Egyptians say, 'It was with evil intent that he delivered them, only to kill them off in the mountains and annihilate them from the face of the earth.'"[35] But the Bible confirms that God is grimly determined to punish the chosen people for their spiritual lapses—and Moses turns out to be his willing henchman. Not long after his stirring speech in defense of the Israelites, Moses organizes what can only be described as a death squad, and some 3000 men and women who joined in the worship of the golden calf are put to the sword for their sin.

"Thus says the Lord, the God of Israel," cries Moses to the men whom he recruits to carry out the killings. "Each of you put sword on thigh, go back and forth from gate to gate throughout the camp, and slay brother, neighbor, and kin."[36]

The unmentioned but unmistakable subtext of these and many other biblical passages is that Yahweh, no less than Aton, is a failure. The God of Israel is rejected by the majority of the Israelites, the very people whom he has chosen as his "treasured possession," and not just at the moment when they worshipped the golden calf but repeatedly over the long and troubled history of ancient Israel. Indeed, the Bible can be read as a bitter song of despair as sung by the disappointed prophets of Yahweh who tried but failed to call their fellow Israelites to the worship of the True God. Fatefully and tragically, the prophets respond to rejection in exactly the same way that God is shown to react to the worship of the golden calf—they are roused to a fierce, relentless and punishing anger toward any man or woman whom they find to be insufficiently faithful.

The Core Value of Monotheism

Here we encounter the core value of monotheism at its most blood-thirsty. Starting with Akhenaton, monotheism has been character-ized by what scholars call exclusivism, the belief that worship is to be offered to a single god to the exclusion of all other gods and god-desses. At its purest expression, monotheism insists that its deity is not only the best of all gods and goddesses, but the one and only god, and that all other deities are false—"no-gods," as the prophet Jere-miah puts it.[37] The most zealous monotheists have always sought to exclude from their ranks anyone who does not share their true belief. And, as we have just seen, some monotheists insist that anyone who dares to offer worship to a false god is worthy of not merely exclusion but death. Indeed, the most militant monotheists—Jews, Christians and Muslims alike—embrace the belief that God demands the blood of the nonbeliever.

The point is made again and again in the Bible. All of Israel is of-fered the opportunity to enter into the covenant that Yahweh made with Abraham, but only a precious few accept the offer and perform their duties with the fidelity that God desires of them. The rest are hopeless sinners, worthy of every kind of suffering that God inflicts on them, sometimes through drought and famine, sometimes plague and pestilence, sometimes through acts of violence by zealous men like Moses and his death squad. According to the worldview of the authors and editors who composed and compiled the biblical text, the whole of humankind can be divided into two categories—on one side, the elect, the blessed, "the holy seed," as the prophet Ezra puts it,[38] and on the other side, the fallen, the accursed, "the wicked and the sinner."[39]

What does God demand of the chosen people that they find so objectionable? Sermonizers over the centuries have suggested that anyone who rejects the True God is rejecting the exalted moral and ethical teachings that are the glory of monotheism. To be sure, the

Bible includes a few sublime passages that encourage us to be kind and gentle, caring and compassionate, not merely in our hearts but in our deeds, and not merely toward our own kin but toward the stranger, too. When Isaiah ponders what God demands of those who seek him, for example, the prophet insists that God himself disdains prayer and fasting: "What is the fast that I desire? It is to share your bread with the hungry, and to take the wretched poor into your home, [and] when you see the naked, clothe him."[40]

To call such teachings the essence of biblical monotheism, however, misses the point that is made so forcefully and so fervently by the most rigorous biblical authors. They do not define wickedness and sin in terms of moral and ethical conduct. Indeed, they are far more concerned with the purity of religion than with the pursuit of justice. The very worst sin of all, as they see it, is not lust or greed, but rather the offering of worship to gods and goddesses other than the True God. Whenever a biblical author is moved to call something "abominable," he is using a code word for every ritual and belief other than his own.

When it comes to spiritual purity, only a few of the Israelites are judged worthy to be counted among the holy seed, and the vast majority are characterized as wicked sinners. "They provoked him to jealousy with strange gods," Moses is made to say of the Israelites in the Book of Deuteronomy. "They sacrificed to demons."[41] And the Bible warns that such sins will bring a terrible punishment: "For a fire is kindled in my anger," announces God. "The sword without, and terror within, shall destroy both the young man and the virgin, the suckling also with the man of gray hairs."[42]

Any misfortune that befalls the wicked and the sinful, according to the cruel logic of monotheism, must be understood as the sure and awful workings of divine justice. Sometimes the instrument of God's will is an angel of death from on high, sometimes an enemy from abroad, and sometimes a fellow countryman or even a blood relation. But, no matter who acts on behalf of the True God, the victim is always regarded as wholly deserving of his punishment. The Bible includes a generous measure of myth and metaphor, but if we read the biblical text literally, as so many rigorists urge us to do, it is clear that the True God is not only "a jealous god"[43] but also a deeply resentful one—and what he resents above all is his own failure to win the hearts and minds of the people whom he has chosen as his own.

The Cuckolded Husband

Nowadays, the most punishing texts of the Bible are mostly passed over in favor of the more elevating and inspiring ones. But the kinder and gentler deity who can be teased out of the scriptures through a selective reading of the text is very different from the jealous and vengeful god who so inspired the rigorists in Judaism and Christianity during the early history of monotheism. They imagined God not as a heavenly father, bland and benign, but rather as a cuckolded husband who is so embittered and enraged by the promiscuities of his spouse that he is moved to torture and murder. Indeed, it is the image of the spurned lover—a favorite and even obsessive theme of the angriest biblical prophets, including Jeremiah, Ezekiel and Hosea—that allows us to feel the visceral emotions that drove (and still drive) the most zealous of monotheists to acts of terror and carnage.

Apostasy and idolatry are the theological equivalent to adultery and harlotry, according to these biblical authors, even if their poetry and prose are so lurid and so literal that the reader may forget that they are expressing themselves in metaphor. Thus, for example, the prophet Ezekiel conjures up a scene in which Jerusalem is likened to a woman who is abandoned at birth and left to die in an open field, then rescued and raised by a kind and caring man and finally— "[when] your breasts became firm and your hair sprouted"—betrothed to her rescuer, who turns out to be God himself. The passage begins like an enchanting fairy tale—"I clothed you with embroidered garments, and gave you sandals of dolphin leather, I decked you out in finery and put bracelets on your arms and earrings in your ears and a splendid crown on your head"—but it ends like a horror story told by the Marquis de Sade.

> Your time for love had arrived, so I entered into a covenant with you by oath. But confident in your beauty and fame, you played the harlot, you lavished your favor on every passerby. You sullied your beauty and spread your legs to every passerby, you multiplied your harlotries to anger me. Yet you were not like a prostitute, for you spurned fees; you were like the adulterous wife who welcomes strangers instead of her husband.[44]

But God is not content with ranting and raving at his faithless wife. As his rage builds to a climax—"Now I will stretch out my arm against you, I will direct bloody and impassioned fury against you"— he spins wildly out of control, and he is moved to threats and acts of violence that are described in near pornographic language:

> I will assemble all the lovers to whom you gave your favors, along with everybody you accepted and everybody you rejected, and I will deliver you into their hands. Then they shall assemble a mob against you to pelt you with stones and pierce you with their swords. They shall put your houses to flames and execute punishment upon you in the sight of many women. Thus will I put a stop to your harlotry.[45]

Here we behold the ugliest face of monotheism, an especially dark and dangerous one. The true believer is taught in the Bible that "the Lord is a jealous and avenging God, vengeful and fierce in wrath."[46] He is shown that God works his will through emissaries and deputies and surrogates of all kinds, and he is encouraged to regard himself as an instrument of God's will. And, once he embraces the idea, he may feel inspired and empowered and even obligated to follow the example of Moses by strapping a sword on his thigh and taking it upon himself to punish the wicked and the sinful, whether they are strangers or "brother, neighbor, or kin."

The impulse to translate an overheated biblical metaphor into an act of violence is self-limiting as long as the rigorists are small in number and lacking in political or military power. They are surely capable of inflicting punishment on those whom they regard as wicked and sinful, but only on a relatively modest scale. When the rigorist is also a king and the power of the state is put in the service of true belief, however, both the risk and the scale of religious persecution are vastly greater. That rude beast slouching toward Bethlehem, as we shall see, is the soldier and the secret policeman, the prosecutor and the public executioner.

CHAPTER TWO

WHAT DID PAGANS DO?

The Case Against Classical Paganism
—and Why It Was Wrong

Ye cannot drink the cup of the Lord, and the cup of devils.
—1 Corinthians 10:21

The biblical condemnation of polytheism, when stripped of its rhetorical overkill, rests on a single theological offense: the pagan commits an unforgivable crime when he or she prays to *any* god or goddess other than the Only True God. Although some of the biblical authors delight in describing (and, of course, denouncing) the exotic and provocative rituals of paganism, the manner of worship ultimately matters less to these ancient rigorists than the deity to whom worship is offered. Indeed, the rituals and practices of classical paganism were very much like those of the faith that is actually described in the Bible.

"Paganism" is a term that is used indiscriminately to describe a vast array of unrelated beliefs and practices, ranging in time, place and expression from the crude burial rites of the Neanderthals to the exquisite statuary and epic poetry of the Greeks and Romans—and much else in between. Among the fantastic variety of pagans who have come and gone over the centuries, to be sure, were men and women whose religious practices were bloody, bizarre and even deadly. But the only thing that all of these pagans share in common is the fact that they did not confine their worship to the Only True God as that deity is variously defined in Judaism, Christianity and Islam.

Because the final and decisive battle in the war of God against the gods was fought in the heart of the Roman empire at the very peak of its power and glory, as the most rigorous Jews and Christians saw it, the principal enemy of monotheism was the high culture of the classical world, a culture that began in Greece, reached its zenith in Rome and spread throughout the Roman empire. "Classical paganism," then, was the official religion of a civilization that is recalled and honored today in the classical texts that are studied in our universities, the statuary that fills our museums and the architectural styles that grace our monuments and public buildings.

Still, the bad odor that clings to paganism begins with the alarming and sometimes revolting depiction of pagan ritual that we find in the Bible—paganism, we are taught, is hopelessly tainted with harlotry, idolatry, sorcery and, at its most wretched, human sacrifice. All of these notes are rung, for example, by Ezekiel in the passage that we considered in the last chapter. When God describes the debaucheries of the fallen woman who symbolizes faithless Jerusalem, he does not confine himself to her "harlotries." Rather, he allows us to understand that her sin is spiritual as well as carnal.

> You took your beautiful things, made of the gold and silver that I had given you, and you made yourself phallic images and fornicated with them. The food that I had given to you—the choice flour, the oil, and the honey—you set it before them for a pleasing odor. You even took the sons and daughters that you bore to me and sacrificed them to those images as food—as if your harlotries were not enough, you slaughtered my children and presented them as offerings![1]

The Bible insists that all the rituals of paganism are "abominations," even the ones that are strikingly similar to the rituals of monotheism, because they honor the wrong deity. And the biblical authors decorate their simple theological argument with atrocity propaganda, insisting that pagans are not only apostates and blasphemers but fornicators and baby killers, too. Indeed, the authors seem to protest too much, and their obsessive concern with harlotry only confirms that the most rigorous of the biblical sources were plainly fascinated by what they claimed to find so abominable.

The temptations of paganism are so powerful that God himself is held responsible for using them to tempt and then punish his chosen people. "They shall be a snare and a trap unto you, and a scourge in your sides, and pricks in your eyes," warns Joshua after the Israelites have yet again driven God into a rage over their stubborn refusal to comply with his sacred law, "until ye perish from off this good land which the Lord your God hath given you."[2]

Still, by late biblical antiquity, the paganism that the prophets found so abominable was something very different from the parade of horribles that is described in the Bible. Paganism in the Mediterranean world was an ornament of what was (and is) regarded as the highest expression of classical civilization. Its scripture consisted of the works of Homer, for example, and its "idols" were the statuary that is today displayed in museums all over the world. What, then, did pagans actually do that the rigorists in Judaism and Christianity found so appalling that they deemed it worthy of death?

The Sacred Whore

Harlotry, as we are asked to believe by both the biblical prophets and some secular historians, was an ancient, enduring and beloved practice of paganism. A "sacred" or "temple" or "cultic" prostitute is understood to have been a man or woman (and sometimes a boy or girl) who offered to engage in sexual intercourse with all comers at the temples of a goddess of love, like the Babylonian goddess Ishtar, or a goddess of fertility, like the Canaanite goddess Astarte. The pious pagan regarded "divine intercourse" as a sacred offering to the goddess in the hope that she would reward the ritual lovers with "abundant harvests and an increase of cattle."[3] And the ancient sources tell of a tradition that required brides to sacrifice their virginity to the goddess by presenting themselves at a shrine to be deflowered by strangers on their wedding nights, although the husband was sometimes allowed to put on a disguise and play the role of the stranger.

Such titillating scenes have always excited the human imagination, not only among strict monotheists like Ezekiel but even among the pagans themselves. The Greek historian Herodotus, writing in the fifth century B.C.E., was already shocking his readers with tales of sexual adventure in the service of the gods and goddesses of the ancient world. Even the high-born matrons of Babylon, he reports, were under a legal duty to serve as temple harlots at least once in their lives: "Such of the women as are tall and beautiful are soon released," he writes with a leer, "but the ugly ones have to stay a long time before they can fulfill the law."[4]

The historical reality, however, may not have been quite so lurid. The "harlotries" that so agitated the prophets may have been mostly or entirely metaphorical. Rituals of sacred sex, if they took place at all, probably consisted of a single act of ceremonial intercourse by a priest and a priestess on a holy day or at a moment of crisis such as a plague, drought or famine. Indeed, some revisionists openly wonder whether the sexual practices of paganism are mostly in the eye of the beholder. They point out that "*qedeshah*," the Hebrew word that is rendered in conventional Bible scholarship as "temple prostitute," literally means "a consecrated woman." A fresh reading of ancient texts and archaeological evidence leads some recent scholars to believe that a *qedeshah* was not a sacred whore at all but a midwife, a wet nurse or perhaps a sorceress. "Tragically," writes Bible critic Mayer I. Gruber, "scholarship suffered from scholars being unable to imagine any cultic role for women in antiquity that did not involve sexual intercourse."

Pagans, in fact, were as intent on imposing sexual law and order on a lively populace as the most rigorous monotheists. The Roman Senate, for example, was outraged by the spectacle of the Bacchanalia, a festival that honored the god of wine, Bacchus (also called Dionysus), with orgiastic bouts of drinking, the display (and use) of phallic icons like the ones that Ezekiel complains about and even the occasional act of public sex, all carried out in plain sight in the streets. By 186 B.C.E., the senators, declaring themselves to be concerned that the initiates were at risk of anal rape, ordered that the Bacchanalia be suppressed by force of arms as a "depraved foreign superstition."[5]

If we take the ancient sources at their word, some goddess-shrines in the more remote corners of the Roman empire served as functional equivalents of brothels. "A school of wickedness for all the votaries of unchasteness" is how the ancient Christian chronicler Eusebius of Caesarea describes the temple of Aphrodite at Aphaca (now Efqa, in Lebanon).[6] The temple, for example, attracted prostitutes of both sexes, among whom were male transvestites—"men undeserving of their name [who] forgot the honour of their sex," as Eusebius puts it, "and propitiated the demon by their effeminate conduct." But the worship of the goddess may have had little or nothing to do with their sexual exploits—the "abandoned votaries of sensuality and impurity," as Eusebius dubs them, may have included ordinary prostitutes offering their services to worshippers who were aroused by the ceremonies that they just attended inside the shrine.[7]

By late antiquity, sex in the sacred precincts of paganism was more a matter of private scandal than religious practice. During the reign of Tiberius (14–37 C.E.), for example, an unsigned note was delivered to a Roman noblewoman called Paulina. She was invited to the temple of Isis, the Egyptian goddess of fertility, where the jackal-headed god Anubis promised to grant her the privilege of bedding down with him. When she dutifully appeared at the temple, the figure wearing the mask of Anubis turned out to be a thoroughly mortal man—a Roman knight who was either the seducer of a gullible woman or the lover of a conniving woman.

Far from confirming the "harlotries" that so concerned the prophets, the incident at the temple of Isis in Rome only suggests that polytheists could be as prudish and puritanical as monotheists: the emperor ordered the crucifixion of a few priests of Isis, according to the Jewish historian Josephus, as a caution against any further sexual outrage in the holy places where the gods and goddesses were worshipped.

A Mirror to Juno

The images of gods and goddesses that so outraged Moses and his fellow monotheists can now be found in museums all over the world, where they are displayed as works of art, historical artifacts or anthropological specimens—and sometimes all three at once. To the propagandists of monotheism, however, they are "idols," and their worship is the emblematic sin of paganism, so offensive to God that the second of his ten commandments is specifically directed against the making of *any* image that might be mistaken for a deity.

The installation of an idol in the temple of the True God reduces the biblical author to a kind of sputtering rage: "The abomination of desolation" is how it is described in the Book of Daniel and echoed in the Gospel of Matthew.[8] And those who make and use idols are the target of open ridicule and bitter irony—the idol maker, says the prophet Isaiah, is a man who chops down a tree and uses some of the wood to build a fire in order to warm himself, and some to bake bread or roast meat in order to feed himself. "Of the rest, he makes a god—his own carving!" scorns Isaiah. "He bows down to it, worships it, he prays to it and cries: 'Save me, for you are my god!' "[9]

But the pagans of high antiquity were not quite so naïve or simpleminded about the use of statuary in rituals of worship. Among some of the more exotic cults, of course, the statues of gods and goddesses were still the object of elaborate rituals in which the priests and priestesses treated them as if they were alive. At the temple of Isis in Rome, for example, the statue of the goddess was awakened every morning, bathed and anointed with oil, "covered with sumptuous raiment and ornamented with jewels and gems," as historian Franz

Cumont puts it, seated at a banquet table and offered meals, and then returned to bed every night.[10]

Such practices, however, had been already regarded with skepticism by Greek philosophers of distant antiquity—and with open ridicule by the more refined and sophisticated pagans of imperial Rome. "We should like to forbid offering linen garments and a stiff brush to Jupiter, and holding up a mirror to Juno," writes the philosopher Seneca the Younger (c. 4 B.C.E.–65 C.E.). "The god needs no domestic servants."[11] And the poet Horace (65–8 B.C.E.), adopting the same stance that we find in the Book of Isaiah, pokes fun at the Greek god of procreation, Priapus, who was symbolized by the figure of an outsized phallus: "Once I was a fig tree's stump, a useless log, then a carpenter, uncertain as to whether he would make a stool or Priapus, decided for a god."[12]

The images of the gods and goddesses were more commonly treated with the same affection and respect that Judaism and Christianity still offer to their own holy objects, and for much the same reason. A pagan entering a house in the ancient Rome, for example, might pause to kiss the image of the goddess-protector that was customarily placed at the threshold just as a Jew in ancient Palestine (or, for that matter, anywhere in the world today) might pause to kiss the *mezuzah* that was customarily mounted on the doorpost. The kiss was intended to show respect and reverence to the deity, of course, but in both cases the gesture also betrays a primitive but enduring and thoroughly human belief, shared by polytheists and monotheists, that a man-made object may possess the miraculous power to bring good fortune.

Similarly, the images of the gods and goddesses were intended to inspire the worshipper as he or she offered prayer and sacrifice in the same way that icons or altar paintings or altarpieces are meant to inspire the worshipper in a Christian church. Indeed, the same can be said of *all* religious art, whether it consists of the letterforms and geometric shapes that adorn Islamic calligraphy and architecture, the golden crowns and silver shields that decorate the scrolls of the Torah, the *Pietà* of Michelangelo at the Basilica of St. Peter in the Vatican— or, for that matter, the statuary of pagan Greece and Rome, which provided Michelangelo with such exalted models when he set his own chisel to stone.

The Three Magicians

Among the most famous—and fiercest—of the laws that Moses is shown to bring down from Mt. Sinai are the ones that criminalize the practice of magic. "There shall not be found among you a soothsayer, or an enchanter, or a sorcerer," decrees Moses. "Thou shalt not suffer a witch to live."[13] Magic working is condemned with equal fervor in the Christian Bible, where it is explicitly linked with all the other outrages of paganism: "The fearful, and unbelieving, and the abominable, and murderers, and whoremongers, and sorcerers, and idolaters, and all liars, shall have their part in the lake which burneth with fire and brimstone, which is the second death."[14]

Ironically, an intriguing and illuminating clue to the function of sorcery in the pagan world is buried away in one of the most beloved passages of the Christian Bible. "Three wise men" come in search of the newborn Jesus, or so goes the conventional English translation of Matthew 2:1–2, "for we have seen his star in the east, and have come to worship him." The "wise men" are plainly called "magi" in the Greek text, the plural form of "magus," a word that was used among the pagans of Babylonia and Persia to identify seers, soothsayers and sorcerers. "Magus" is the root of "magic," and so we might more accurately call the men who followed a star to Bethlehem the three magicians.

"Magus" came to be used in Jewish and Christian circles as a derogatory term to describe someone who trafficked in black magic: a sorcerer, a deceiver, even a poisoner. But the original meaning of the word in the pagan world was honorable and even exalted—it was used to identify a teacher or a physician, an interpreter of dreams, an astrologer or an augur, all of whom were regarded throughout antiquity as wholly trustworthy practitioners. They were experts in the ancient equivalent of "information technology," as historian Robin Lane Fox puts it, a set of tools and techniques that were believed to reveal (and, sometimes, to bend) the will of the gods.[15] Indeed, the Gospel of Mark allows us to glimpse the workings of pagan magic—the three wise men are, among other things, astrologers who observe the night sky, see the star over Bethlehem, and recognize it as the sign of the birth of the "King of the Jews."

To be sure, the magi of antiquity were the inventors and users of what we would today call magic tricks. At some shrines and temples, the priests used smoke and mirrors, quite literally, to amaze and bedazzle the worshippers—the arrival and departure of the god would be simulated with fireworks or flashes of torchlight reflected from a temple ceiling or a pool of water. An initiate into a mystery religion might be conducted through an underground passage and into a subterranean shrine, and his senses would be stimulated first by foul odors, then the aroma of incense and finally by light bursts and trumpet blasts. One famous magus was credited with causing the torch held by a statue of Hecate, a goddess of sorcery, to burst into flame, a feat that surely owed more to chemistry than the black arts. At a temple to Apollo, the priests would carry an idol of the god into his shrine on a litter, and the idol appeared to rise of its own accord as it passed through the threshold—the idol was fashioned out of iron, and a magnet was apparently installed in the lintel.

"[W]orship involved the chanting of hymns and secret formulae, the lighting of torches and burning of incense, sudden blazes of light, obsessive music, theatrical effects—moving statues, doors opening of their own accord, and so on—and it normally took place in underground chambers," writes historian Robert Browning about the cult of Cybele. "It sounds trivial, like something from the fairground. But so does almost any other religion, described from the outside."[16]

Such acts of legerdemain were not intended to entertain the worshippers, of course, but rather to put them into an appropriate state of awe and wonder and thus prepare them for the offering of prayer and sacrifice to the gods. The point was made by modern archaeologists at work in Greece, who discovered an ancient marble bust with a curious funnel-shaped opening at the mouth—they contrived to attach a length of bronze tubing to the opening in the bust, and they found that when someone spoke into the tube, his voice seemed to come from the statue's mouth. "[T]he effect was powerful and strange," the archaeologists explain, "a voice which would sound to an emotional mind both weird and mysterious."[17]

To ancient monotheists as well as modern skeptics, the wonder-working priests and priestesses were resorting to cheap tricks to exploit the fearful and needy men and women who gathered in their shrines and temples. But there is quite another way to understand the use of "special effects" in the rituals of paganism. The ancients were taught by poets and playwrights, as well as priests and priestesses, to believe that gods and goddesses routinely manifested themselves in the here and now. Perhaps they were willing to go along with the trick in much the same way that modern audiences happily pay for the opportunity to momentarily suspend their disbelief in a Las Vegas magic show or a movie full of special effects.

"Because men expected their gods to be 'present and manifest,' who could blame the priests if they helped the gods live up to expectations?" proposes Fox. "Again, the line between religion and magic vanishes."[18]

Spilled Guts and Startled Birds

Sorcery was not always or only a matter of dazzling the crowds at a pagan shrine. More commonly, sorcery was put to use in paganism in the effort to answer the fundamental questions of *all* religion: What does the deity want of us? What is the deity willing to do for us? And how can we persuade the deity to do our bidding, whether we seek a happy marriage, a healthy child, a successful career, a safe journey or the cure of a disease? Such are the concerns of ordinary men and women, no less in ancient times than in our own.

The ancients resorted to fortune-telling at every opportunity. The scheduling of a haircut, a manicure or a bath might be submitted for approval by an augur or an astrologer. For an emperor, the will of the gods was believed to be a matter of life and death—the imperial fortune-tellers, known as the College of Haruspices, were always consulted before any new undertaking, whether it was a matter of setting off on a voyage or marching off to war. That is why soothsaying will figure as prominently and crucially in the lives of both Constantine and Julian, a Christian and a pagan, as it did in the lives of kings and commoners alike throughout the ancient world.

The tools and techniques that were used by magi of various kinds strike us today as crude or weird or perhaps even slightly pathetic. They would examine the spilled guts of an ox that had been sacrificed to the gods to see what meanings they could read in the lobes of a fresh liver. They would ponder the significance of the place and timing of a lightning strike, the direction of a startled bird's flight, the posture of the corpse of someone who had dropped dead in the street. They would consult the vast libraries of oracular writings— the so-called Sibylline books were only the most famous example— and extract a revelation from the ambiguous words and phrases that they found there.

The seers were credited with the ability to wring meaning out of every happenstance, or so we are asked to believe by the ancient historians. Alexander the Great always had an augur at his side, and he was said to heed the augur's readings of what might strike us as random and unremarkable events. A swallow that landed on Alexander's head and then rose again, for example, was said to be a sign that he would survive a conspiracy against his life. An eagle that perched on the railing of a warship predicted victory in an upcoming battle. And when a pair of crows were spotted in a sandstorm in the deserts of Egypt, they were identified as pathfinders sent by Zeus to guide

Alexander to the shrine where he would be hailed as the son of the god.

The most famous soothsayers of all were the strange but powerful women who secreted themselves in shrines and grottoes, put themselves into a deep trance and channeled the eerie voices of the gods and goddesses: the oracles of Eleusis and Delphi, Claros and Miletus, are perhaps the single best example of "the conjunction of an uncanny place and a canny person."[19] Their voices were meant to sound weird and spooky, and their utterances were intentionally vague, thus allowing the hearer to find meaning in bursts of gibberish—the oracles at the shrine of Apollo at Didyma, who worked in a laurel grove enclosed by an elaborate temple, were called "the Grunters."[20]

Indeed, the ancients may not have always been wholly credulous when they beheld one of the oracles as she grunted out the words of a god. The term "Pythia," for example, was originally the title of the oracle at Delphi who was believed to give voice to the utterings of Apollo himself. The name refers to the Python, a dragonlike serpent whom Apollo, according to myth and legend, battled and slew at the site of the oracular shrine. Even in antiquity, however, the word came to be used to identify a stage ventriloquist who threw his voice for the amusement of the crowds.

The Royal Road

More than one form of "information technology" favored by the ancients was also used by enemies of paganism—and many of them are still in use today. Just as Freudians regard dreams as the "royal road" to the revealed wisdom of psychoanalysis, for example, the ancients were convinced that gods and goddesses spoke to both kings and commoners as they slept. Both Constantine and Julian insisted that they had been granted visions and revelations in their dreams, and their claims were perfectly plausible to their contemporaries. Indeed, no single experience of life was freighted with greater or more various meaning in the ancient world than a recollected dream.

Some pagan temples, in fact, were equipped with dormitories where a troubled man or woman would spend the night in the earnest hope that the god would appear in a dream or a vision, a practice that is known by the technical term "incubation." On the advice of the priests, they would fast for days in advance and then sleep in the cured skins of a sacrificed beast, all in the hope of inducing an especially rich and meaningful dream. Back at home, a man might finger the figurine of a god or goddess before going to bed for the same purpose. "Dream-seeking" and "dream-sending" potions were prescribed,[21] and Plutarch preserves the recipe for a concoction of sixteen spices that were burned as incense to encourage such dreams, although modern science has proven that they were not hallucinogenic or even intoxicating.

Artemidorus of Daldis, a kind of a proto-Freudian, compiled a series of dream-books in which he painstakingly records the most intimate details of the dreams reported to him by his contemporaries, and then offers a key to the interpretation of dreams. A dream about Aphrodite in which the goddess appears bare-breasted, he insists, is an omen of good things to come, but the appearance of the goddess fully nude is a bad omen to all dreamers except working prostitutes. And if the dreamer engages in sexual relations with the goddess, the meaning of the omen depends on whether or not the encounter was pleasurable.[22]

What did these earnest seekers want from the gods? A few of them sought nothing less than an epiphany—a physical encounter with the god or goddess—or a revelation of the secrets of the cosmos. But, according to the books of oracles that have been preserved from distant antiquity, a far greater number asked questions that were touchingly ordinary, the same kind of questions that are posed nowadays to tarot readers and telephone psychics: "Will I receive my wages?" "Will I get a holiday?" "Will I be successful" Other questioners were afflicted with even more poignant concerns: "Will I be divorced from my wife?" "Will my son be born with a big nose?" The most dire question turns out to be a highly practical one: "Have I been poisoned?"[23]

One of the less celebrated furnishings of a typical pagan temple helps us to understand the poignance of the encounter between pagan men and women and the deities whose care and comfort they sought. Along with the statuary that depicted the gods and the goddesses in all of their glory, the domed sanctuaries where the priests and priestesses conducted the solemn rituals of worship, and the altars where incense was burned and libations were poured, some temples included an oversized model of an ordinary human ear, fashioned out of plaster or clay or stone. Worshippers were invited to whisper their most intimate questions and their most urgent pleas into the ear—and then they hastened back to their homes, to sleep and perchance to dream.

The God of the Hanged

Of all the supposed sins of paganism, according to the Bible, the primal offense was human sacrifice. "They shed innocent blood, even the blood of their sons and of their daughters," writes the Psalmist, "whom they sacrificed unto the idols of Canaan; and the land was polluted with blood."[24] And archaeological evidence confirms that the offering of human flesh and blood to the gods and goddesses is a practice that dates back to the beginnings of the human race. Human beings, it seems, have always convinced themselves that killing a fellow human being and offering the corpse as a gift is the best way to soothe the anger of a vengeful deity or win the goodwill of a mercurial one.

"[B]lood and violence lurk fascinatingly at the very heart of religion," writes anthropologist and historian Walter Burkert. "*Homo religiosus* acts and attains self-awareness as *homo necans*"—that is, "Religious man" can also be regarded as "Man the killer."[25]

Some of the most common examples of human sacrifice are among the most horrifying and heartrending: the burial of a child in the foundation of a new building, the drowning of a virgin in a river or stream, or the mass cremation of slaughtered babies, all in an effort to please or appease some god or goddess. Such may have been the fate of the two six-year-olds whose blackened skeletons were uncovered at the sanctuary of Gezer or the fifteen-year-old girl whose remains were dug out of the foundations of an ancient building at Megiddo, both sites located in Israel and dated back to the biblical era, or the hundreds of urns containing the charred remains of children that were uncovered at the site of Carthage, which may have been the farthest outpost of the Middle Eastern god known in the Bible as Moloch.

Men and women all over the world have been inspired to perform the same rites, of course, the Incas of South America no less than the Carthaginians of North Africa. Stripped of the ghastly details, however, the underlying transaction was always the same: the goodwill of the gods was purchased at the price of human life. "Human sacrifice," argues anthropologist and philosopher Edward Westermarck, "is essentially a method of life-insurance—absurd, no doubt, according to our ideas, but not an act of wanton cruelty."[26]

One crucial benchmark in the history of religion, of course, is the shift from human sacrifice to animal sacrifice, a phenomenon that can be found in both monotheism and polytheism. The Bible depicts the very moment when God is first shown to express a preference for animals rather than human beings as sacrificial offerings—he demands that Abraham slay his own son, Isaac, and offer the corpse on the altar fire, then changes his mind even as Abraham is holding a knife over his son's throat, finally providing the dutiful Abraham with a ram as a replacement.[27] Thereafter, Yahweh demands only the sacrifice of animal life and the cutting of human flesh in the ritual of circumcision, a practice that may have originated as a surrogate form of sacrifice in which the foreskin of the male infant, rather than the whole child, is offered to the deity.

But monotheism cannot claim a monopoly on the replacement of human beings with animals as acceptable offerings on the altar of sacrifice. According to Greek myth, Agamemnon, who has managed to offend the goddess Artemis by hunting down a stag that she holds sacred, is warned by a soothsayer that the goddess will afflict his army with pestilence and his navy with an unnatural calming of the winds unless he offers his virgin daughter, Iphigenia, as a sacrifice. Agamemnon, just like Abraham, finds the demand to be unremarkable and is perfectly willing to comply. At the last moment, the goddess Artemis—like the God of Israel—spares the young woman and provides a young deer to take her place on the altar fire.

The myth suggests that human sacrifice was already in decline in the Greco-Roman world in distant antiquity. The Vestal Virgins, for example, engaged in a ritual of sacrifice to Vesta, the Roman goddess of the hearth, but they used straw effigies rather than human beings when they symbolically cast thirty sacrificial offerings into the Tiber on the Ides of May. By 97 B.C.E., when the Roman Senate formally adopted a law that criminalized the offering of human victims, animal sacrifice had long before replaced the offering of human flesh and blood to the gods and goddesses of Greece and Rome.

Thus, for example, a hecatomb might be offered to Apollo, one hundred oxen slaughtered, quartered and put to the flames in a single offering, with a few pieces cast on the altar fire as a sacrifice to the high god and the rest offered to the celebrants as a pious feast. More exotic sacrifices depended on the tastes of the particular deity— Artemis, regarded as the protector of women ever since that episode with Agamemnon and his daughter, was believed to favor offerings of eggs, dates or the testicles of stallions. Priapus was thought to prefer a whole donkey. But human flesh was no longer on the divine menu.

Indeed, classical paganism prided itself on its highly civilized rituals of worship. Among the distinctions that the ancient Romans drew between themselves and the "barbarians" who threatened their empire was the *absence* of human sacrifice in their own religious practices. They were as shocked and disgusted as any of the biblical prophets at the tribes of northern Europe, who believed that the high god called Odin preferred to see his sacrificial victims put to death by strangulation and thus dubbed him "the god of the hanged,"[28] or the Celts of Britain, who enclosed their human offerings in wicker baskets fashioned in the image of a god and then lowered the basket into a bonfire. Such pagan luminaries as Pliny and Cicero condemned these practices, and the Roman generals who conquered the barbarians and occupied their tribal lands expended much effort in suppressing the practice of human sacrifice.

Of course, some of the citizens of civilized Rome may have been as reluctant as the "stiff-necked" Israelites to give up the old ways of worship. A century after the first laws against human sacrifice were enacted by the Senate, the emperor Hadrian (76–138) deemed it necessary to issue a new edict against the same practice. "The very laws which the Romans drew up against certain kinds of human sacrifice," observes historian Nigel Davies, "are the surest proof they existed."[29] As late as the third century, the Roman historian Porphyry was still fretting over the occasional lapses: "Who does not know that to this day, in the great city of Rome, at the feast of Jupiter Latiaris, they cut the throat of a man?"[30]

Then, too, some of the most familiar scenes of ancient Rome represent the survival of human sacrifice in a slightly different form. The famous gladiatorial combats in the Colosseum and other arenas all over the Roman empire were, in fact, religious ceremonies in which the victor was understood to dedicate the vanquished to the honor of the gods. Even a common criminal might be seen as a kind of sacrificial victim—if a man were arrested and convicted for the offense of stealing grain, for example, he suffered a death sentence that was understood to be both a criminal penalty and an offering to Ceres, the Roman goddess of agriculture.

But classical paganism cannot be charged with the practice of human sacrifice of the kind that is described in the Bible, and even the offering of animal sacrifice was in sharp decline by the beginning of the Common Era. The imperial cult of ancient Rome was satisfied with ceremonies that required only the offering of wine and cakes or the casting of a pinch of incense on the altar fire rather than the cutting of flesh or the spilling of blood, human *or* animal. Indeed, as we shall see, the emperor Julian was famously heartbroken when he visited a temple of Apollo in the hope of witnessing one of the legendary hecatombs about which he had read in the *Iliad*, which served some of the same functions in classical paganism that the Bible serves in monotheism, and found only a solitary priest chasing a single forlorn goose.

Goddesses and Priestesses

From its very earliest stirrings, of course, paganism envisioned the various deities as both male and female and afforded a place for both men and women in its rites and rituals. Against the Only True God of monotheism—a masculine deity, both a bachelor and a loner—and his exclusively male priesthood, the traditions of polytheism recognized and honored the fact that human beings are distinguished by gender. Some of the most beguiling and beloved of the pagan deities, in fact, were female. The tutelary spirit known as Tyche or Fortuna, who was thought to embody the "genius" and good luck of a city, was regarded as feminine, for example, and so were all the deities of love and fertility: Aphrodite and Athena, Ishtar and Astarte.

Flesh-and-blood women, too, were afforded a crucial and prominent place in paganism. They served as priestesses, presiding over cults that consisted wholly of other women or sometimes men and women alike. Some cults, like that of the goddess Vesta, required priestesses to be virgins, while others, like that of the god Dionysus, restricted the most elevated roles to women who were married. Women participated in many of the pastimes that were dedicated to the gods and thus amounted to sacred rituals—singing and dancing, oratory and recitation, athletic games and contests. Women were initiated into the highest orders of some, if not all, of the mystery cults, and they were granted the power to initiate others into the same mysteries.

Some of these women served in roles that are among the most famous and most familiar expressions of paganism: the Vestal Virgins, for example, who tended the altar fire of the goddess of the hearth; the Pythonesses, who spoke in the voice of the gods at Delphi and Eleusis; and the Sibylline oracles, whose collected writings served as the basic text of pagan prophecy. But others have been wholly forgotten—some nameless women, for example, competed in the games that were dedicated to the goddess Hera as a kind of female counterpart to the ancient Olympiad, and others actually put on armor, picked up a weapon and entered a coliseum to fight as gladiators in the formalized public combat that served as a ritual of worship in ancient Rome. But, far more often, goddesses and priestesses focused on the most basic human experiences—"childbirth, puberty, marriage, serious illness, and death," according to Ross Shepard Kraemer[31]—and the most fundamental human yearnings for comfort and cure.

"Female deities were extolled as healers, dispensers of curative herbs, roots, plants and other medical aids," explains Merlin Stone in *When God Was a Woman*, "casting the priestesses who attended the shrines into the role of physicians of those who worshiped there."[32]

Pagan women were commonly accused of bad motives and bad conduct by both Jewish and Christian sermonizers. If a woman presided over the ritual of worship to a goddess of love, for example, she was condemned as a whore. If she concocted one of the brews and potions that were thought to cure illness and promote conception, she was condemned as a witch. But the priestesses and prophetesses, seeresses and sorceresses, can also be seen as practitioners of something far more benign: "Even the witches of Thessaly, whom people credited with the power of making the moon descend from the sky," allows Franz Cumont, "were botanists more than anything else, acquainted with the marvelous virtues of medicinal plants."[33]

Pagans as Puritans

To be sure, the pagans of imperial Rome indulged in some of the practices that are harshly condemned in the Bible. Prostitutes were readily available, male and female alike, and slave owners were not reluctant to bed down with their female slaves. A Roman patrician might dally without censure with a beautiful young boy, a beautiful young girl or both. Even the sexless were sometimes put to use as sexual objects: "[T]he emperors of the Late Empire employed the services of eunuchs," explains historian Pierre Chuvin, "and sometimes their bodies when they were attractive."[34]

Homosexuality, bisexuality and prostitution all served a dual purpose—they were sources of sexual pleasure and, at the same time, they functioned as a form of birth control, which may have been one reason that they were tolerated. Abortion, too, was available, and the most appalling form of family planning was the exposure of infants—an unwanted baby, especially a baby girl, might be abandoned in some out-of-the-way place and left to die. Abandoned babies were sometimes snatched up and later sold off as slaves—the Greek surname Kopreus, which means "off the dung-heap," was sometimes taken as a sign that its bearer had been abandoned at birth and then rescued.[35]

But paganism had its prudes, too. Pagans in polite society placed a high value on virginity, and women were expected to refrain from sex until they married. Adultery was regarded as a sin and even a crime. One temple in ancient Pergamum, for example, required a worshipper to wait for one full day to pass after having sex with his wife before he was permitted to participate in the ritual of sacrifice— and two full days after having sex with someone else's wife. Tellingly, the dream collector Artemidorus, anticipating Kinsey as well as Masters and Johnson by some eighteen centuries, confirms that men who paid for the services of prostitutes reported that they experienced feelings of shame and remorse and, not incidentally, a pinch on the pocketbook.

Nor were the rituals of worship in classical paganism the scenes of orgiastic excess that are depicted in both religious tracts and Hollywood movies. Priests and priestesses in many of the pagan cults were expected to remain celibate—the virgins who tended the altar of Vesta in ancient Rome were the most famous example but hardly the only one. Indeed, the priests of Isis and Cybele were expected to castrate themselves to remove any possibility of breaking their vows of celibacy. If some of the worshippers of Bacchus or Cybele were prone to public displays of sexual excess, the more refined polytheists were just as scandalized as the monotheists. The Bacchanalia, as we have seen, was banned by the Roman senate precisely because it was regarded as an offense against pagan morality.

Contrary to what we have been encouraged to believe by the teachings of monotheism, the phrase "pagan morality" is *not* a contradiction in terms. The pagans may have been guilty of hypocrisy, praising virginity and fidelity while indulging in sexual adventures of various kinds, but they were no more hypocritical than worshippers of the Only True God who have shown themselves to be equally capable of failing to practice what they preach. Indeed, the moral aspirations and the moral failings of polytheism and monotheism—the longing to lead a decent life in the face of the thoroughly human tendency to do otherwise—were often one and the same. Thus did the pagan emperor Julian echo the prophet Isaiah when he describes the ideal pagan ruler as "one who is just, kind, humane, and easily moved to pity" and one who champions "the poor against those who are strong, dishonest, and wicked."[36]

"The Jews Agree with the Gentiles"

The awkward and ironic truth is that the rituals against which the biblical authors rant and rave bear a striking resemblance to some of the approved beliefs and practices of monotheism as they are depicted in the Bible. What pagans did, as it turns out, was not so very different from what the pious worshippers of the Only True God did.

The prophets and kings who are depicted in the Bible, for example, used the "information technology" of divination to communicate with the God of Israel. Moses, Saul and David are shown to resort to divination by the casting of lots—the mysterious Urim and

Thummim that are mentioned (but not described) in the Book of Exodus, for example, appear to have been the paraphernalia for the casting of lots that yielded yes or no answers to the questions that were posed to the God of Israel. And the worshippers of Yahweh were no less convinced than the worshippers of Apollo that dreams were the likeliest way to receive a divine revelation: "If there be a prophet among you," says Yahweh, "I the Lord do make myself known unto him in a vision, I do speak with him in a dream."[37]

Even magic working is among the practices of otherwise pious worshippers of the God of Israel—Moses himself makes and uses a bronze serpent to cure snakebite, as we have seen, and the curious object is preserved as a cherished relic in the Holy of Holies at the Temple in Jerusalem. Among the otherwise humane and progressive laws that Moses is shown to bring down from Mt. Sinai is one that prescribes a weird ritual of sympathetic magic for determining whether a woman has committed adultery. The priest is to write out a series of curses, wash the ink into an earthen vessel with "holy water" and make the suspected adulteress drink the potion. If she is guilty of the crime, the Bible assures us, "her belly shall swell and her thigh shall rot."[38]

Above all, the daily rituals of blood sacrifice to the God of Israel that are described in such exacting detail in the Torah were very nearly identical to the ones practiced in honor of the gods and goddesses of paganism. Monotheists, like polytheists, favored the offering of animals that were good to eat—oxen, sheep and goats—and the offerings were an important source of sustenance for the men who served in the priestly castes. And the sacrifices carried out by the priests of Yahweh were, if anything, even more frequent and far bloodier than the ones conducted by their pagan counterparts: "Then shalt thou kill the ram," goes one of the passages in the Book of Exodus, describing the duties of the very first high priest of Yahweh, "and take of its blood, and put it upon the tip of the right ear of Aaron, and upon the tip of the right ear of his sons, and upon the thumb of their right hand, and upon the great toe of their right foot, and dash the blood against the altar round about."[39]

The irony was not lost on Julian, the most civilized of pagans and one who delights in taunting the rigorists of monotheism in his own writings: "The Jews agree with the Gentiles except for the fact that they believe in one God," Julian points out in a tract titled *Against the Galilean.* "We have all else in common—temples, sacred precincts, altars for sacrifice, and purifications, in all of which we differ not at all from one another."[40]

Spiritual Overinsurance

The attitude that Julian displays here, so characteristic of the core value of polytheism, was quite as obnoxious and off-putting to the true believers of monotheism as the supposed sins of harlotry, sorcery, idolatry and human sacrifice. Paganism, as we have noted, was "a spongy mass of tolerance and tradition,"[41] according to historian Ramsay MacMullen, a phantasmagoric collection of gods and goddesses, rituals and beliefs, art and iconography, and nothing was alien to it except the very notion of apostasy: "Everyone was free to choose his own credo," explains MacMullen. "[A]nyone who wished could consult a priest, or ignore a priest, about how best to appeal to the divine."[42]

Thus, for example, a pagan might be a devotee of the stately old gods of Rome and Greece whom Homer calls "the Olympians"— Apollo and Zeus, Aphrodite and Athena—and, at the very same time, a worshipper of the Syrian goddess known as the Great Mother, the Persian god called Mithra or the newfangled cult that conjoined the Egyptian goddess Isis and a freshly minted god called Serapis, a conflation of two older Egyptian deities. One famous pagan called Praetextatus, a contemporary of both Constantine and Julian, is described on his epitaph as a proud collector of pagan priesthoods and initiations of all kinds: "high priest of Vesta, high priest of the sun, a priest of Hercules, an initiate of the mysteries of Dionysos and Eleusis, priest and temple guardian in the mystery of Cybele, and Father in the mystery of Mithras."[43] It says as much about paganism as about Praetextatus that he used to joke with the pope that "he might be tempted to become a Christian by the prospect of being Bishop of Rome."[44]

So welcoming was polytheism that even the holiest figures of monotheism were recruited into Greco-Roman paganism. One emperor, who could readily hold in his mind the thought of a supreme god and a whole gang of lesser gods, all living in peaceful coexistence with one another, adorned his private chapel with "statues of Abraham, of Orpheus, of Apollonius, and of Christ," writes Edward Gibbon of Alexander Severus (208–235), "as an honour justly due to those respectable sages who had instructed mankind in the various modes of addressing their homage to the supreme and universal deity."[45]

Even Yahweh, regarded by the strict monotheists who wrote the Bible as the one and only god, was made over into the deity called Iao and given a place among the many gods and goddesses of paganism. The Romans who sought the blessings of the God of Israel meant only to pay their respects to yet another deity whom they had encountered among the colorful and diverse peoples they ruled. Isis of the Egyptians, the Great Mother of Syria, and Yahweh of the Jews were all regarded with both curiosity and a certain measure of awe and fear, and they wanted to make sure that they did not forfeit the blessing of the *right* god by making sure to worship to *all* gods—a practice that the historian Robin Lane Fox describes as "spiritual over-insurance."[46]

An intriguing example of spiritual overinsurance at work in the pagan world can be teased out of a passage in the Christian Bible, where we are given an account of Paul's mission to Athens, the seat of classical paganism. "As I passed by, and beheld your devotions," Paul says of the pagan worship that he witnessed, "I found an altar with this inscription: *To the Unknown God.*" Paul believes that the poor benighted pagans are unwittingly offering worship to the Only True

God, even though they are ignorant of his identity—and he proceeds to reveal it to them: "The unknown God is the one I proclaim to you," declares Paul. "Since the God who made the world and everything in it is himself Lord of heaven and earth, he does not make his home in shrines made by human hands."[47]

No pagan altar has been found with the inscription that Paul describes, but there is an abundance of archaeological evidence for an ever-so-slightly different inscription: "*To the Unknown Gods.*" The inscription that Paul saw in Athens probably referred to "gods" in the plural, thus attesting to the anxiety that prompted the pagans to offer worship not only to the hundreds of gods and goddesses whose names they knew but also to deities who were unknown to them. A sacrifice offered at an altar dedicated to the "unknown gods," as historian Hans-Josef Klauck points out, is like a letter addressed "To whom it may concern."[48]

"Whilst all nations and kingdoms honor their respective gods, the Romans respect the gods of all the others, just as their power and authority have reached the compass of the whole world," boasts the pagan orator Caecilius. "They search out everywhere these foreign gods, and adopt them for their own; nay, they have even erected altars to the *unknown* gods."[49]

But the open-mindedness of the pagan world was regarded by those who worshipped Yahweh as the True God as its very worst sin. It is exactly what Ezekiel means when he likens Israel to a promiscuous woman who "poured out your harlotries on everyone that passed by," and it is what prompted the author of the Book of Revelation to characterize Babylon—a code word for Rome—as "the mother of harlots and the abominations of the earth.[50] By a bitter irony, it was the open-minded and easygoing attitude of paganism that roused the rigorists in both Judaism and Christianity to their hottest and ugliest expressions of true belief.

CHAPTER THREE

TERROR AND TRUE BELIEF

The Jewish King Who Reinvented
the Faith of Ancient Israel

Now go and smite Amalek, and utterly destroy all that they
have, and spare them not; but slay both man and woman,
infant and suckling, ox and sheep, camel and ass.

—1 Samuel 15:3

At certain sublime moments in the Bible, the spirit of toleration
that was the core value of paganism is celebrated by some of the
kinder, gentler biblical authors. The Israelites are commanded
by God not only to respect and protect the "stranger"—a word that
refers to anyone who does not belong to the Chosen People—but to
love him, too. "The stranger who settles with you in your land shall be
treated as the native-born among you," says Moses in the Book of
Leviticus, uttering the very first biblical expression of the "golden rule"
that was later embraced by Jesus of Nazareth. "You shall love him as a
man like yourself because you were strangers in the land of Egypt."[1]

Here we find the deeply empathetic teaching that prompts us to
characterize Judaism, Christianity and Islam as "ethical monotheism." Over the centuries and millennia that have passed since these
words were first recorded in the Bible, all three of the great monotheisms have struggled to put them into practice. And the majority of
Jews, Christians and Muslims in the modern world embrace the values of respect, toleration and compassion that can be found in their
sacred texts. Rigorism and all that it implies—fundamentalism,

fanaticism and religious terrorism—are found only on the ragged fringes of all three faiths.

Still, the worst excesses of monotheism are also plainly and sometimes even proudly recorded in the Bible. Some of the biblical authors adopt a punishing attitude toward the stranger, including all of the peoples of Canaan except the Israelites, and all gods and goddesses whom they worship. And some passages seem to pronounce a death sentence on any man, woman or child who dares to follow any deity other than Yahweh. The most heated and hateful passages of the prophetic writings can be explained away as rhetorical and metaphorical excess, of course, but the equally bloodthirsty accounts that we find in Exodus and Numbers and Deuteronomy, Joshua and Samuel and Kings, are presented as works of history.

If we read the Bible literally, as the rigorists ask us to do, some of the earliest accounts of monotheism depict what is today called genocide, and it is a genocide carried out in the name of the Only True God.

Fear and Dread

"By war, and by a mighty hand, and by an outstretched arm, and by great terrors" is how Yahweh promises to bring the Israelites out of Egypt and into the land of Canaan. "This day will I begin to put the dread of you and the fear of you upon the peoples that are under the whole heaven, who, when they hear report of you, shall tremble and be in anguish."[2]

The military operations of the army of Israel that crosses the frontier of Canaan, as described in the Bible, can be understood as a war of conquest. God is shown to charge the Israelites with the task of defeating the native-dwelling peoples and establishing their own sovereignty by force of arms, and he points out that he is bestowing upon the Israelites not an empty wilderness but "great and goodly cities, which you did not build, and houses full of good things, which you did not fill, and vineyards and olive-trees, which you did not plant."[3]

The war of conquest is also explicitly described as a war of extermination. "You shall save nothing alive," God commands the Israelites, "but you shall utterly destroy them."[4] And the Israelites take
of God at his word: "And we utterly destroyed every city, the men,
and the women, and the little ones," says Moses in the account of one
campaign as recorded in the Book of Deuteronomy. "We left none
remaining."[5]

Above all, the war of conquest and extermination is justified as a
war on paganism. "You shall tear down their altars, smash their images, and cut down their Asherim"—that is, the upright posts or living trees by which the Canaanite goddess Asherah was worshipped.[6]
Crucially, all of the acts of violence carried out by the Israelites are attributed to the God himself. Among the many titles and honorifics
used to describe the God of Israel is *Elohim Yahweh Sabaoth*, which is
usually translated as "Lord of Hosts" but also means "Yahweh, the
God of Armies."[7] Although the soldiers of Israel will actually wield
the weapons of war, they are encouraged to regard themselves as the
instrument of the divine will: "The Lord your God," declares Moses,
"it is he that fights for you."[8]

Priests and prophets, kings and commoners, are shown to carry
out the will of God with the same bloodthirsty zeal against both the
pagans and the Israelites who find the pagan gods so alluring. On the
long march from Egypt to Canaan, for example, a man called Phinehas discovers that an Israelite prince named Zimri has taken a Midianite woman as a lover—and he is inspired to kill both the prince
and his lover with a single spear thrust, a feat that suggests they were
engaging in an act of love, belly to belly, at the moment of their
death.[9] The Bible reports that God is well pleased by his act of zeal:
"Phinehas turned my wrath away from the children of Israel," God is
made to say, "in that he was zealous for my sake, so that I consumed
not the children of Israel in my jealousy."[10]

The same zeal moves Moses to send an army of 12,000 soldiers to punish the Midianites *en masse* for a similar sin on an even greater scale—the women of Midian have lured the men of Israel into their shrines *and* their beds. When the army returns in victory, the commander reports to Moses that every man among the Midianites has been slain, and their women and children taken as prizes of war. Moses, however, is angered by the very sight of the captives: "Have ye saved all the women alive?" he demands. Then he orders that all of the women and male children be put to the sword, too, sparing only the virgin girls and condemning them to a lifetime of slavery.[11]

Not only does God sanction such acts of violence, according to the sternest biblical sources, but he is moved to wrath whenever his worshippers do not carry out his commands with sufficient promptness, precision and ruthlessness. King Saul, for example, is ordered by God to "go and smite Amalek," an ancient tribal enemy of Israel, and the Book of Samuel confirms that he "utterly destroyed all of the people with the edge of the sword"—but Saul, in a moment of *noblesse oblige*, takes it upon himself to spare the enemy king. To punish him for his lack of zeal, God withdraws his favor from Saul and drives him to despair and even madness by refusing to grant him any further oracles. God orders the prophet Samuel to anoint a new ruler of Israel—David, the warrior-king, whom the Bible approvingly describes as both "a man after [God's] own heart" and "a man of blood."[12]

"Defiance of God is as sinful as witchcraft, and stubbornness as evil as idolatry," Samuel scolds Saul, characterizing his decision to spare a single human life as an act of apostasy because God had decreed the death of *all* the Amalekites, man, woman and child. "Because you have rejected the word of the Lord, he has rejected you."[13]

Thus does the Bible provides both the vocabulary and the theological rationale of a new kind of rigorism. Yahweh is a jealous and wrathful god—he is moved to a murderous rage when any other god or goddess is worshipped, whether in place of him or merely in addition to him. Of his own worshippers, he demands not merely faith but zeal—he is not satisfied with good intentions and an earnest effort. Anything less than abject submission to the divine will is as sinful as sorcery and idolatry. And what is God's will? It is to punish "with the edge of the sword," sometimes wielded by a single zealous man and sometimes by a whole army, anyone and everyone who refuses to worship him as the Only True God.

We have a phrase to describe the kind of war that is fought according to these rules of engagement: it is the blight on human history called holy war, and it begins here.

The Man Who Invented Biblical Israel

Whether the wars of conquest and extermination that are described in such gruesome detail in the Bible actually took place is a matter of debate. According to modern biblical scholarship, the Israelites may not have conquered the land of Canaan at all—rather, they may have migrated to Canaan gradually and peacefully, or they may have been there all along. If so, what we are invited to regard as the very first holy war in recorded history is wholly mythical, a work of imagination by one or more of the biblical authors who sought to inspire and motivate the worshippers of the True God.

Indeed, the whole point of such mythmaking would have been to strengthen the idea of "chosenness," to physically separate the Yahweh worshippers from everyone else in the land of Canaan, and to discourage the Chosen People from indulging in the pagan rituals of their friends and neighbors. The most bloodthirsty passages of the Bible, according to the consensus of modern scholarship, can be seen as the handiwork of a faction of fundamentalists that emerged in the seventh century B.C.E. and carried out a bloody purge of Judaism as it was then practiced. If so, they can be understood to have picked up the flag of monotheism where Akhenaton dropped it and to have passed it along to the generations that followed them, all the way down to Roman emperors who achieved the final victory in the war of God against the gods.

The crucial figure in the making of Jewish monotheism, according to the revisionists in Bible scholarship, is the king called Josiah (c. 648–609 B.C.E.), a sixteenth-generation descendant of David, the greatest of all the biblical kings. No less than Akhenaton, Josiah was a visionary and a revolutionary who resolved to repudiate the oldest traditions of the land that he ruled and impose a new set of rituals and beliefs on his subjects. And Josiah was remarkably successful in doing so. According to the latest theories of biblical authorship, the Bible as we know it and the faith of ancient Israel as it is described there were the result of the crusade of religious reform that King Josiah carried out.

Before the reign of Josiah, we are invited to imagine, the majority of ancient Israelites mixed and matched their religious beliefs and practices, just like the pagans among whom they lived, and strict monotheists represented only a tiny minority of the Chosen People. But Josiah rejected the easygoing ways of his fellow Israelites and devoted himself to the worship of Yahweh as the Only True God. He allied himself with the most rigorous of the priests who served at the Temple of Solomon in Jerusalem, and he granted them a measure of power and privilege that they had never before enjoyed.

The tale is told in the Bible itself. Josiah is only eight years old when his father is assassinated, the victim of a conspiracy among his own courtiers, and he ascends the throne as king.[14] Presumably, the boy king rules under the regency of his mother, Jedidah, but the spark of true belief is already burning within him by the age of sixteen, when he wakes up to the spiritual failings of his fellow Israelites and "began to seek after the God of David." At the age of twenty, he commences the first of a series of purges: "He began to purge Judah and Jerusalem from the high places, and the Asherim, and the graven images, and the molten images."[15] Later, at twenty-six, he piously resolves to refurbish the Temple of Solomon in Jerusalem, and he sends carpenters and stonemasons into the ancient shrine to make repairs. At that moment, according to the Bible, Josiah is granted a revelation from on high.

"A Pious Fraud"

The high priest reports to the young king that something remarkable has been discovered in the Temple—a long lost scroll of the Torah. When Josiah opens the scroll, he is so alarmed at what he finds there that he rips his own garments in a gesture of grief and terror. The scroll, as it turns out, includes a set of laws that do not appear in the other four books of the Torah, the only ones known to the Israelites until the discovery of the lost scroll. If the missing fifth book of the Torah is authentic, Josiah realizes, the Israelites have been unwittingly breaking the sacred law of Yahweh for several hundred years.

What are the laws that came as such a shock to Josiah? Most of the text of the lost scroll simply restates the laws that appear in the earlier books of the Torah, including all of the commandments against "that which is evil in the sight of the Lord"—that is, the practices that the Israelites have borrowed from their pagan neighbors. But one point of law is wholly new—the scroll declares that God will accept sacrifice from only a single site in all of ancient Israel, the Temple of Solomon in Jerusalem. Elsewhere in the Bible, of course, it is reported without comment or criticism that altars have been erected and sacrifices have been offered to Yahweh at sites all over the land, ever since the God of Israel first revealed himself to Abraham. But now the Israelites discover that Abraham, Isaac and Jacob, Moses and Joshua, Saul and David, among many others, were defying the sacred law of God when they did so.

Josiah sends the scroll to a prophetess called Huldah for authentification—one of the few instances in the Bible in which a woman is afforded a decisive role in the spiritual life of ancient Israel. The prophetess declares the scroll to be genuine, and so the young king resolves to strictly enforce the new set of laws by, among other things, suppressing the offering of sacrifices to Yahweh at any site except Jerusalem, which happens to be the capital city of his kingdom. Indeed, as it turns out, the newly discovered scroll is perfectly consistent with Josiah's own understanding of what God wants of the Israelites. It is precisely this coincidence that prompted one nineteenth-century Bible scholar to call the lost scroll—which scholars believe to have been most or all of what we know today as the Book of Deuteronomy—"a pious fraud."[16] Fraud or not, however, the scroll allows Josiah to claim that he is acting on specific instructions from God in escalating and expanding the purge that he has been carrying out with such zeal.

The reformer-king orders the destruction of all sanctuaries outside Jerusalem where sacrifices have been offered to the God of Israel in unwitting defiance of the newly discovered laws. Idols and other paraphernalia for the worship of pagan gods and goddesses are dragged out of the Temple and burned down to ash—"all the objects for Baal and Asherah and the host of heaven."[17] The red-light district that has grown up around the Temple, where "sodomites" ply their trade as prostitutes, sacred or otherwise, and women fashion the ornaments and hangings that adorn the pagan shrines, is razed to the ground.

All over the land of Israel, pagan statuary and the altars where they have been put to use, including the ones installed by the anointed kings of Judah, are burned and beaten into dust. Even the shrines erected by King Solomon for the pleasure of his pagan wives and concubines—"for Ashtoreth, the abomination of Sidonians, and for Chemosh, the abomination of Moab, and for Milcom, the detestable thing of the Ammonites"[18]—are pulled down. At the height of the holy war that Josiah conducts within his own realm, all priests who offer sacrifice to any god other than Yahweh are put to death on their own altars.

Judaism as a faith of strict monotheism can be said to begin with King Josiah. His purge "dramatically changed what it meant to be an

Israelite," according to archaeologist Israel Finkelstein and his collaborator, Neil Asher Silberman, in *The Bible Unearthed*, "and laid
the foundations for future Judaism."[19] Thanks to his discovery of the
lost scroll of the Torah that turned out to be the Book of Deuteronomy, Josiah can be said to have added to the Bible a strong measure
of zeal that is quite at odds with those biblical authors who are perfectly willing to show Yahweh siring a brood of randy godlings, Moses
making a magical bronze snake and David keeping a few household
idols on hand.

But King Josiah was more than a religious reformer. The young
king saw clearly how the idea of a single all-powerful god in heaven
implied the appropriateness of a single all-powerful king on earth—
an idea that would continue to exert a powerful appeal for kings and
men who would be kings down through history, including Constantine and his fellow Christian emperors. "One God, worshiped in one
Temple, located in the one and only capital, under one king of the
Davidic dynasty," explain Finkelstein and Silberman, "were the keys
to the salvation of Israel."[20]

The Son of Amon and the Son of Zeus

Josiah's reign was brought to an abrupt end before he reached the age
of forty. The tiny kingdom of Judah was caught between two rival su-
perpowers, Egypt and Assyria, and Josiah sided with the Assyrians.
When the pharaoh and his army crossed through the land of the Jews
on the way to do battle with the Assyrians on the far banks of the Euphrates, Josiah loyally came to the assistance of his ally. At a place
called Megiddo—the site where, according to biblical prophecy, the
apocalyptic battle of Armageddon will take place—Josiah mounted a
war chariot and led an attack on the Egyptians in 609 B.C.E. An arrow
fired by an enemy archer struck him, and he fell from his chariot.

"Have me away," cries the king in the battle report that we find in
the Bible, "for I am sore wounded."[21]

His comrades in arms rescued Josiah and carried him back to

Jerusalem, but he succumbed to his wound. His purge, as it turned out, was incomplete and ultimately ineffective—Jewish kings and commoners alike hastened to take up the very practices of paganism that Josiah had tried to eradicate. Archaeologists at work in modern Israel, for example, have recovered numerous examples of statuary that depict a woman cupping her breasts in her hands—she is believed to be the goddess Asherah, a figure the women of ancient Israel continued to revere, despite the best efforts of their reformer-king.

Within a quarter century after Josiah's death, the dynasty that began with David finally died out and Jewish national sovereignty was extinguished. Jerusalem was conquered by the Babylonians in 586 B.C.E.; the Temple was destroyed and the rest of the ruling class were marched off to Babylon. When the exiles were allowed to return to Jerusalem some fifty years later by the Persian conquerors of Babylon, they regarded themselves as the "Holy Seed" and they insisted on separating themselves from the rest of the Jews who had been allowed to remain behind. The returned exiles, for example, refused to allow the so-called *Am Ha'aretz*—"the people of the land"—to join them in the task of rebuilding the Temple of Yahweh in Jerusalem, where the strict and pure monotheism of Josiah was put back into practice.

Invasion, conquest and exile failed to exterminate the hardy monotheists of the Holy Land. Indeed, as we shall shortly see, the argument can be made that oppression and persecution are the ideal conditions for the flourishing of true belief. Far more dangerous to fundamentalism, as it turns out, are the seductions of peace, freedom and prosperity. And so the faith that survived the destruction of the Temple, the conquest of Jerusalem and the Babylonian Exile was put to its greatest trial when confronted with the changing tide of classical paganism that began with a young Macedonian general called Alexander.

Alexander the Great (356–323 B.C.E.) was so successful in his own wars of conquest that he was famously said to have wept when he ran out of worlds to conquer. But his greatest conquest was achieved without force of arms: wherever Alexander and his armies marched, he introduced his new subjects to the language, philosophy, literature, religion and other institutions of Greek civilization, leaving behind cities and towns in the Greek style that endured long after he was gone. Indeed, Alexander was dead at the age of thirty-three, but he was still revered six centuries later by the Roman emperors, who followed his example in matters of both religion and statecraft.

The Greek culture that Alexander carried around the world is known as Hellenism, and it played the same role in the ancient world that American culture plays in our own. Just as the world covets the weapons, medicines, machines and amusements that America produces, the ancient world aspired to copy the Greek style of dress and manners, arts and letters, athletics and education, weaponry and military tactics. The Greek language, like English today, was the *lingua franca* of international commerce and diplomacy. Above all, the world embraced the Greek pantheon of gods and goddesses and the Greek way of worshipping them. The people whom we call "pagans" called themselves "Hellenes."

The religion of Hellenism was the highest expression of the openness that had always characterized paganism. Alexander may have waged war with cruelty and brutality, and he may have made slaves of those he conquered, but he did not punish anyone for holding a belief in one god rather than another. Indeed, he displayed a lively interest in the gods and goddesses who were worshipped in the lands that he conquered, and he followed the old pagan practice of adding the deities of his new subjects to his own traditional pantheon. Thus, for example, Alexander advertised himself as the begotten son of a god whom he identified with both the Greek deity Zeus and the Egyptian deity Amon. The conflation of gods from two different cultures, the mixing and matching of beliefs and practices, is an example of what historians of religion call syncretism, and it is the essential feature of classical paganism as it was embodied in Hellenism.

Alexander brought Hellenism to the land of the Jews when he replaced the defeated Persian emperor as its overlord. Much to the horror of the Jewish rigorists, the Chosen People promptly showed themselves to be no less vulnerable to the charms and attractions of Hellenism than they had been to the "abominations" of their pagan seducers in distant biblical antiquity. By the second century B.C.E., the city of Jerusalem boasted its own gymnasium, where Jews studied the Greek language and practiced the athletic skills that were put on display in Olympic-style games. Not only did they insist on competing in the nude, aping the traditions of ancient Greece, but some of them resorted to a primitive form of plastic surgery to conceal the fact that they were circumcised—an act that was regarded by the rigorists as the ultimate betrayal of the God of Israel.

We cannot know how Judaism would have fared if the Jews of antiquity had been free to choose between their own traditions of monotheism and the attractions of Hellenism. Then, as now, the lure of assimilation was so powerful that no amount of scolding or sermonizing was effective in preventing defections from the oldest and strictest traditions of Judaism. But, as it turned out, the Jews did not enjoy the freedom to choose between the worship of one god or many gods. Rather, after the death of Alexander and the disintegration of his empire, they found themselves under the rule of a pagan ruler so harsh and so punishing on matters of faith that he more closely resembled a monotheist like Akhenaton or Josiah than any of his fellow pagan kings.

The Mad King

Alexander the Great believed that Hellenism would win the hearts and minds of the people he conquered by its own undeniable superiority and its own powerful allure. But one of the men who inherited a portion of his empire, Antiochus IV (c. 215–164 B.C.E.), lacked the open mind that was the hallmark of Hellenism. He was disgusted and enraged by the stubborn refusal of the most observant Jews—known as the Hasidim ("Pious Ones")—to pay respect to the pantheon of Greek gods and goddesses, and he resolved to impose Hellenism on all of his unruly Jewish subjects by force of arms.

Antiochus looted the gold and silver treasures of the Temple at Jerusalem. He defiled the Holy of Holies—the inner chamber that only the high priest of Yahweh was permitted to enter—by installing a statue of Zeus. He banned the fundamental rites of traditional Judaism, including circumcision, the observance of the Sabbath and the dietary laws of *kashrut*. He forbade the offering of sacrifices to the God of Israel, and he compelled the offering of sacrifices to the gods and goddesses of the Greek pantheon. To make the offerings especially offensive, he commanded that only the animals that Jewish law regarded as ritually impure could be offered to the pagan deities—a pig was to be slaughtered on the holy altar of Yahweh, its flesh was to be eaten in public by the high priest and its offal was to be poured over the scrolls of the Torah.

But Antiochus was not content with merely suppressing the practice of Judaism and compelling the practice of polytheism in its place. Antiochus sent his soldiers into the land of the Jews to carry out a massacre. His death squads sought out the Pious Ones and put them to death—men, women and children alike. Special tortures were reserved for those who were caught with Torah scrolls: "They were whipped with rods," reports the ancient Jewish historian Josephus, "and their bodies torn to pieces." Mothers who dared to defy the royal decree against circumcision were strangled together with their circumcised sons, and the dead child was hung from the neck of his mother, "as they were upon the crosses."[22]

The pagans of the ancient world were capable of inflicting terrible cruelties on their fellow human beings, especially criminals, prisoners of war and conquered peoples. But they did not engage in the kind of religious persecution that Antiochus inflicted on his Jewish subjects. Only rarely did the ancient pagans attempt to suppress the practice of a religion, and even when they did, they displayed a degree of restraint that seems almost quaint from our vantage point. Thus, if the atrocities carried out by Antiochus were an assault on the values of monotheism, they were also a betrayal of the values of polytheism.

The grotesqueries of Antiochus's war against the Jews inspired a subtle act of resistance by his victims. Antiochus had adopted the pious title Epiphanes, which means "the Manifestation of God," but the atrocities that he committed against his Jewish subjects were so senseless that they called him Antiochus Epimanes—"Antiochus the Madman." The moniker reminds us that Antiochus violated the canons of the very civilization that he claimed to champion and thus crossed from mere cruelty into mental aberration.

Zealous for the Law

Even if the account of the conquest of Canaan by the Chosen People as depicted in the Torah is mostly or only a myth, it served its purpose during the reign of Antiochus the Madman. Inspired by the stirring examples of zealotry that they found in the Torah, the Jewish rigorists banded together in a guerrilla army, rose up in open rebellion against Antiochus and eventually inflicted a defeat on both their foreign overlords and those of their fellow Jews who had embraced the pleasures of Hellenism. Significantly, the very first casualties in their campaign were a Syrian and a Jew.

An old man of priestly descent called Mattathias and his five sons, according to a tale that is cherished in both Jewish and Christian tradition, are the first to take up arms. Mattathias has been ordered by a Syrian officer to offer a sacrifice to the pagan god, and when he refuses, a more willing Jew steps forward to comply. "Fired with zeal," Mattathias steps forward and strikes down both the Syrian officer who gave the order and the Jew who was willing to obey it, leaving their dead bodies on the altar of sacrifice. "Follow me, every one of you who is zealous for the Law and the Covenant," cries Mattathias, whose tale is told in the Book of Maccabees. "Thus Mattathias showed his fervent zeal for the law, just as Phinehas had done by killing Zimri."[23]

The author of the Book of Maccabees is reminding his readers of an incident in the Book of Numbers—the slaying of the the Israelite prince who took a pagan woman as a lover. Significantly, Phinehas is the same man who commands 12,000 soldiers of God on a punitive expedition that ends with the mass murder of the men, women and male children of Midian. Thus did the Maccabees take up the tradition of holy war as they found it in the pages of the Torah.

Mattathias and his sons put themselves in command of an army of Jewish partisans and conducted a sustained campaign of guerrilla warfare against the Syrian invaders. The battlefield commander was one of Mattathias's sons, Judah, whose toughness and tenacity earned him the nickname Maccabee ("hammer"), and the Jewish resistance movement came to be known as the Maccabees. Under Judah and his successors, the Maccabees defeated the armies of Antiochus and restored the sovereignty of the Jewish homeland for the first time since the Babylonian conquest in 586 B.C.E.

But the struggle of the Maccabees was more than a war of national liberation—it was also a holy war. They fought against the armies of the Syrian king with the sure conviction that God was on their side, and they enjoyed the tactical advantage that is bestowed upon any soldier who is willing and even eager to die. But the pagan army from beyond the borders was not the only enemy. The Maccabees and their successors targeted not only the Syrian overlords but also their fellow Jews, punishing the Jewish assimilationists and collaborators who were deemed too friendly with the army of occupation.

Among the less celebrated exploits of the Maccabees, for example, was a campaign of forcible circumcision that was directed against any Jew, whether infant or adult, who had neglected the ancient and all-important rite. Some of the Jewish fathers and mothers who failed to circumcise their sons, of course, were merely seeking to spare their lives by complying with the royal decree of Antiochus that criminalized the practice. Others, as we have seen, were seeking to ape the ways of Hellenism and perhaps even to conceal their Jewish origins so they could pass into the pagan world. To the rigorists, however, it

did not matter whether the failure to circumcise was the result of coercion or collaboration—it was an act of disobedience to Yahweh,
and disobedience, as the prophet Samuel put it, is the theological
equivalent of sorcery and idolatry.

No single point of conflict between the rigorists and the assimilationists in Judaism offers a clearer example of what was at stake in
the larger conflict between monotheism and polytheism. Circumcision was an unmistakable and ineradicable sign of membership in
the Chosen People, a sign that is literally carved into the flesh. As the
Jewish rigorists saw it, circumcision at the point of a sword was "not
an act of tyranny," explains historian Steven Weitzman, "but an act
of zeal required to restore the social boundaries between Jews and
Gentiles in the Holy Land."[24] The God of Israel, according to the
strictest practitioners of monotheism, required nothing less of his
worshippers.

The Invention of Holy Martyrdom

The war that the Maccabees fought against Antiochus ended in victory. But, significantly, the Book of Maccabees preserves the memory
of those moments when the worshippers of Yahweh were victims
rather than victors. It is a collection of stomach-turning and
heartrending accounts of the Pious Ones who preferred to perish by
fire or by sword rather than break faith with the Only True God. The
most horrific of these tales shows us the ordeal of a mother who is
forced to witness Antiochus's torture of her seven sons in the hope
that she will persuade at least one of them to comply with the king's
command to taste a morsel of pork. How she responds to the king's
cruel demand marks the beginning of something new and crucial in
the history of monotheism—the invention of the holy martyr.

The author spares his readers no gruesome detail in describing
the ordeal of the Jewish mother and her sons—that's the whole point
of telling the tale in the first place. The seven brothers are beaten with
whips and straps, but they are resolute: "We are ready to die," declares

one of the brothers, "rather than break the laws of our fathers." The outraged king orders that his tongue be cut out, his scalp torn from his skull and his body mutilated. At last, what is left of the young man, still alive, is roasted in a cauldron. One by one, the brothers suffer the same horrific fate until only the youngest remains. The king, maddened by their defiance, demands that the woman use her motherly wiles to persuade her last surviving son to swallow a bite of pork and thus save himself.

She pretends to agree, but when she addresses her son—speaking in her native tongue so that the king will not understand what she is saying—the heroic mother delivers a very different message. "Do not be afraid of this man," she boldly counsels her seventh son before the both of them give up their lives. "Accept death and prove yourself worthy of your brothers."[25]

Here we are witnessing the birth of a tradition that is absent from the triumphal passages of the Torah where Yahweh, the God of Armies, decrees a holy war against the abominations of paganism. It is the Maccabees, insists Rabbi Emil L. Fackenheim, a Holocaust survivor and a contemporary Jewish philosopher, who literally "invented martyrdom."[26] And martyrdom, as we shall see, is the moral counterweight of holy war. The soldier of God may delight in taking the enemy's life, but when the battle turns against him, he must be equally willing to offer his own life, all in the name of the True God. Holy war is the weapon of the powerful and the victorious; martyrdom is the weapon of the weak and the vanquished. Both will be wielded in the war of God against the gods.

The Jewish War

The Maccabees defeated the army of Antiochus in 164 B.C.E. and promptly set up the first independent Jewish state since the last descendant of King David had been dragged from the throne in Jerusalem some four hundred years before. The new Jewish kings are known as the Hasmonean dynasty, a term that derives from Hasmon, the family name of Mattathias, Judah and his brothers. But the new Jewish commonwealth was not the theocracy that the Maccabees had fought to establish. The Hasmonean kings were accommodationists and assimilationists who made their peace with the pagan world of Hellenism, adopting Greek names, titles, dress and manners. By then, both Judah the Maccabee and Antiochus the Madman were dead, and their successors were far more inclined to compromise, thus proving that rigorism in both religion and politics burns so hot that it sometimes burns itself out.

Indeed, the victory of the Maccabees did not erase the old struggle between the Pious Ones and the less rigorous Jews who preferred the pleasures of Hellenism, and a civil war broke out in the little Jewish kingdom in the first century B.C.E. By now, a new superpower dominated the ancient world—the empire of pagan Rome—and each of the warring Jewish factions struggled to win the support of the Roman emperor. But the Romans, who sought to impose the so-called *Pax Romana* ("Roman Peace") on the whole of the known world, refused to be drawn into the treacherous politics of the tiny Jewish state. Instead, a Roman army marched into Judea in 63 B.C.E., conquered Jerusalem and ultimately installed a king to serve as both "King of the Jews" and a client of pagan Rome.

The new king was Herod (73–4 B.C.E.), a man of Arab descent whose family had been converted to Judaism during the reign of the Hasmoneans. Herod had come to the attention of the Roman authorities when, as a provincial governor in the Galilee, he was charged with the task of searching out and exterminating the latest generation of Jewish rigorists who challenged the occupation of their homeland by the Roman legions. He found out for himself that some of the Jewish partisans who had taken up arms against Roman occupation were perfectly willing to martyr themselves in defense of their faith and their country. During one operation, for example, he pursued a band of resistance fighters to a cliffside cave and contrived to lower a few of his soldiers from the cliff top in baskets so they could haul out the fugitives. One man sheltering inside the cave was seen to cut the throats of his wife and children before taking his own life, preferring to die by his own hand rather than surrender to Herod's army.

Herod was no mere puppet king, and he earned the same title that was bestowed upon Alexander before him and Constantine after him: "the Great." His army managed to suppress the Jewish rigorists who still sought a purer form of Judaism and a free Jewish state, and he succeeded in brokering an uneasy peace between his unruly Jewish subjects and his Roman overlords, who followed the customary pagan practice of letting the locals worship as they pleased. A golden eagle, the symbol of Rome, was mounted on the gateway to the Temple, but—quite unlike Antiochus—the Romans declined to defile the inner chambers of the Temple itself with pagan imagery. So deferential were the Romans to Jewish sensibilities, in fact, that a Roman legionnaire who defied the Jewish prohibition against entering the inner courtyards of the Temple in Jerusalem could be put to death for the offense.

"Even the Jews, a wretched people as they are, and separate from all other nations, certainly worship but one God," allows one ancient writer who disdains the theology of Judaism but recognizes something familiar in the Jewish rituals of worship. "Yet they do it openly, they do it in temples, they do it with altars, sacrifices and ceremonies." [27]

The Temple remained the single most important site in Jewish observance, a place where thousands of sheep and goats were sacrificed to Yahweh according to the rituals that are prescribed in the Torah. Herod expanded and enhanced the Temple, enclosing the old structure that had been rebuilt when the exiles returned from Babylon inside a vastly larger construction that aped the architecture of Greece and Rome and was regarded as one of the wonders of the ancient world; indeed, the Temple was a kind of tourist attraction. But the Temple was not the only monument to Hellenism—Herod built amphitheaters and stadiums, baths and gymnasiums, all the facilities that the Greco-Roman culture demanded. Fatefully, he also built for himself a fortified palace in the desert wilderness at a place called Masada.

The Fire Within

After the death of Herod in 4 B.C.E., Rome left his sons in charge of various provinces of his kingdom, but the whole of Judea was now under Roman occupation. The Romans discovered that Jewish resistance was still alive. Just as one person's "terrorist" is another person's "freedom fighter," the Romans called them "brigands" and "bandits," but they regarded themselves as holy warriors in a struggle to restore Jewish sovereignty in the land of the Jews. Just like the Maccabees, they resorted to what we would today call acts of terrorism against both the Roman overlords and those of their fellow Jews who were deemed too friendly toward the occupation authorities.

The so-called Sicarii, for example, were urban guerrillas who adopted the tactic of slipping into a crowded public square in Jerusalem, drawing close to some Jewish collaborator, striking him down with the stealthy blow of a dagger (*sica*) and then disappearing into the crowd again. Precisely because they embraced the old traditions of holy war—like Phinehas and Mattathias, they were "zealous for the Lord"—the ancient Jewish historian Josephus coined a new term to describe the Jewish partisans who resisted the Roman occupiers and their Jewish collaborators. He called them Zealots.

The Zealots rose up in open rebellion against Rome in 66 C.E., a guerrilla army challenging a superpower. For four years, the Zealots and their allies managed to keep the most formidable army in the ancient world at bay. But, unlike the holy war that the Maccabees conducted against Antiochus, the latest war of national liberation ended in defeat. In 70 C.E., Roman legions fought their way into Jerusalem, destroyed the Temple and put to death all but a remnant of the resistance fighters. Perhaps a thousand survivors of the siege of Jerusalem sought refuge in the palace Herod had built for himself in the Judean desert—the mountaintop fortress called Masada—where they held out for another two years. But Jewish armed resistance and Jewish political sovereignty had been crushed by the weight of Roman arms. All that was left was the opportunity for martyrdom.

Masada, of course, is the ultimate and enduring symbol of martyrdom in Jewish history. Surrounded by a Roman army, watching Jewish prisoners at work on an earthen ramp that would allow the legionaries and their siege engines to reach the walls of the fortress and awaiting the inevitable moment of defeat and death, the defenders of Masada chose to slay themselves rather than be slain by their enemies. Or, perhaps more accurately, the most zealous of their leaders made the choice on their behalf. On the night before the final assault by the Roman army, lots were cast to determine who would put nearly one thousand Jewish men, women and children to the sword before taking their own lives.

"[W]hen ten of them had been chosen by lot to be the executioners of the rest," reports Josephus, "every man flung himself down beside his wife and children where they lay, put his arms round them, and exposed his throat to those who must perform the painful office."[28]

The ten executioners drew lots again, and one of the ten was selected to cut the throats of the other nine. At last, only a single man remained alive atop Masada. As his last act of defiance, he set fire to the palace of Herod, "and, summoning all his strength, drove his sword right through his body and fell dead by the side of his family." When the Roman soldiers finally reached the summit of Masada at dawn, fully expecting a last stand by the most zealous of the Jewish freedom fighters, they found only corpses: "Dreadful solitude on every side," as Josephus recalls it, "fire within, and silence."[29]

The Turncoat General

Jewish armed resistance against Rome did not come to a final end at Masada. Another major insurrection against Roman occupation took placed under Bar Kokhba in the second century C.E., and Jewish uprisings on a more modest scale continued to flare up now and then over the next several hundred years. But Judaism was ready to make its peace with pagan Rome. Indeed, the ancient historian who recorded the events of the Jewish War, including the last hours of the martyrs of Masada, offers a good example of the spirit of compromise that replaced the spirit of zealotry that had exhausted itself in the war.

He is remembered as Flavius Josephus, but he was born in Jerusalem about 37 C.E. as Yoseph Ben Mattiyahu. A wealthy and aristocratic Jew of priestly descent, Josephus was called upon to serve as governor general of Galilee, and he was placed in command of a Jewish army at the outset of the uprising against Roman occupation. But he counseled his fellow Jews against making war on Rome, and he surrendered to the Roman general Vespasian after surviving his first and only battle. Notably, Josephus declined to embrace the ideal of martyrdom as espoused by the Maccabees and the Zealots, and he contrived to escape the fate of his comrades in arms, who committed suicide *en masse* rather than be taken prisoner by the enemy.

The turncoat Jewish general put himself at the service of the Roman conquerors. He frankly depicts himself standing beneath the walls of besieged Jerusalem and calling on his fellow Jews to join him in surrender. For changing his colors, Josephus was rewarded with an apartment in the imperial palace at Rome and a life of leisure that afforded him the opportunity to write the histories and memoirs where some of the most crucial events in the history of Judaism and Christianity are recorded. He was exactly the kind of "Hellenized" Jew whom the Zealots would have deemed worthy of death, and yet it was Josephus and not the Zealots who lived to tell about the experience of the Jewish War.

Much of what we know about the Zealots, in fact, comes from the war memoir in which Josephus offers an eyewitness account of the siege of Jerusalem and the destruction of the Temple. He may have set himself against the "brigands" and "bandits" of the Jewish resis-

tance, but he betrays a grudging admiration for the self-willed martyrs of Masada, praising "the nobility of their resolve" and their "utter
contempt of death."[30] Still, the writings of Josephus amount to a kind
of epitaph for the doctrine of holy war that begins in the Hebrew
Bible but now disappears from Jewish history.

"God takes care of mankind," muses Josephus on the futility of a
war undertaken in the name of Yahweh, "but men perish by those
miseries which they madly and voluntarily bring upon themselves."[31]

Josephus was proud of his Jewishness, and he used his writings to
defend the Jewish people and explain Judaism to the pagan world.
And yet, as a former politician and general, he understood the *realpolitik* that now governed the fate of the Jews in the Roman empire. A
Jewish king like Josiah was able to carry out a purge of Judaism only
because he commanded the power of the state. At his decree, rival
sanctuaries for the worship of the God of Israel were closed and
sealed, pagan shrines and statues were burned to ash and any priest
who did not conform to his kind of Judaism was put to death. A Jewish general like Judah Maccabee was able to compel the forcible circumcision of his fellow Jews only because he commanded an army.
The same resources, of course, are required in order to go to war, holy
or otherwise, against a foreign enemy. Once the Jewish state was dismantled and the Jewish army was demobilized by victorious Rome,
holy war was no longer an option.

The Rabbi in the Coffin

Now that the once glorious Temple that Herod had built was only a
pile of broken stones, the sacrifice of animals that Yahweh is shown
to demand in the Torah could no longer be offered. God, as King
Josiah had determined when he found the lost scroll of the law, would
not accept sacrifice from any place other than the one where "the
Lord your God shall cause his name to dwell"[32]—that is, the Temple
at Jerusalem. So Judaism was forced to reinvent itself yet again.

The study of the sacred writings of Judaism—the Bible and, later, the anthology of religious law, legend and lore known as the Talmud—wholly replaced the rituals of blood sacrifice. Rabbis took the place of the hereditary male priests who once served at the Temple in Jerusalem as the spiritual leaders of the Jewish people. "Rabbi" literally means "my master," and a rabbi functioned not only as a prayer leader but also as a teacher, a preacher, a scholar, a judge. Worship could be offered anywhere in the world where a *minyan* of ten Jews gathered.

The revolution in monotheism that followed the destruction of the Temple is summed up in a tale that is told about Yohanan ben Zakkai, a revered figure in the history of rabbinical Judaism. One of his fellow rabbis insists that the Jews are doomed because, now that the Temple is gone, they can no longer atone for their sins by offering sacrifices to Yahweh. "My son, be not grieved," says Yohanan ben Zakkai, who goes on to quote some of the softer words of the prophet Hosea. "We have another atonement as effective as this, and what is it? It is acts of loving-kindness, as it is said, 'For I desire mercy and not sacrifice.' "[33]

Yohanan ben Zakkai, in fact, is the emblematic figure in the new kind of monotheism that constituted the practice of Judaism after the destruction of the Temple. He was a contemporary of Josephus, and he, too, made a separate peace with Rome. Yohanan ben Zakkai smuggled himself out of besieged Jerusalem in a coffin, placed himself under the protection of the same Roman general to whom Josephus surrendered, and asked his captor only for a safe haven where he could establish a rabbinical academy to preserve and study the sacred law of Judaism. Just as Josephus was granted refuge in the imperial palace in Rome, where he wrote his memoirs, Yohanan ben Zakkai was permitted to establish a *yeshiva* at a place called Yavneh, where the writings that constitute the Hebrew Bible were finally canonized in 90 C.E.

So a strictly observant Jew like Yohanan ben Zakkai, no less than a "Hellenized" Jew like Josephus, demonstrates exactly how and why Judaism made its peace with paganism. The call to zealotry is replaced by the celebration of "acts of loving-kindness," and rigorism is confined to the study and observance of religious law. The rabbis whose teachings are collected in the Talmud are *not* Bible literalists or religious fundamentalists: they preserve the passages of the Torah that command a faithful Jew to keep the Sabbath and the dietary laws of *kashrut,* but they overlook the passages that call on a faithful Jew to take up arms against the "abomination" of paganism. The pious rabbi and the turncoat general, as it turns out, adopt the very same stance toward pagan Rome.

"Pray for the peace of the ruling power," advises Rabbi Hanin, one of the contemporaries of Yohanan ben Zakkai whose words are recorded in the Talmud, "since but for the fear of it men would have swallowed each other alive."[34]

The ruling power, of course, was pagan Rome, which had just inflicted upon Judaism its cruelest defeat and greatest humiliation. Perhaps one million Jewish men, women and children died in the Jewish War, a casualty figure that prompts Bible critic Jack Miles to call it "the Roman Shoah" in *Christ: A Crisis in the Life of God.* The land of the Jews was reduced to the status of an occupied territory, and its name was changed from Judea to Palaestina, a reference to one of the traditional enemies of the Jewish people, the Philistines. Jerusalem was renamed Aelia Capitolina, a tribute to the family name of the reigning emperor, and a shrine to Jupiter was erected on the site where the altar of Yahweh once stood. And yet, remarkably, the Roman authorities and the Jewish people found a way to forgive and forget.

"A Craze for Judaism"

The Jews were not universally loved in ancient Rome. Pagans, who were respectful toward the gods and goddesses of the people they conquered, resented the Jewish claim to be the "Chosen People" of the "Only True God." The characteristics of Judaism that pagans found so obnoxious were only reinforced by the rite of circumcision, the dietary laws of *kashrut* and the strict observance of the Sabbath, all of which tended to keep the Jews to themselves. However, for exactly these reasons, Judaism was not regarded as much of a threat to paganism—few Roman men were willing to submit to circumcision, and neither men nor women were eager to give up the banquets for which Rome was so celebrated in order to keep the laws of *kashrut*.

In fact, despite all of these disincentives, the strange new idea of the Only True God began to exert a certain appeal to pagans, who were starting to entertain the notion of a supreme god even within the context of polytheism. Then, too, the pagans were impressed by the fact that the history of Judaism was fully as ancient as their own, and they were intrigued by the Jewish emphasis on the study of the Torah and other ancient texts. Tellingly, the very first translation of the Hebrew Bible into Greek—the so-called Septuagint—had been completed in the second century B.C.E. in Alexandria, the seat of Hellenistic civilization, and its translators had been commissioned by the pharaoh of Egypt, one of the rulers of the former empire of Alexander the Great.

By the first century of the Common Era, Rome was undergoing "a 'craze' for Judaism," as historian and biographer A. N. Wilson puts it in *Paul: The Mind of the Apostle*. Curious pagans who attended Jewish services—the so-called God-fearers—were numerous enough that some synagoges were outfitted with special galleries to accommodate spectators.[35] And the Jews were treated with a marked degree of respect and tolerance when it came to participation in the rituals of emperor worship that had become a kind of loyalty test in the Roman empire—the worshippers of the Only True God were officially permitted to pray *for* the emperor rather than *to* the emperor, a theological nicety that reveals something profound about the capacity of both Judaism and paganism to take a step back from rigorism.

Thus did a certain kind of zealotry pass out of Jewish tradition. The Jewish people, of course, would continue to provide martyrs in terrible abundance. But they would be men, women and children on whom martyrdom was imposed rather than besieged and defeated soldiers, like the Zealots at Masada, who preferred suicide over surrender. And the future martyrs were not victims of paganism; rather, by a terrible irony, their oppressors and persecutors would be fellow worshippers of the Only True God. For now, however, the Jewish people and pagan Rome made their peace with each other, and it was the soldiers of Christ who took up the banner of holy war and carried it into battle.

CHAPTER FOUR

CONFESSORS AND TRAITORS

Pagans and Christians Go to War in Ancient Rome

**All degraded and shameful practices eventually
collect and flourish in Rome.**

—Tacitus

By the first century of the Common Era, just as Rome was reaching the high-water mark of its worldly empire, the classical paganism of Greece and Rome was already in decline. The old gods and goddesses were regarded by sophisticated Romans as the stuff of fairy tales and folklore rather than objects of awe and wonder: "That there is a subterranean kingdom, a ferryman with a long pole, and black frogs in the whirlpools of the Styx, that so many thousand men could cross the waves in a single boat," writes the Roman poet Juvenal about the pagan myth of the underworld, "today even children refuse to believe."[1] Many of the minor deities had been reduced to bloodless and disembodied abstractions such as Victory and Fortune. And so the spiritual appetites that ordinary men and women have always experienced, and still do, went mostly unsated by the stately rituals of the official cults.

But, then, the ceremonies of worship conducted by the priestly colleges were never intended to meet the intimate spiritual needs of the citizenry of ancient Rome. Rather, they were designed to earn divine favor for the Roman empire in all of its power and glory. The proper sacrifices offered in the proper way, it was hoped, would ensure the life and health of the emperor, the safe arrival of grain ships from Africa and victory in battle for the Roman legions against the "barbarian" tribes threatening the border provinces in western Europe and the armies of the Persian empire, the rival superpower on the eastern frontier. What we call religion was regarded by the ruling class of ancient Rome as a civic duty and an essential component of statecraft.

That is why, for example, the *Pontifex Maximus*—the high priest of the state religion of ancient Rome—was the emperor himself. His priestly duties were intended to preserve the so-called *Pax Deorum*, or "peace of the gods," the deal by which the Romans purchased divine protection with the currency of smoke from burning incense and blood of slaughtered cattle. For the ordinary man or woman who sought some kind of comfort from the gods, the high ceremonials of imperial cult had little or nothing to offer. "Never did a people of advanced culture have a more infantile religion," declares the historian Franz Cumont. "In Greece as well as Rome, it was reduced to a collection of unintelligible rites, scrupulously and mechanically reproduced without addition or omissions because they had been practised by the ancestors of long ago."[2]

But paganism is a term that encompasses far more than the worship of the Olympian gods and goddesses who enliven the pages of the *Iliad* and the *Odyssey*. In the backwaters and byways of the Roman empire, a phantasmagorical assortment of odd and beguiling deities were offered prayer and sacrifice, and the rituals by which they were worshipped were as strange and exotic as the gods and goddesses themselves. As Rome conquered new lands and peoples, as the network of Roman roads and the routes of Roman trading ships reached out to link the farthest stretches of the sprawling empire to the imperial capital, many of these new beliefs and practices began to catch the attention of the Roman citizenry.

Rome was the center of gravity of the ancient world, its commercial and diplomatic capital, a rich source of patronage for arts and letters, a market for goods and services of all kinds and a magnet for fortune seekers from every far-flung province of the empire. Rome was crowded with people who brought with them the languages and folkways of countless different cultures—diplomats and traders from all over the ancient world, soldiers and sailors who had served in the remote outposts of the empire and slaves who were imported from conquered lands to work in the imperial capital. The cultural baggage that they carried with them included an astounding array of spiritual beliefs and practices, all of which were offered in the Roman marketplace of religion like so many intriguing baubles.

"Who can tell," muses Cumont, "what influence chambermaids from Antioch or Memphis gained over the minds of their mistresses?"[3]

Soldiers of Christ

Precisely because the oldest traditions of classical paganism seemed so hollow and brittle to so many of the Romans, the acolytes of new and exotic gods and goddesses found an attentive audience. Because many of the most beguiling new faiths originated in the eastern stretches of the Roman empire, they are known in older works of scholarship as "Oriental" or "Asian" religions. Because they promised to reveal to their initiates the divine secrets that are hidden from ordinary human beings, they are also called mystery religions. Among the most provocative—and, for that reason, among the most popular—of the Eastern mystery religions that reached ancient Rome were the cults of the Persian god Mithra, the Syrian goddess *Magna Mater*, the Great Mother of the Gods, and the Egyptian goddess Isis.

But these three pagan imports were not the only "Oriental mystery religions" on offer in Rome. From the newly subjugated province of Palestine came the worshippers of the god called Yahweh, and their insistence on offering prayer to one god alone was so intriguing that their synagogues were crowded with the curious pagans who came to be known as "God-fearers." By the first century, in fact, perhaps 10 percent of the population of the Roman empire was Jewish, and the readership of prominent Jewish authors like Josephus and Philo of

Alexandria, who explained the history and beliefs of Judaism in language that a Hellenist could understand, including the ruling class of pagan Rome.

Nor was Judaism the only monotheism from the Middle East that offered its teachings to the pagan world. In the first century, the practitioners of a new faith that embraced Jesus of Nazareth as a God-sent savior—a figure known in Jewish tradition as the Messiah (literally, "Anointed One")—reached the imperial capital. "Messiah" is translated into Greek in the Septuagint as "*Christos*," and so the followers of Jesus came to be called "Christians." They had started out as one of the dozens of sects and schisms within Judaism as it was practiced in Palestine, but now they insisted that they alone knew the proper way to worship the Only True God.

Here we see the first stirrings of a new kind of rigorism that was ready to erupt into the pagan world. As Christianity emerged from Palestine and spread throughout the Roman empire, the beliefs and practices of the early Christians remained in a state of revolutionary flux. The very idea of Christianity—and, therefore, the organization, leadership and rituals of the Christian church—were something wholly new, and even a theological question as fundamental as whether Jesus of Nazareth was the Son of God or God himself would still be hotly debated by Christians three centuries after his crucifixion. But the one belief shared by all of the early Christians distinguished them from all the other men and women of the Roman empire except the Jews: they were strict and uncompromising monotheists.

Paganism can be likened to a noisy and colorful bazaar where merchants hawk their wares, each one declaring the superiority of the god or goddess whom he or she is offering to the crowd—Apollo or Aphrodite, Mithra or Isis, and countless others, too. They might try to outshout one another, but they do not engage in brawls. The earnest advocates of the Only True God, however, enter the bazaar with the sure conviction that all other gods and goddesses are not merely inferior but counterfeit. Significantly, they call themselves Soldiers of Christ, and they see the encounter between monotheism and polytheism not as a competition of ideas and values in the marketplace of religion but as nothing less than a holy war.

"Call Me by My True Name"

All the so-called mystery religions, whether they advertised one god or many, appealed to the jaded spiritual appetites of pagan Rome with novel, colorful and highly provocative rituals and beliefs. All of them sought to restore a sense of mystery to the practice of religion. They did not neglect the intimate and practical concerns that moved their congregants to prayer—happiness in marriage, healing of illness, safety while traveling, a full purse and a full belly—but they also offered answers to a question that has always plagued humankind: How can a mortal man or woman secure the favor of the invisible power that rules our fate? Above all, they all held out the tantalizing and even thrilling opportunity of achieving, if only for a moment, a direct encounter with the divine.

The worshippers of Mithra, for example, were initiated into their new faith in the ritual of the taurobolium, a so-called baptism of blood that reenacted a key event in the myth that had been imported from Persia along with the god himself—the slaying of a sacred bull by Mithra. The initiate was conducted into an underground shrine in which a wooden platform had been erected; a bull was made to stand on the platform, and the initiate stood beneath it; when the bull was sacrificed to Mithra by the priest, its blood poured down through an opening in the floor of the platform and literally showered the initiate. The "red baptism," as Franz Cumont describes the ritual of the taurobolium, was not meant to promote the health of the emperor or the security of the empire.[4] Rather, it was an act of personal salvation, and the initiate who underwent the ritual of the taurobolium was believed to experience "the new birth to eternal life."[5]

The taurobolium was also employed in the worship of the *Magna Mater*, a goddess of love and fertility who had been imported from Phrygia in Asia Minor in the late third century B.C.E. and granted a place in the pantheon of Hellenism—she was dubbed Rhea by the Greeks and Cybele by the Romans. According to one version of the myth that came to be associated with Cybele, the goddess fell in love with a young shepherd called Attis and sought to prevent his marriage to a mortal woman by sending him into a frenzy of desire for Cybele on his wedding day, but he frustrated her efforts by committing suicide in an act of self-emasculation; the grief-stricken goddess then prevailed on the high god Zeus to restore Attis to life. The ritual of initiation into the cult of Cybele included a period of fasting, followed by the consumption of libations with high alcoholic content and, finally, a spell of music, drumming and dancing. At the climax of the ritual, the most frenzied celebrants castrated themselves with axes or swords in imitation of Attis, thus performing what historian Jocelyn Godwin delicately calls "the irreversible act."[6]

A less delicate account of the same bloody spectacle is provided by James Frazer, who allows us to see exactly how and why the mystery religions appealed to a citizenry that was jaded and bored by the formulaic rites of classical paganism. "While the flutes played, the drums beat, and the eunuch priests slashed themselves with knives," he writes in *The Golden Bough*, "the religious excitement gradually spread like a wave among the crowd of onlookers."[7]

Man after man, his veins throbbing with the music, flung his garments from him, leaped forth with a shout, and seizing one of the swords which stood ready for the purpose, castrated himself on the spot. Then he ran through the city, holding the bloody pieces in his hand, till he threw them into one of the houses which he passed in his mad career. The household thus honoured had to furnish him with a suite of female attire and female ornaments, which he wore for the rest of his life.[8]

A third mystery religion that came to Rome—perhaps the most successful of them all—was the cult of Isis and Serapis, which began in Egypt and spread all over the empire. Isis, of course, was a prominent and powerful member of the pantheon of ancient Egypt. According to sacred myth, Isis restores life to Osiris, her brother and lover, after he has been murdered and dismembered by a third sibling called Seth. Isis gathers up all of the body parts except the penis, which she replaces with a prosthetic device fashioned out of wax and spices, and restores her dead sibling-lover to life. By tradition, each reigning pharaoh was regarded as the living embodiment of the son of Isis and Osiris, the demigod called Horus.

After the conquest of Egypt by Alexander the Great, however, one of his successor-kings seized upon the myth of Isis and Osiris and made it over into a Hellenistic cult. The beguiling Isis survived intact, but Osiris was conflated with another Egyptian god and transformed into a new deity called Serapis. "We need not wonder, then, that in a period when traditional faiths were shaken, when systems clashed, when men's minds were disquieted, when the fabric of the empire itself, once deemed eternal, began to show ominous rents and fissures," writes Frazer, "the serene figure of Isis should have appeared to many like a star in a stormy sky, and roused in their breasts a rapture of devotion not unlike that which was paid in the Middle Ages to the Virgin Mary."[9]

These three mystery religions are all examples of syncretism at work, the mixing and matching of religious beliefs and practices that was the hallmark of high paganism. The taurobolium was borrowed from the worship of the Great Mother and put to use in the worship of Mithra. The cult of Isis and Serapis was an act of pure invention, the mating of an ancient Egyptian goddess with a hybridized Hellenistic god. The Great Mother originated in Phrygia but, as we have seen, she was identified with the Greek fertility goddess called Rhea and her Roman counterpart, Cybele. In fact, *all* of the many goddesses of sex, love and fertility whose worshippers were found in the backwaters and byways of the ancient world were eventually hailed in some pagan circles as incarnations of one great goddess.

The universality of Isis is affirmed in *The Golden Ass*, a rather bawdy work of literature dating from the second century C.E., and one of the precious few examples of pagan writing that survived the Christian censorship of pagan texts after the triumph of Constantine. The tale is told by a young man who is turned into a donkey by a sorcerer and then restored to human form by a savior-goddess. In a passage that shows exactly how syncretism worked in the ancient world, the goddess catalogues her many names and guises before revealing her true identity.

> [T]he Phrygians call me Mother of the Gods. The aboriginal races of Attica call me Minerva. The Cyprians call me Venus. The Cretans call me Diana. The Sicilians call me Proserpine. The Eleusinians call me the ancient goddess Ceres. Some call me Juno. Some call me Bellona. Some call me Hecate. But those who are enlightened by the earliest rays of that divinity the sun, the Ethiopians, the Arii, and the Egyptians, who excel in antique lore, all worship me with their ancestral ceremonies and call me by my true name, Queen Isis.[10]

Roman paganism was proud of its willingness to honor the vast array of gods and goddesses as equally authentic expressions of divinity: "The Romans respect the gods of all the others," affirms Caecilius, "just as their power and authority have reached the compass of the whole world."[11] But it is also evidence of a movement in the direction of monotheism that was already in progress in the pagan world when it first encountered Judaism and then Christianity. One could readily imagine a convergence of monotheism and polytheism if only the easygoing pagans of antiquity had been allowed to find their own way to the worship of one high god. Indeed, some of the oldest and most civilized traditions of paganism had already arrived at a kind of monotheism of their own.

Philosophers and Jugglers

Yet another voice that could be heard, quite literally, in the market-place of ancient Rome belonged to the philosopher. Nowadays, philosophy has come to be regarded as an intellectual pastime that has little to do with the practice of religion—and nothing at all to do with real life. But the philosophers of pagan antiquity were the functional equivalent of what we would today call theologians: they pondered the beginning and ending of the world, the nature and destiny of humankind, the identity and will of the divine. For the same reason that some of the ancients found more spiritual meaning in the mystery religions than in the staid ceremonies of the official cults, others placed themselves under the tutelage of philosophers who offered to reveal the arcane secrets of the cosmos.

Philosophy was fully as diverse as any other expression of paganism. Just as one might worship one or another of the many gods and goddesses, one might study and practice the teachings of the Stoics or the Epicureans, the Skeptics or the Cynics, the Peripatetics or the Pythagoreans or the Platonists. And, like the mystery religions, the philosophers offered something that the priests in the official cults ignored—a concern for the happiness and fulfillment of the men and women who placed themselves under their tutelage. "[T]hey specialised in an activity that one could call in modern language pastoral care, life counseling or psychotherapy," explains historian Hans-Josef Klauck.[12]

While the *Pontifex Maximus* and the lesser priests and priestesses of the official cults called upon the old gods and goddesses of the Greco-Roman pantheon to preserve the empire, the philosophers were offering advice to ordinary men and women about how to live a decent life. Here is another example of the moral and ethical concerns that were among the core values of classical paganism—the philosophers instructed their followers on "what is honourable and what is shameful, what is just and what is unjust," according to one ancient orator, "how a man must bear himself in his relations with the gods, with his parents, with his elders, with the laws, with strangers, with those in authority, with friends, with women, with children, with servants."[13]

The most accomplished philosophers held forth in the academies, the houses of wealthy patrons or the royal court—King Philip of Macedon set the standard when he engaged Aristotle as the tutor for his son, the future Alexander the Great—but others plied their trade in public, wandering from town to town and collecting the odd coin in an outstretched bowl. Bearded, cloaked in a toga and holding a staff—the standard iconography of a working philosopher—they would deliver their oratory at the gates of a pagan temple, in the public baths or amid the bustle of the marketplace. Not unlike a stand-up comic, a philosopher had to work the crowd and cope with hecklers: "What, is a juggler coming on?" was one common taunt as reported by an ancient source.[14]

Some of the most colorful trappings of paganism were regarded with skepticism and even contempt by the most sophisticated philosophers. The gods and goddesses of myth and legend, so prone to sexual adventure and other human passions, were already something of an embarrassment. So was the belief that the deities routinely revealed themselves to ordinary human beings, a notion that was openly ridiculed by pagan philosophers even before it was lampooned in the Christian Bible in a scene where Paul and Barnabas are mistaken for Mercury and Jupiter by a crowd of benighted pagans.[15] "Plato complained of Homer's support for such absurdities," observes historian Robin Lane Fox, "and was inclined to see them as a particular delusion of women."[16]

Indeed, philosophy was already moving toward what we would today call ethical monotheism. All of the gods, goddesses and godlings of paganism, some philosophers suggested, ought to be understood as fanciful ways of describing the various attributes or manifestations of a single high god—the "Great Ruler of Intelligent Beings," as Plotinus (c. 205–270) dubs the deity.[17] "[I]t makes no difference," insists Celsus, writing in the first century of the Common Era, "whether one calls god Zeus or Adonai or Sabaoth or Ammon such as the Egyptians do."[18]

Just like Akhenaton, the world's first monotheist, some polytheists adopted the single brightest object in the sky as an austere and elegant symbol for the supreme divinity—King Helios ("Sun King") or *Sol Invictus* ("Unconquered Sun") came to be used in some pagan circles to identify the high god, and figured importantly, as we shall see, in the lives of both Constantine and Julian. "If the sun is the ruler of the other lights of the heavens," reasoned one ancient philosopher, "the sun must then be the lord and author of all."[19] Above all, the pagan moralists insisted that the supreme deity demanded that ordinary men and women strive toward goodness as well as godliness: "Without real moral strength," insists Plotinus, "*God* is only a word."[20]

The Philosopher and the Magus

One school of philosophy, however, was not content with such abstract and elevated notions. Like the priests of the mystery religions, the practitioners of a school of philosophy that came to be known as Neoplatonism offered something far more thrilling, a potent blend of mystery and philosophy that originated in Alexandria and soon reached Rome. Echoing ideas that were first expressed by Plato in the fourth century B.C.E., the Neoplatonists taught that mortal human beings possessed a divine soul that was capable of achieving union with the "One Supreme Being."[21] But they, too, were syncretists, and they borrowed much of the mysticism and magic that suffused the other mystery religions of Rome.

Along with a single high god, for example, the Neoplatonists believed in the existence of a vast but invisible population of demigods, some good and some evil, a concept borrowed from the elaborate system of angelology and demonology that originated in Persia. They taught that the power of the god on high could be invoked for practical purposes down here on earth by use of "theurgy," a kind of white magic that was attributed to the Chaldeans of the ancient Near East;

indeed, the word "Chaldean" was now a synonym for "magician." They also engaged in mystical rituals that were designed to send the participants into a state of ecstasy and thus provide them with insights into the secrets of the cosmos or even a glimpse of the divinity.

Neoplatonism, then, engaged in practices that were as eerie as anything offered by the imported mystery religions—a "strange mixture of lofty speculation and superstition," according to historian Samuel Dill.[22] Although it was later hailed as "the 'highest' and most philosophical variety of paganism," according to historian Diana Bowder, its rituals can be seen as "really nothing more than an exalted and exotic form of magic."[23] And yet, precisely because it catered to the human appetite for mystery and ecstasy, Neoplatonism was a powerful competitor in the pagan world—"a world tantalized by a belief that some men at least had seen God and had found in the vision the sum of human happiness," as historian K. E. Kirk puts it, "a world aching with the hope that the same vision was attainable by all."[24]

"Neither Jew nor Greek"

When the Roman historian Tacitus (56–c. 120) complains that "[a]ll degraded and shameful practices eventually collect and flourish in Rome," he is referring to not only the strange kinds of polytheism that came from Egypt and Phrygia and Persia, but also the even stranger kind of monotheism that came from the unruly Jewish province of Judea—the so-called Christians.[25]

At first, the followers of Jesus were only one of the many "Judaisms" of the ancient world—the Talmud counts twenty-four Jewish sects and schisms during the period of Roman occupation, most of which are now only historical curiosities. And the same fate might have befallen the first Christians if they had remained a sect within Judaism. But the Christians, still small in number but already diverse in opinion, soon began to fight among themselves; one faction insisted that anyone who wished to embrace the teachings of Jesus must embrace the Jewish faith, too, and the other faction insisted with equal fervor that it was unnecessary to convert to Judaism in order to call oneself a Christian.

The defining moment came when the two factions argued over the fundamental question of whether to require pagan converts to Christianity to undergo the ancient Jewish rite of circumcision and to comply with the strict dietary laws. Such practices had always tended to keep the Chosen People apart from the pagans among whom they lived, which is precisely what they were intended to do, and thus reassured the Roman authorities that Jewish monotheism did not pose a threat to polytheism; after all, who would voluntarily submit to circumcision and forgo the pleasures of the banquet table? Now the followers of Jesus debated the same question among themselves—how could they carry the "good news" about Jesus to the pagans if, at the same time, they were obliged to deliver the bad news about the burdens that Judaism imposed on its converts?

The debate among the first Christians, as reported in the Christian Bible, turns on the old issue of rigorism. James, the brother of Jesus, refuses to sit down at the dining table with non-Jews who do not observe the Jewish dietary laws. Paul, by contrast, regards the rites and rituals of Judaism as an affliction—"Christ," he argues, "has redeemed us from the curse of the Law"—and he recognizes that the old ways must be discarded if the Christians hope to win converts outside Judaism. Paul prevails over the "Judaizers," as they came to be called in Christian tradition, and he is set free to preach the new faith without having to explain why a pagan needs to be a good Jew before he can be a good Christian.

Paul was born a Jew, but he revolutionized early Christianity by carrying it far beyond the confines of the Jewish world: "There is neither Jew nor Greek, there is neither bond nor free, there is neither male nor female," he famously announces, "for you are all one in Christ Jesus."[26] Paul's missionary travels amount to a grand tour of the eastern Roman empire, and his last stop is the imperial capital. The final destination is crucial and fateful—Paul, who boasts of his

Roman citizenship, regards it as his sacred duty to win converts among the pagans in Rome itself.

"As you have testified of me in Jerusalem," God is shown to instruct Paul, "so must you bear witness also at Rome."[27]

Paul and his fellow missionaries discovered that Rome's willingness to tolerate and even embrace strange new gods and goddesses, an old and honorable tradition in paganism, did not extend to the Only True God. Indeed, pagan Rome was offended by the Christian claim that the deities of the Greco-Roman pantheon were not merely inferior to the Christian god, not merely false gods, as the Jews claimed, but demons in disguise: "The things which the Gentiles sacrifice," insists Paul, "they sacrifice to devils."[28] Thus provoked by the uncompromising zeal of the Soldiers of Christ, according to Christian tradition, the Roman authorities arrested Paul and sentenced him to death during the reign of the emperor Nero. Ironically, one of the privileges that Paul enjoyed as a Roman citizen was immunity from crucifixion; therefore, he was beheaded.

While Rome Burned

Jesus and his followers went largely unnoticed by the ancient chroniclers who were at work in pagan Rome during the period that is described in such detail in the Christian Bible. Josephus, for example, makes only a passing reference to "Jesus, a wise man, if indeed one ought to call him a man," and the authenticity of even these few words has been the subject of hot debate among scholars for several centuries. Suetonius (c. 69–c. 122), the Roman biographer and historian, was so unfamiliar with the Christians that he seems to have been under the impression that Jesus himself was living in Rome and stirring up trouble in the Jewish neighborhoods in the middle of the first century C.E.

But the Christians passed into the bright light of history in 64 C.E., when a fire of suspicious origin raged through the imperial capital and Nero cast about for someone to blame for starting it. The emperor himself was suspected of the deed, accused of fiddling while Rome burned, and he tried to deflect the accusations by casting suspicions on another culprit: the tiny, obscure and powerless community of Christians that had only recently appeared in Rome. Until Nero called attention to them, in fact, the only violence that touched the Christians in Rome were the occasional fisticuffs with the Jews, a settling of old theological scores by two communities that both claimed to worship the same god.

Now Nero singled out the Christians and decreed that they should be punished. According to secular historians, however, the punishment had nothing to do with their strange new faith. Nero was familiar with the fabulous array of exotic rites and rituals that were on display in Rome—his own wife was reputed to be one of the "God-fearers" who attended services at the local synagogues—and he was probably untroubled by the religious practices of a sect as small and obscure as the Christians. Rather, the pagan emperor condemned the Christians as common criminals, guilty of the crime of arson, and he sentenced a few of them to the standard penalty for arson in Roman law, death.

Some of the Christians were crucified, a form of capital punishment that was commonly used throughout the empire. Others were bound in the skins of wild animals and sent into the gladiatorial arenas, where the crowds watched as they were attacked by packs of hungry dogs. A few were put to more exotic forms of torture and death in the gardens of Nero's imperial palace—they were sheathed in leather, painted with pitch, hung from crosses, and set afire, thus serving as human torches to illuminate a garden party hosted by the emperor. But their deaths started a very different kind of fire—Christian tradition sees them as the first casualties in a holy war against paganism, the first Christian men and women to suffer martyrdom in the cause of the Only True God.

The Peace of the Gods

Once Nero chose to blame the Christians for the burning of Rome, they became the object of ever closer scrutiny by the imperial authorities. What troubled the pagan magistrates was not their theology or their religious practices—far stranger rites, as we have seen, were tolerated and even embraced by pagan Rome—but their stubborn refusal to participate in the rituals of worship that were regarded as the civic obligation of every loyal citizen of the Roman empire. As the pagans saw it, the *Pax Romana* depended on the *Pax Deorum*, and the "peace of the gods" depended on paying the proper respect to the old gods and goddesses. By shunning the imperial cult, the Christians were calling their own patriotism in question, and the pagan authorities regarded Christianity as a security risk.

After all, the pagans reasoned, the rituals did not require much of an effort—a few grains of incense cast on the altar fire or a few words of prayer uttered before the image of the deified emperor were sufficient to discharge one's civic duty. As long as the gesture was made, as long as respect was paid to the old gods, one was perfectly free to worship the deity of one's own choosing. Since the Christians insisted that they were *not* Jews, they did not enjoy the dispensation that had been granted to the Jewish community, and so they were expected to do their part to preserve the *Pax Deorum* like every other Roman citizen. More than a few Christians, in fact, did what was expected of them in public and then retreated to the home churches where they prayed privately and discreetly to the Only True God.

But the old rigorism that is written so deeply into the Bible stirred the true believers in Christianity as it had once stirred the Maccabees and the Zealots. They regarded a few grains of incense or a mumbled prayer offered to the pagan gods not as a gesture of civic virtue but as an act of apostasy and betrayal. The most zealous among them saw it as their solemn duty to make a public display of their faith even if it meant arrest, torture and death—significantly, the original meaning of the Greek word "martyr" is "witness." A few of the Soldiers of Christ actively sought martyrdom by charging into the shrines and temples of the pagan gods, smashing the statuary and overturning the altars, as they were instructed to do by their own scriptures: "You shall break down their altars, and dash in pieces their pillars, for the Lord is a jealous God."[29]

The offense that the Christians committed against Roman law and tradition was not called or punished as heresy—the whole vocabulary of true belief was alien to paganism. Rather, the Christians were suspected of subversion and treason, and they were accused of acts against public order and civic virtue. A Christian could escape arrest and punishment by turning over his Bible and offering a sacrifice to the gods, thus demonstrating his loyalty and good citizenship. Still, the most pious pagans were outraged by the theological rationale of Christianity, and they roused themselves to a certain rigorism of their own in defense of the *Pax Deorum*. Like true believers in monotheism, the persecutors of the Christians coined a new word to describe those who denied the very existence of the old gods and goddesses—the Christians were condemned as "atheists."

The Shameless Darkness

Christian "atheism" excited rumor and speculation among the pagans, who were baffled by what Christians believed and curious about what Christians did. The atrocity propaganda that was directed against Christianity was all the more plausible because monotheism itself was such a strange idea in the pagan world. After all, if a man or woman was capable of publicly denying the thousand-year-old traditions that had established and preserved the culture of Hellenism and the Roman empire, what else might he or she do in secret?

The mystery was only deepened by the fact that Christian rituals were, by legal and practical necessity, conducted in private. The Christian church was not recognized as a corporate body by Roman law and thus could not own property, and so Christians were forced to use private residences as their gathering places. Later, when Christians found themselves at risk of arrest and imprisonment for the practice of their faith, they were even more secretive—Christian services took place only in hidden rooms and only during hours of darkness. And so, ironically, the pagans suspected the Christians of the same acts of sexual excess and bloody human sacrifice that so obsessed the biblical prophets.

"[T]hey make love together before they know one another," goes one especially agitated pagan tract, "for there is a certain amount of lust mixed up with their religion, and they promiscuously call themselves brothers and sisters." Their rituals of worship were said to include "reverencing" the genitals of their priests, and a jackass "is most improperly consecrated to I cannot imagine what kind of worship." After feasting and drinking, "[p]eople of every age and sex . . . couple in abominable lust in the shameless darkness." At the most horrific moment in the initiation ceremonies, a sacrifice is offered in a "suitably corrupt and vicious way" to Jesus of Nazareth, "a man punished for his crimes by the supreme penalty":[30]

> A baby is smothered with flour and . . . offered to one to be initiated, who kills it with blows on the floury outer surface. They lap the blood up thirstily and eagerly share out the limbs.[31]

Demonizing one's theological adversaries begins in the Bible, as we have seen, but it can be found in paganism, too. Such slanders are what provoked the official campaign against Christianity, and they were later used to justify even the worst atrocities against the Christians. The gruesome garden party that took place in Nero's palace, where Christians were burned alive as human torches, is recalled as the first persecution of Christianity by pagan Rome. And Christian tradition counts a total of ten persecutions, ending only with the so-called Great Persecution conducted by the emperor Diocletian (245–316) in the opening years of the fourth century.

Combs and Seashells

Roman justice was notoriously cruel, and accused criminals were routinely tortured, sometimes to extract a confession, sometimes as a
form of punishment and sometimes just to satisfy the impulse to inflict pain that is, sadly, one of the characteristics of the human species.
A man might be scourged with whips, his bones shattered with rods,
his eyes gouged out with hooks. He might be flayed until he was literally skinned alive, or his skin might be scraped off with iron combs or
the sharp edges of seashells. Many of the implements of torture that
figure so prominently in the practices of the Holy Office of the Inquisition were first invented and perfected in pagan Rome.

Indeed, the principal method of capital punishment under
Roman law, crucifixion, was essentially a kind of torture that was
specially and ingeniously designed to make a public display of the
whole process. Once nailed or tied to the cross, the victim was allowed to hang for days. If he appeared too comfortable, he might be
poked or slashed with a spear, but if he appeared likely to die too
soon, his executioners would refresh him with a beverage in order to
prolong his suffering. At the end, the weight of his own body would
make it impossible for the victim to breathe, and he would die slowly
of asphyxiation. For the crucified, death was a welcome relief.

Criminals who were spared the death penalty and survived the
torture sessions might be put to work in mines or galley ships. They
might be confined in prison or exiled to some especially unwelcom-
ing backwater of the Roman empire. They might be branded on the
forehead, outfitted with an iron collar or draped with heavy chains.
Their goods might be confiscated and—under some circumstances—turned over to the informers who carried the accusations to
the imperial authorities in the first place. And the conduct that put an
ancient Roman at risk of punishment included not only petty theft
and other minor crimes but such private moral lapses as adultery and
seduction.

A Christian might suffer any or all of these afflictions if he or she defied the imperial order to make an offering to the gods or refused to surrender a cherished copy of the Bible. But the tortures that were inflicted on the Christian martyrs were even more sadistic—or so we are asked to believe by pious Christian sources. The atrocities that are preserved in the Book of Maccabees, where the tradition of martyrdom begins, are far exceeded in sheer gruesomeness by the hagiographers who describe the ordeal of the Christian martyrs for the edification and inspiration of their fellow believers.

The Christians and the Lions

A Christian martyr, we are told, might be made to seat himself on an iron chair or stretch out on an iron bed that had been heated until it glowed red, thus roasting to death for the amusement of the pagan executioners. Molten lead might be poured down the throat or funneled into another and even more sensitive bodily orifice. A victim, male or female, might be sawn in half, or tied up in a bag and thrown to the bulls, or slowly carved up into tiny morsels that would be tossed to a caged beast. One old bishop was smeared with honey, suspended in a cage and exposed to a swarm of wasps that slowly stung him to death.

Other accounts of martyrdom as preserved in Christian tradition are faintly pornographic—virgins were dragged to temples of Venus and offered the choice of either sacrificing to the goddess of love or submitting to forcible rape on her altar. The ordeals of Christians who were, quite literally, thrown to lions are rendered with heart-tugging but heroic details—when a highborn Roman matron called Perpetua and her slave-girl, Felicitas, were sent into the arena to be ravaged by wild beasts, for example, the crowd could plainly see that "one was a delicate girl, the other fresh from childbirth with her breasts still dripping with milk."[32] And the pagan spectators who crowded into the coliseums and circuses of ancient Rome are said to have been as bloodthirsty as the beasts and the gladiators:

"Well-washed, well-washed" was the sarcastic cry that went up in the arena when Christian blood began to flow, a phrase that was customarily used as a friendly greeting in the public baths.[33]

The pagans, we are asked to believe, were provoked into such outrages by the courage and conviction of the willing Christian martyrs. Ordinary torture was not enough to satisfy their blood-lust—the Romans set their practical skills and their sadistic imagination to the task of devising new and ever more terrible ways of tormenting and murdering their enemies, and all because they were so addled and demon-ridden that they failed to recognize the self-evident truth of the Christian faith in the Only True God. But it is also true that the Christians had learned the propaganda value of martyrdom from the Jewish zealots who were the authors of the Book of Maccabees—if the human imagination is capable of devising ever more sadistic tortures, the human heart is stirred to ever greater passion by the example of such atrocities. Significantly, the most ardent of the new converts to Christianity submitted to baptism during the hottest periods of persecution.

"Horrid and Disgustful Pictures"

Whether the gruesome accounts of Christian martyrdom are works of history or works of propaganda, however, is still an open question. Writing in the late eighteenth century, Edward Gibbon was already suggesting that the most bloodcurdling examples of torture originated in the imaginations of monks who sat safely in their cells and entertained themselves by inventing "extravagant and indecent fictions."[34] Few of the details that decorate ancient Christian writings can be confirmed in the pagan histories that have survived, and secular historians ever since Gibbon have taken a skeptical view of the martyrologies.

"It would have been an easy task . . . to collect a long series of horrid and disgustful pictures, and to fill many pages with racks and scourges, with iron hooks, and red-hot beds, and with all the variety of tortures which fire and steel, savage beasts and more savage executioners, could inflict on the human body," writes Gibbon. "But I cannot determine what I ought to transcribe till I am satisfied how much I ought to believe."[35]

A rather less frightful picture of the persecution of Christians can be pieced together from the ancient sources. Here and there across the vast empire, a few especially hateful magistrates carried out the imperial decrees with real sadism. Elsewhere, the same harsh decrees were enforced only halfheartedly or not at all. A Christian might be permitted to prevail upon a pagan friend or neighbor to make a sacrifice in his place, and an officer who came to seize a forbidden copy of the Christian scriptures might be willing to take a bribe and leave the Bible behind. Some magistrates literally begged the Christians who were brought into their courts to go through the motions of pagan sacrifice in order to provide an excuse for sparing them. "In these relatively favoured circumstances," observes Robin Lane Fox, "it takes two to make a martyr."[36] And so, on the occasion when a Christian was actually put to torture and death, his or her own zeal was a necessary element of martyrdom.

"Unhappy men!" cried one frustrated Roman proconsul to the defiant Christians. "If you are thus weary of your lives, is it so difficult for you to find ropes and precipices?"[37]

Confessors and Traitors

Among all the Christians who lived through the ten persecutions by the authorities of pagan Rome, only a modest number were martyred; Gibbon, for example, speculates that the victims of the so-called Great Persecution amounted to only two thousand or so, and Will Durant insists that fewer Christians died at the hands of pagans during *all* ten pagan persecutions than at the hands of fellow Christians during the two hottest years of the theological civil war that would later be fought within Christianity over various beliefs condemned as heresies and apostasies.

We do not know the number of Christians who saved their lives by abjectly surrendering their Bibles for burning and sacrificing to the pagan gods. Surely the vast majority of Christians were neither zealots nor cowards, and they managed to survive with their bodies and their souls intact. But, as we shall see, it was the example of the heroes and villains, the contrast between zealotry and cowardice, that shaped the revolution that Christianity was ready to work in pagan Rome.

The persecution provided a new vocabulary to describe the heroes and the villains. A Christian who served the faith by proudly confessing to the crime of Christianity and suffering the consequences, willingly and even joyously, was called a "confessor." A Christian who betrayed the faith was called a *"traditor"*—the Latin word literally means "one who hands over" and refers to those who handed over Christian writings and artifacts to the Roman soldiers who enforced the imperial decrees that criminalized the practice of Christianity. From the word *traditor* comes a more familiar English word: "traitor."

A confessor who endured and survived the persecutions of pagan Rome was lionized by his fellow Christians—he was regarded as a veteran of the holy war against paganism, a living example of what it meant to be a Soldier of Christ, and his wounds and scars were seen as badges of honor. A *traditor*, by contrast, was the object of contempt and disgust among the uncompromising Christians—the polytheist saw nothing unusual and nothing wrong in offering sacrifice to more than one god, but the monotheist was taught that nothing was a greater "abomination" in the eyes of the Only True God.

By the opening years of the fourth century, when the greatest of the persecutions was in progress, the war of the Only True God against the many gods and goddesses of paganism seemed to be a lost cause. The apostle Paul, as we have seen, believed his destiny—and the destiny of Christianity—lay in the imperial seat of the Roman empire, but history seemed to prove him wrong. So far, Rome had served only as a place of torture, death and burial for Christian confessors for nearly 300 years. "They have shed the blood of saints and prophets," writes the author of Revelation, who likens Rome to a woman on whose forehead is written "mother of harlots and abominations of the earth," a woman who is "drunken with the blood of the martyrs of Jesus."[38]

Yet Paul turned out to be right, although for reasons and under circumstances that he never predicted and could not have imagined. Christianity was about to be elevated from a despised and persecuted cult to the state religion of the greatest superpower of the ancient world. A single man was responsible for the revolution in pagan Rome, but he was neither a confessor nor even a Christian during the Great Persecution. By a strange irony, the "Soldier of Christ" who was single-handedly responsible for the triumph of monotheism in Rome was born and raised a pagan, and the argument can be made that he remained one until the day of his death.

BOOK TWO

THE WAR OF GOD
AGAINST THE GODS

*For although there may be so-called gods in heaven or
on earth—as indeed there are many "gods" and
many "lords"—yet for us there is one God.*

—Paul, 1 Corinthians 8:5–6

◆

CHAPTER FIVE

"IN THIS SIGN, CONQUER"

The Curious Encounter of Christ and Constantine in the Struggle for the Roman Crown

> What god was it that made you feel that the time had come
> for the liberation of the city against the advice of men and
> even against the warning of the auspices?
>
> —Panegyric to Constantine
> after the Battle of the Milvian Bridge

The remarkable saga of how Christianity rose from a persecuted cult to the state religion of imperial Rome begins with a
slightly bawdy tale about a general and an innkeeper's
daughter.

Inns, as it happens, were a feature of the famous system of roads
that was one of the greatest achievements of ancient Rome. First con-
structed to permit the speedy movement of the Roman legions across
the vast stretches of the empire, the network of roads was also used
by imperial agents, diplomatic couriers and travelers of all kinds—
"All roads lead to Rome" is the old aphorism that describes its essential function, and stretches of the ancient roadway can still be seen all
over Europe. To serve the needs of those who traveled over the roads
by foot or horseback, cart or carriage, a service industry was established in the form of way stations called *stabula*, where the travelers
refreshed themselves with food and drink, spent the night and set out
again with fresh mounts.

Innkeepers, then as now, always seek to keep the customers satisfied, and the *stabula* offered all of the services that a weary traveler

demanded—the young women who poured the wine and filled the trenchers surely provided other services, too. And the Roman legionnaires who were the principal users of the roads were their best customers. For that reason, some pagan chroniclers have charged that a Roman soldier by the name of Flavius Valerius Constantius (c. 250–306) availed himself of something more than food and drink when he stopped at a way station on the Roman road and first encountered the publican's daughter who is known to history as Helena.

The commander's striking visage, pale and drawn, earned him the nickname Constantius Chlorus—"Constantius the Pale"—and his complexion has been explained by the ancient sources as "a symptom of the intense energy which he put into the struggle for survival and self-advancement," according to historian John Holland Smith.[1] Constantius demonstrated these qualities in combat against the so-called barbarian tribes that continually threatened the frontiers of the Roman empire, the Franks and the Alemanni, ancestors of the Germans. Although a genealogy was later invented to link him to the oldest and most aristocratic families of old Rome, Constantius is reputed to have been the son of a peasant, born in some Balkan backwater of the Roman empire. Ultimately, it was his exploits in battle, rather than his imaginary family history, that brought him the political clout that sometimes turns common soldiers into emperors.

The lowborn but combat-hardened soldier, in fact, rose to the highest circles of power in the Roman empire, but not before he had taken up with the innkeeper's daughter, and she had given him a son—the baby boy was named Constantine. Pious historians insist on referring to their union as a marriage, and one overenthusiastic medieval historian even claimed that Helena was the daughter of the British king who is immortalized in the nursery rhyme "Old King Cole." The fact is, however, that Helena was a commoner, and the ancient chronicler Eutropius hints at the real state of affairs when he characterizes her relationship with Constantius as "a marriage of the more obscure kind."[2] Ancient pagan sources boldly call Helena a concubine, and some of them even claim that she served as a prostitute in her father's inn before she met Constantine's father.[3]

Helena's questionable origins and the dubious nature of her relationship with Constantius apparently rendered her unsuitable to her husband's upwardly mobile career in public service. The ruling class of pagan Rome was, contrary to twenty centuries of Christian moral censure, rather fussy and even puritanical on the subject of sex, especially in outward appearances. Once he was raised to imperial rank, Constantius separated from the innkeeper's daughter—"dismissing" her, as befits a concubine, rather than divorcing her—and made an advantageous marriage with the stepdaughter of the emperor Maximian (c. 240–310), a woman of noble birth called Theodora.

Son of the God

When Constantius the Pale was "raised to the purple"—the phrase refers to the color that was reserved for use in the apparel of royalty and worn as a badge of high office by kings and emperors throughout the ancient world—he was only one of four men who ruled the Roman empire. Thanks to an elaborate system of power sharing invented by Diocletian, no single one of them could claim to be *the* emperor of Rome. Indeed, just as pagan Rome recognized the divine authority of a great many gods and goddesses, the Romans submitted to the political authority of a great many men.

Here we encounter another core value of polytheism, one that is expressed in politics rather than religion. Some of the oldest and most revered political traditions of Rome, like those of Greece, were based on the simple idea that no single man was entitled to rule as an autocrat. Greece was the birthplace of a primitive form of democracy, and Rome deposed its last reigning king in favor of a republican government in 509 B.C.E. Of course, neither of these early forms of democracy were very democratic in the modern sense—political power was shared only by wealthy and highborn males who enjoyed the privilege of sitting in the assemblies and making decisions that were binding on everyone else, including the women, the poor and the slaves who made up the majority of the population. But the proto-democracies of the ancient world embodied one of the fundamental assumptions of paganism—just as the pagans of Greece and Rome did not worship a single all-powerful god, they did not submit to a single all-powerful king.

But, significantly, the old assumptions began to change shortly before the radical new idea of Christian monotheism first appeared. Octavian, a grandnephew of Julius Caesar, prevailed over Marc Antony in the civil war that followed his great-uncle's assassination and elevated himself to the rank of emperor in 27 B.C.E. The newly minted emperor began to call himself Augustus ("Sacred One"), a term that would later be used as a title of office by his successors on the imperial throne. He followed the example of Alexander the Great in accepting an honor previously afforded only to deities and dead emperors—statues were fashioned in his image, and worship was offered to him as a living deity.

Even so, Octavian dared not abolish the Senate, which retained much of its old prestige and many of its old privileges, and he never repudiated the republican traditions of Rome. The very first Roman emperor, according to law, ruled not as an all-powerful autocrat but as the *Princeps*—that is, the "first man" but not the *only* man to exercise political authority in Rome. Octavian accepted worship as "son of [the] god," a reference to the fact that his great uncle (and adoptive father) had been deified after death, but it never occurred to him or anyone else to suggest that the newly divinized emperor—or *any* of the many other gods and goddesses—was the *only* deity worthy of worship.[4]

Indeed, it was under Octavian that an altar to the Goddess of Victory was installed in the chambers of the Senate, a neglected temple of the Magna Mater, the Great Mother of the Gods, was restored and the Greek god Apollo, long worshipped in Rome, was formally added to the Roman pantheon with the construction of a temple in his honor on the Capitoline. Not until the victory of monotheism did the notion of the Only True God find its political equivalent in the Roman empire in the notion of a single and all-powerful monarch.

Lord and Master

By the reign of Diocletian, Rome had been ruled (or misruled) by a long succession of men who claimed the rank of "Augustus." Few of them, however, enjoyed the success in war and diplomacy that had been achieved by Octavian. The Roman empire reached its high watermark during the first century c.e., when the *Pax Romana* stretched from Mesopotamia to Britain, from Gaul to Carthage. But the zenith of imperial Rome passed quickly, and the next three centuries were memorably characterized by Gibbon as its "decline and fall." The emperors who followed Octavian to the throne were forced to contend with a series of seemingly apocalyptic woes—famine and drought, plague and pestilence, earthquakes and volcanic eruptions, wars and rumors of wars, the threat of both "barbarian" hordes and Persian armies on the frontiers of the far-flung empire, not to mention such thoroughly modern problems as consumer price inflation and currency devaluation.

A few of the emperors who presided over the decline of the Roman empire were men of accomplishment and even brilliance— Marcus Aurelius (121–180) distinguished himself as a philosopher as well as a statesman—but most of them ranged down the scale from mediocrity to outright incompetence or abject madness. Nero for example, is recalled as a demonic sadist who was believed to have engaged in incest with his own mother during the riotous days of the Saturnalia, the festival in honor of the god Saturn, and reputedly kicked to death his pregnant wife. But not even the worst of them ruled over the Roman empire as an absolute monarch. Nero declined an offer from the Senate to be officially deified and worshipped: "The Princeps does not receive the honour of a god," he demurred, "until he has ceased to be among men."[5]

Diocletian was markedly less modest than Nero on the question of his own divinity. A commoner from one of the Balkan provinces, reputedly the son of an emancipated slave, he rose through the ranks of the Roman legions and was boosted onto the imperial throne in a coup d'état carried out by his fellow officers. Once enthroned, he did not hesitate to put his new wealth and authority on lavish display. He was not content with a mantle of imperial purple; his garment was hemmed in gold and even his slippers were bejeweled. He crowned himself with a diadem, a circlet of gold and gemstones that prefigured the more elaborate headgear of future kings. On the rare occasion when he granted an audience to one of his subjects, the petitioner was required to prostrate himself. He was the first Roman emperor to adopt the titles of Lord and King, which created something of a scandal among those who still honored the republican traditions of ancient Rome and disdained such exalted titles for the "first man" of the empire.

"Two hundred and fifty years earlier," writes historian John Holland Smith, "when Tiberius had once been called 'Lord and Master' he had claimed that he was being deliberately insulted."[6]

Still, Diocletian did not repudiate all of the stately traditions of pagan Rome. Tellingly, he renounced the newfangled cult of *Sol Invictus*, the Unconquered Sun, which dressed up the idea of monotheism in the garb of paganism, and he sought to polish up the Roman pantheon and restore the old gods and goddesses to their primacy in the official rituals of worship. Indeed, the anxieties that prompted Diocletian to order the torture and mutilation of Christians who refused to join in the pagan rituals of worship—and, along with them, the followers of the Persian mystic called Mani—were stoked by his conviction that the various imported cults posed a distinct and growing threat to the empire itself.

Thus, while Diocletian still offered worship to Mithra—the Persian god especially favored by the Roman legions from which Diocletian had risen to power—he reserved the greatest honors for the old pantheon of Greco-Roman gods, Jupiter and Hercules among them. He may have been an *arriviste* and a self-made man, a reformer who tinkered with the old institutions of the Roman empire and invented entirely new ones, but he regarded himself as the savior and protector of the *Pax Deorum*—the "peace of the gods"—on which the empire was believed to depend for its very survival. Indeed, as if to replicate the rule of the many gods, Diocletian devised a new system of imperial rule that came to be called the Tetrarchy, a kind of imperial civil service that divided the office of emperor among four men.

Two members of the Tetrarchy held the higher rank of Augustus, and two held the lower rank of Caesar, both titles derived from names used by the very first Roman emperor, Octavian. One pair of emperors—an Augustus and a Caesar—ruled over the western provinces of the Roman empire, and the other ruled over the eastern provinces. Although Diocletian was still the first among the coemperors, the edicts and decrees now carried the names of all four. Diocletian envisioned that the officeholders would gather seniority based on their years of service, the junior Augustus replacing the senior Augustus when he died or retired, thus providing an orderly succession in place of the intrigue and violence that had long characterized the imperial politics of Rome.

The theological underpinnings of the Tetrarchy were specifically polytheistic. Diocletian, as the senior Augustus, claimed the high god Jupiter as his tutelary deity; the junior Augustus, Maximian, claimed the demigod Hercules; and the two divinities symbolized the power sharing that was so characteristic of paganism. And so, when Constantius the Pale was first raised to the purple in the western half of the Roman empire in 293, his title was Caesar, and he was second in rank to Maximian. Their counterparts in the east were Diocletian and Galerius, who served as his Caesar.

The Fortunate Son

When Constantius put away Helena, the innkeeper's daughter, and took Theodora, the emperor's stepdaughter, as his wife—all at the urging of the senior Augustus, Diocletian—he was engaging in the ancient and enduring act of self-promotion known as marrying the boss's daughter. Helena is suddenly eclipsed by Theodora in the ancient chronicles, although she will ultimately reappear as the single most powerful woman in the life of her son, Constantine. But Constantius did not distance himself from his firstborn. While three more sons and three daughters were born to Constantius and his new wife, Theodora, it was Constantine whom he regarded as his favorite son and future heir, even though he may have been, strictly speaking, a bastard.

Young Constantine was born in one of the military encampments where Constantius spent his early career as a soldier on campaign, although we do not know exactly where. By tradition, the year was 274, although the date of his birth, too, is the subject of speculation. Constantine may have been raised in Gaul, his father's base of operations against the barbarians and later his seat of government as Caesar, or in the unknown provincial backwater where his mother had been sent to live, or—perhaps most likely—he shuttled between both places during his unsettled childhood.

The details of Constantine's upbringing have not been preserved, if only because they were regarded in retrospect as awkward and embarrassing for a man hailed as "the Great." He was "less than well educated," as one ancient source delicately puts it,[7] and the best evidence is found in the oratory, decrees and letters that can be shown to have originated with the emperor himself rather than one of his servitors—Constantine's work is characterized by "clumsiness" and "childish silliness," according to historian Andrew Alfoldi.[8] We know that Constantine grew up speaking Latin, the *lingua franca* of the western Roman empire and the language used in matters of state; his command of Greek—the language of high culture in the Hellenistic world—was notoriously and even laughably poor.

What instruction Constantine received in matters of religion is a subject of much speculation. His father was a worshipper of *Sol Invictus*, a fact that prompts some historians to regard Constantius the Pale as a kind of proto-monotheist or even a secret Christian. One of his daughters by Theodora, for example, was named Anastasia ("Resurrection"), a name with powerful resonance in Christian tradition. The stern decrees of Diocletian against the practice of Christianity went mostly unenforced in the provinces of the Roman empire where Constantius reigned as Caesar, and his court was known as a place of refuge for high-ranking officials who happened to be Christians. But it is unlikely that Constantine or anyone else in his family were, as yet, practicing Christians. "If the sacrifice to the Genius of Empire that was the test of loyalty was ever demanded of them, they must have offered it unhesitatingly," writes John Holland Smith, "otherwise Eusebius would have written not the *Life of Constantine* but the *Acts of Constantine the Martyr.*"[9]

Still, Constantius came under suspicion in the court of Diocletian for his distinct lack of fervor in seeking out and punishing the Christians who refused to demonstrate their good citizenship by offering sacrifice to the deified emperor and the other pagan gods. When young Constantine and his mother were summoned by Diocletian, abruptly and without explanation, the senior Augustus may have been seeking to hold Constantine as a hostage to ensure his father's loyalty. And the ploy was successful in provoking the concerns of Constantine's father—Constantius monitored his son's welfare, seeking reports from his own sources in Diocletian's court about how Constantine was faring in the treacherous world of imperial politics.

Constantine, it turned out, was faring remarkably well. Diocletian was impressed by the young man, who grew up strong, fit and handsome—the surviving busts of Constantine give him even features, a strong jaw and a cleft chin—and the emperor groomed him for a career in imperial service. At the age of nineteen, Constantine was granted his first commission as an officer in the Roman legions. A year later, he was betrothed to Fausta, the daughter of Maximian, the western Augustus under whom his father served as Caesar. By the age of twenty-two, Constantine had been promoted to tribune first class, a rank roughly equivalent to a colonelcy, in the palace guard that attended Diocletian, and he traveled with the imperial entourage on a campaign to Syria to suppress the unruly Saracens on the eastern fringe of the Roman empire. Later, he campaigned with distinction against the enemies of Rome in far-off Egypt, on the long embattled Persian frontier and in various hot spots where barbarian tribes threatened Roman outposts in Britain and Gaul.

In fact, young Constantine may have been rather *too* successful for his own good. He was "matched by none in grace and beauty of form, or in tallness, and so surpassed his contemporaries in personal strength that he struck terror into them," writes the church historian Eusebius of Caesarea, a contemporary of Constantine and an eyewitness to many of the events he describes in detail in his *Life of Constantine*. So the superior qualities of the eldest son of Constantius the Pale excited jealousy rather than admiration among the other members of the Tetrarchy: "The ruling emperors, noting his virile and vigorous appearance and enquiring mind, were moved to jealousy and fear, and they carefully watched for an opportunity to inflict a damaging wound on his character."[10]

Among the tales that came to be written into Constantine's biography by Christian chroniclers are accounts that could (and may) have been drawn from various episodes in the biblical account of Samson and David. Constantine, it is said, was dispatched by a jealous Galerius to command the legions in places where the fighting was hottest, thus exposing him to the heightened risk of a convenient death in battle. On one occasion, Galerius set the young Constantine in single combat against an especially fierce prisoner of war taken in battle against the barbarians of the Danube Valley. According to another tale, young Constantine was so eager to prove himself—and so little able to control his formidable temper—that his comrades in arms baited him into taking on a wild lion. As if to prove Constantine's kingly qualities, the lion was the loser.

The War on Monotheism

On February 23, 303, after consulting an oracle of Apollo and receiving what he believed to be encouragement from on high, Diocletian issued an edict that formally criminalized the practice of Christianity, and the so-called Great Persecution—the last and most extensive of the ten persecutions that started with Nero—began in earnest.

Diocletian had been moving toward open persecution throughout his reign. Only a few years earlier, for example, he had convened a conference at Antioch to consider a grave problem: when he sacrificed to the gods to obtain their advice on military operations against the enemies that surrounded and threatened Rome on all sides, the priests who studied the livers and other viscera of the slain animals were repeatedly unable to find clear answers to his questions.

The problem, said the chief soothsayer, was that Christians among the imperial servants and the palace guard were secretly crossing themselves at the moment of sacrifice. Christian magic, as the pagans saw the gesture, was so offensive to the gods and goddesses that they were shocked into silence. "Those Christian brethren, by signing their brows with the Cross," explains the church father Lactantius, "put the gods to flight, so that they could not reveal the future from the entrails of the beasts."[11] Diocletian promptly ordered everyone in the imperial court to prove his piety and loyalty by offering a sacrifice in the pagan manner—anyone who refused was flogged, and the soldiers among them were stripped of their rank.

The most zealous of the Christians posed an even more direct threat, one that reminds us of the Maccabees and the Zealots. The Christian community in Syria, for example, rose up in open resistance against the imperial decrees that were meant to intimidate them into abandoning their new faith. And when a fire broke out in the bedchamber of Diocletian's palace at Nicomedia, Diocletian suspected that it was an act of terrorism by a pair of eunuchs in imperial service who had been seduced into converting to Christianity. The eunuchs, he feared, had been persuaded by "desperate fanatics" among their fellow Christians to assassinate both Diocletian and Galerius, and the fire in his bedchamber represented their earnest if failed effort to do so.[12]

The soothsayers who blamed the Christians for their inability to see the future in a mess of guts were clearly playing on the mounting anxieties of the emperor. Every misfortune that befell Rome—every spike in the price of grain, every drop in the value of the coinage, every skirmish with a barbarian tribe on the embattled borders, even the bolts of lightning that struck the imperial palace—were seen as ominous and compelling evidence that the "atheists" were threatening the "peace of the gods" that had previously preserved the empire. The refusal of the Christian rigorists to afford even a simple gesture of respect to the deities of the Roman pantheon was seen as mad, demonic or subversive, and possibly all three at once.

Diocletian was also urged toward open war on monotheism by his second in command, Galerius, a man of barbarian descent who showed himself to be so brutal and so coarse that the troops under his command dubbed him "the Drover."[13] His own hatred of Christianity was stoked by his mother, a priestess in one of the pagan cults, who complained bitterly to her son about the poor turnout of Christians at the sacrificial rites over which she presided. Long before Diocletian issued the harsh decrees that have come to be called the Great Persecution, Galerius was ready to carry out an even more bloodthirsty purge—he urged the senior Augustus to decree that any Christian who refused to sacrifice to the pagan gods and goddesses be burned alive.

So the Great Persecution was Diocletian's declaration of war on monotheism—the spirit of religious toleration that had always characterized paganism was withdrawn from Christianity, and the Christians returned the favor by refusing to acknowledge the pagan gods and goddesses. Christian churches were to be closed down, and Christian writings were to be seized and burned. Christians were forbidden to hold public office or testify in court. Any Christian who refused to demonstrate loyalty to the emperor and the state by turning over his or her Bible and dropping a pinch of incense on the altar fire was liable to torture, disfigurement or death.

"[C]onfessors for the faith," writes Lactantius, a pagan who embraced Christianity during the Great Persecution out of admiration for the courage of the martyrs, "had their ears and nostrils slit, their hands and feet cut off, and their eyes gouged out."[14]

Thus did the rigorism that inspired some zealous Christians to seek martyrdom find its counterpart in some zealous pagan magistrates who were perfectly willing to make martyrs of them. Gibbon, as we have seen, estimates that a couple of thousand Christians were put to death during the reign of Diocletian, and thousands more may have endured the elaborate forms of torture that are recorded in Christian accounts of the Great Persecution, although the most grotesque examples go unnoticed by pagan historians.

The Great Persecution was meant to exterminate, once and for all, the Christian god, if not the Christians themselves. Here was a decisive clash between two forms of extremism, one pagan and one monotheistic—Diocletian was determined to suppress the practice of Christianity under threat of death, and the willing martyrs within the community of Christians were just as determined to die rather than submit to his decree. Here and there throughout the empire, pagan magistrates showed themselves willing to oblige, as when one Roman governor in the province of Spain cruelly taunted a Christian bishop in the very moments before he was sent to be burned at the stake.

"You are a bishop?"

"I am."

"You were."[15]

Still, if Diocletian was a zealous persecutor of Christians, he was no megalomaniac. He was perfectly willing to share the office of emperor with his fellow tetrarchs, and he ultimately seemed to lose the will to rule at all. He abandoned the city of Rome, traditional capital of the empire, and moved his seat of government to Milan and later

to Ravenna. He abruptly called off the games that were held to celebrate the twentieth anniversary of his reign, an act of lassitude that
was regarded as an insult to Rome itself and the tutelary gods of the
Roman empire.

The downward spiral of pagan Rome, according to the ancient
historian Zosimus, began when Diocletian denied the citizenry the
opportunity to celebrate his long reign with the customary ceremonies, combats, and contests. When the emperor fell ill with fever
in the winter of 304–305, he simply surrendered to his fate. On May
1, 305, at the age of fifty-five, the senior Augustus abruptly abdicated,
retreating to his estate on the shores of the Adriatic Sea and an-
nouncing his intention to live out his life tending his garden as a gen-
tleman farmer.

Ironically, although Diocletian had succeeded in imposing order
on the chaos that characterized imperial politics in ancient Rome, his
willing abdication prompted a frantic new round of conspiracy and
open conflict among the men who sought to seat themselves on the
throne in his place. At first, Galerius succeeded Diocletian as Augustus in the east, and Constantius the Pale replaced Maximian, who
had been coerced into joining Diocletian in retirement, as Augustus
in the west. But the unsettled state of affairs prompted a series of pretenders and usurpers to make their own claims over the next several
years. At one dizzying moment in 309, no fewer than eight men
claimed the exalted title of Augustus. Among the contenders was
Constantine.

The Fugitive

By 305, Constantine had gathered yet more honors in campaigns
against the restive barbarian tribes along the northern frontier of the
empire and the Persians who threatened to the east. As an officer
whose courage, skill and ruthlessness had been proven in battle—and
as the eldest son of the western emperor—he might have expected to

be raised to the Tetrarchy during the game of musical chairs that followed the retirement of Diocletian. But Constantine had lost the latest round and—for that reason—he was regarded by the winners as a disgruntled and thus dangerous rival.

One intriguing clue to Constantine's status in imperial circles can be found in his own early choice of a mate. Constantine, as we have seen, was betrothed when he was still an adolescent to Fausta, daughter of Maximian, the emperor under whom his father had served as Caesar. Still, as late as 305, Constantine had not yet actually married Fausta. Rather, he had followed his father's example yet again by first taking up with a lowborn woman called Minervina, who is described by Christian sources as his wife and by pagan sources as his concubine. Her name means "household slave of Minerva," the Roman goddess of art and war, and some sources suggest that she was a barbarian woman who was born into slavery or taken as a prize of war in one of the campaigns against the frontier tribes. Thus, again like his own father, Constantine's first love may have been an illicit one.

Constantine could not have endeared himself to the emperor Maximian by spurning Fausta and choosing Minervina as his mate. Even after Maximian was replaced as Augustus in the western empire by Constantius the Pale, his own father, the upwardly mobile Constantine found himself stalled in his imperial career at the very moment when a seat in the Tetrarchy seemed to open up. The point is made in a tale told by Lactantius, who dresses up Constantine as a figure of courage and daring that, once again, may be intended to remind his readers of how the intrepid young David put himself beyond the reach of a murderous King Saul.

As an officer attached to the imperial court of Galerius, the successor of Diocletian as Augustus in the eastern empire, so the story goes, Constantine required the formal permission to leave the palace at Nicomedia and join his father, the western Augustus. Constantine was anxious to do so, and Galerius was just as anxious to keep him within the earshot of his own spies and informers. Petitions from both Constantine and his father were repeatedly refused or ignored until one evening when Galerius, his mood elevated and his senses blunted by a sumptuous banquet and an abundance of wine, finally relented.

Galerius signed the order that permitted Constantine and his entourage to leave the palace and join Constantius the Pale on a voyage to the distant Roman colony of Britain. Galerius was in such an expansive mood that he permitted Constantine to travel at imperial expense on one of the mail coaches that crisscrossed the empire on those storied Roman roads. When Galerius awoke the next morning, perhaps a bit hung over but thinking more clearly about the threat that Constantine represented, he revoked the travel orders, issued a warrant for his arrest and sent a search party on horseback in hot pursuit.

But Constantine, a canny and decisive player of imperial politics, had not tarried at the palace—he was already on his way to join his father when Galerius changed his mind. A detachment of imperial cavalry was sent after him, but when they arrived at the first way station, they discovered that Constantine and his men had taken fresh horses for themselves and hobbled the rest of the mounts to prevent any pursuers from following them too closely. Thus did Constantine make his getaway from the court of Galerius, join his father at the port of Gesoriacum in Gaul (now the French city of Boulogne) and voyage with him to the westernmost outpost of the western empire.

Bastard Son

When father and son reached Britain, they promptly set out on a campaign against the Picts, one of the troublesome tribes that threatened Roman sovereignty in the settled areas of the British Isles. The emperor Hadrian had built the famous wall that still bears his name in order to keep these tribes at bay a couple of centuries earlier, but the mighty Roman legions were never able to fully suppress the barbarians on the vast and far-flung frontiers. Now Constantius and Constantine rode out at the head of an army to push the Picts back beyond the wall, and they returned in triumph to the western emperor's base of operations at York. The expedition against the Picts was the last victory on the battlefield for Constantius, who sickened shortly after their return to base. On July 25, 306, barely fourteen months after being raised from Caesar to Augustus, Constantius the Pale was dead.

No sooner had Constantius passed his last breath than an urgent question presented itself: Who would succeed Constantius as Augustus in the west? According to the elaborate mechanism of the Tetrarchy as designed by Diocletian, the title of Augustus should have passed to a man called Severus, who served as Caesar under Constantius. A rival claim might have been expected by one of the legitimate sons of Constantius by his wife, Theodora. But it was the dead emperor's illegitimate son, the rough-and-ready Constantine, who enjoyed the decisive advantage—he was hardened in battle, savvy in politics, driven by his own urgent ambition and, above all, he found himself at the head of his father's own army, fresh from victory on the field of battle and far from the reach of the senior emperor, Galerius.

The Roman legions and the assorted allies and mercenaries who served with them had been the makers and breakers of Roman emperors for centuries, which explains why commoners and outsiders like Constantius and Diocletian had risen to imperial rank in the first place. Now it was the king of a barbarian tribe who played a crucial role in elevating Constantine to the imperial throne. King Crocus commanded a detachment of cavalry in the Roman campaign against the Picts, and he roused his own soldiers into declaring Constantine as the new Augustus.

The tale was spun by later chroniclers to show Constantine as an unassuming and an even unwilling object of the spontaneous acclaim of his late father's barbarian allies. Constantine "put spurs to his horse" to put himself at a distance from the soldiers who were, in

136   GOD AGAINST THE GODS

fact, carrying out a coup d'état, according to an ancient panegyrist who composed the account in honor of the new emperor. But they rode after him, gently but insistently escorted him back to camp and compelled him to accept the purple mantle that signified his new imperial rank.[16]

The reality is that Constantine was an active participant in "a deliberate act of open rebellion," as historian John Holland Smith puts it.[17] Indeed, Constantine demonstrated his own willfulness and sheer impudence in the official communiqué that he sent back to Galerius. The courier carried news of the death of Constantius and a gift from Constantine to Galerius—an official portrait of Constantine in the garb of his new rank as Augustus, hung with a wreath of bay leaves that signified his imperial rank. The very sight of the portrait reduced Galerius to a state of sputtering rage, according to one ancient historian; he ordered the wreath and the portrait to be burned and spent the rest of the day in bed.

Pretenders and Usurpers

When he finally rose from his sickbed, Galerius was prepared to grant Constantine a place in the Tetrarchy, although he recognized Constantine only as a Caesar, not an Augustus, and the lowest-ranking of the four tetrarchs. And, at least for the moment, Constantine decided not to insist on the higher rank. After all, the man whom Galerius recognized as the legitimate successor to Constantine's father, Severus, did not enjoy much real authority in the land over which he supposedly reigned as Augustus. Constantine was the *de facto* ruler of the western reaches of Roman empire from the Alps all the way to Hadrian's Wall.

But the deadly game of imperial politics was still very much in play. Maximian, who had been forced into retirement along with Diocletian, now sought to reclaim the title of Augustus from Severus, the man who had lawfully succeeded him. A whole gang of pretenders and usurpers, including Maximian's own son, put themselves in contention for the crown. Amid the clamor for the imperial crown, Constantine showed exactly how cunning and cruel he could be.

At first, Constantine and Maximian entered into an uneasy alliance in support of each other's claim to imperial rank. Constantine had been betrothed to Maximian's daughter for more than a decade without bothering to actually marry her, but now he decided to put politics ahead of love. Minervina may have been Constantine's lawful wife, but no divorce is recorded, and so it is possible that Constantine simply "put away" Minervina in the same way that Constantius the Pale had once "dismissed" Constantine's mother. Once free of Minervina, Constantine promptly married Fausta—the wedding, an occasion for a public display of martial splendor, took place at the town of Augusta Treverorum (now Trier, Germany) on March 31, 307. Constantine recognized his father-in-law's claim to the rank of senior Augustus, and Maximian returned the favor by elevating his son-in-law to the rank of junior Augustus.

But his marriage to Maximian's daughter and his alliance with Maximian did nothing to blunt Constantine's own ambition. The whole arrangement, in fact, can be seen as a cunning and even cynical ploy by a master strategist who aspired not to be one of four emperors but rather the one and only emperor. Constantine waited and watched, for example, while his father-in-law fought to defend his claim to the title of Augustus against Severus, the lawful western emperor.

Severus marched on Rome, but his army was bribed into defecting *en masse* to Maximian, and he surrendered on the promise of a safe refuge. When Maximian broke his promise and put Severus under house arrest, the defeated emperor begged for an honorable death by execution. Maximian refused, apparently concluding that Severus was far more valuable as a hostage than as a corpse. Severus, however, ultimately won the battle of will by taking his own life.

Maximian now decided to make a preemptive move against his son-in-law. Lactantius, who delighted in decorating the life of Constantine with dramatic but surely legendary exploits, reports that

Maximian asked his daughter to assassinate her husband by stabbing him to death in bed. When Fausta refused, or so the story goes, Maximian resolved to strike the blow with his own hand.

He presented himself at Constantine's palace in the middle of the night, persuaded the bodyguard to let him into the imperial bedchamber by insisting that he had a strange and perplexing dream to share with his son-in-law and then plunged a dagger into the sleeping figure that lay in the bed. At that moment, we are asked to believe, Constantine stepped out from the curtain behind which he had concealed himself—Fausta had warned him of her father's plot, and he had arranged for one of the eunuchs to take his place in bed. Then and there, Constantine ordered that the neck of the would-be assassin be broken.

Another ancient source offers an account that is more restrained but not entirely lacking in drama. While Constantine was away from his palace on yet another punitive expedition against an unruly barbarian tribe, Maximian circulated the false rumor that he had fallen in battle and offered the troops that remained behind a rich gift in exchange for putting themselves in his own service. Constantine's troops, however, remained loyal to their beloved emperor, and they set out on a fast march across Gaul toward Marseilles, where Maximian was besieged, defeated and captured. Constantine either permitted or compelled Maximian to take his own life, depending on what version one chooses to credit with historical truth.

The death of Maximian in 310 put Constantine in a commanding position in the struggle among the rival emperors. Galerius died of a wasting disease in 311—Christian historians delighted in the gruesome details of his final illness and saw it as a particularly satisfying form of divine vengeance against a persecutor of Christians. Constantine now sought to consolidate his imperial power by moving against yet another rival—Maxentius, the son of Maximian, who had been acclaimed as emperor by the praetorian guard in Rome.

At the head of an army that had repeatedly proved both its ferocity and its loyalty in battle against Romans as well as barbarians, Constantine marched south from Gaul, taking town after town in what he saw as a war of liberation rather than conquest. As he approached Rome, Maxentius and his army hunkered down behind the fortified walls of the ancient capital, a seemingly impregnable position in which they could have comfortably waited out a siege by Constantine's much smaller expeditionary force.

Maxentius, like all pagan emperors and generals, consulted the gods for advice on his military operations. One characteristically vague line of text from one of the Sibylline books predicted that "an enemy of the Roman people" would meet his destruction on October 28, the same date on which Maxentius had been first declared emperor of Rome six years earlier. Whether it was Constantine or Maxentius whom the gods regarded as the enemy was not clear, but Maxentius chose to regard the oracle as a good omen. And so, on October 28, 312, the gates of Rome were opened, and Maxentius marched out to fight his brother-in-law, thus staking the imperial crown on a single clash of arms.

"In This Sign, Conquer"

Constantine, too, yearned for divine favor in the battle to come. He was driven by the sure conviction that skill, strength and daring ultimately mattered less than the will of the powers on high—a notion that lay at the very heart of pagan rituals of worship and sacrifice. If a mortal caught the attention of the right deity with a proper display of piety—and, crucially, if he earned the goodwill of the god with a generous sacrifice—then he would surely prevail against his enemies. If he forfeited the divine favor, then he was doomed to defeat. The whole enterprise depended on picking the right god.

Until now, Constantine had courted the same gods and goddesses as every other contender for imperial rank in the Roman empire. Following his father's example in matters of faith as he did in matters of love, he sought the special patronage of the high god known as King Helios or *Sol Invictus*, the Unconquered Sun. Constantine, according to a panegyric delivered in his imperial court, had been granted a divine vision during a visit to a shrine of Apollo, the Greek god who had long been associated with the sun in the iconography of pagan Rome. The god manifested himself in Constantine's presence, accompanied by the Goddess of Victory, and they presented him with a crown on which the Roman numerals XXX were etched—the figure was understood to represent the divine assurance of a long life and a long reign.

Some historians have argued that his allegiance to the solar god meant that Constantine, like Akhenaton in Egypt some 1600 years earlier, was a monotheist in pagan garb. But the evidence suggests that he was still a convinced and committed pagan on the eve of his battle with Maxentius. After all, he embraced the deification of his late father, who was regarded as having been elevated to "the celestial abode at the heavens' very heart," according to a court poet in service to Constantine, and thus entitled to worship as "Constantius the Divine."[18] And the coinage of his early reign—a highly visible and enduring medium for imperial propaganda, both pagan and Christian—featured not only *Sol Invictus* but Jupiter, Hercules and Mars, sometimes in the very act of receiving the kind of pagan sacrifice that offended Christians so grievously that they were willing to die rather than offer it.

Even as he marched toward Rome, according to the ancient sources, Constantine was seized with anxiety over the outcome of the decisive battle to come. He regarded Maxentius as a magus with the skill to compel the attention and sympathy of the old gods and goddesses, and he worried that they would side with his enemy in the impending battle. He pondered the vexing question of which deity among the many gods and goddesses might be persuaded to break ranks and bestow favor on his army. Just as he had followed his father's example in so many other ways, Constantine thus turned to the pagan deity whom Constantius the Pale had singled out for worship in preference to the other divinities of the traditional Greco-Roman pantheon—*Sol Invictus*.

But, as it turns out, Constantine did *not* need to rely on the patronage of the Unconquered Sun. The man who had once seen Apollo and Victory with his own eyes was now granted another divine vision—but, fatefully, it was not one of the pagan gods or goddesses whom he beheld. On the day before the decisive battle, Constantine looked up into the sky above his encampment and saw something new and remarkable—the symbol of the crucified god of the Christians, and the letters that spelled out the message *In Hoc Signo Vinces* ("In this sign, conquer").

What Did Constantine See?

No single event in the history-making and history-changing life of Constantine the Great has provoked quite so much scrutiny and speculation as the question of what he actually saw in the midday sky outside the walls of Rome on the day before the battle with Maxentius. For true believers, it was the sign of the cross, miraculously displayed in the heavens, and no further explanation is necessary. For some secular scholars, it is more convincingly explained as the play of light on ice crystals in the atmosphere, a phenomenon that can produce the effect of a cross superimposed on a halo. For the most demanding observers, the whole incident is a pious fairy tale or something even more cynical.

Several versions of Constantine's curious vision have been preserved, and—intriguingly—two are the work of contemporaries who may well have heard about the incident from Constantine himself. The first account was set down by Lactantius, who was serving in Constantine's court within a year or so after the battle with Maxentius. The second account is found in an edition of *Life of Constantine* by Eusebius, written nearly thirty years after the fact by a man who was an intimate adviser of Constantine and an eyewitness to many other events in his life.

Lactantius refers to a dream rather than a vision. On the night before the battle with Maxentius, Jesus appears to Constantine in a dream and tells him to mark the shields of his soldiers with a "heavenly sign" of a very curious kind, a figure that resembles the letter P superimposed over the letter X. The same two letterforms are known in the Greek alphabet as *chi* and *rho*, and Lactantius explains the figure as "the monogram of Christ," that is, the first two letters of *Christos*, the Greek word that meant "Messiah" and now unambiguously referred to Jesus of Nazareth. Thus did the symbol enter Christian iconography, where it is known as the *chi-rho*. "By this sign," Jesus tells Constantine in his dream, "you shall be Victor."[19]

Eusebius preserves a different and more familiar version of Constantine's epiphany, although he sets it during the march through the Alps from Gaul into Italy rather than on the eve of battle outside the gates of Rome. Constantine looks up into the sky and sees the figure of a cross and Greek letters spelling out the memorable phrase that has come down through history: "In this sign, conquer!" Still very much a pagan, Constantine is confounded by the sight, and his bafflement is only deepened when, the next night, he is instructed in a dream to inscribe the sign on a battle standard. When he awakens from the dream, he tells his courtiers about his strange dream, and a Christian among them explains that what Constantine has seen in the sky symbolizes the cross on which Jesus of Nazareth, the son of the Christian god, had been crucified. Constantine summons one of the craftsmen attached to his army and orders him to fashion a battle standard, known as a *labarum*, to rally the troops.

The classic version, however, offers its own puzzling flaws and inconsistencies. Constantine needs a Christian to explain the significance of the cross that he has seen in the sky even though he had witnessed the Great Persecution, an empire-wide campaign of state terror that supposedly began when Christians in the court of Diocletian angered the gods by making the sign of the cross during rituals of pagan sacrifice. Even then, Constantine adopts the *chi-rho*, not the cross, as the emblem of the Christian god. Intriguingly, the *chi-*

rho was not yet a Christian symbol when Constantine first uses it to decorate his *labarum*—it was more commonly employed by pagan scribes as an abbreviation for the Greek word *chreston* ("good") in the margins of manuscripts to mark passages that they regarded as noteworthy or memorable.[20]

"Did the Emperor's advisers suggest this clever abbreviation for 'Christ' ('Chrestos')?" muses historian Robin Lane Fox. "Like other symbols in the years after the conversion, it had a double meaning, one for pagans, one for Christians."[21]

Still, we are invited by Eusebius and other Christian sources to imagine that, when Constantine marched out to do battle with Maxentius, his troops carried shields that were marked with the cross, and they followed a battle standard that was decorated not with the golden eagle of pagan Rome but with the *chi-rho* in its new function as a sign of the Christian god. Eusebius describes the *labarum* that was displayed at the court of Constantine in detail, although the one he saw was surely fashioned after the fact—it was gilded with pure gold, surrounded by a laurel wreath, adorned with precious stones and surmounted with a portrait of Constantine himself.

"[A]ssuming the Supreme God as his patron and invoking Christ to be his preserver and helper, and setting the trophy of victory, the saving symbol, in front of his legions," writes Eusebius, subtly conflating *Sol Invictus* and Jesus Christ, "[Constantine] marched with his whole forces in an attempt to regain for the Romans the freedom which they had inherited from their forefathers."[22]

The Head on the Lance Point

On one point of historical fact, however, no debate is necessary. On October 28, 312, the armies of Constantine and Maxentius finally closed with each other—and the army that fought under the symbol of Christ was victorious, an event with profound implications for both Constantine and Christianity. Not even the most pious hagiographer claims that a deity, Christian or pagan, manifested in visible form on the field of battle. Indeed, Constantine's victory can be attributed to the thoroughly human qualities that he had demonstrated in all of the military adventures that he had undertaken while still a pagan: he was a courageous, inventive and determined general who was capable of inspiring impressive feats of arms in the men who served under his command.

Then, too, the incident that resulted in the death of Maxentius can be understood as the result of a simple human error. To permit the army of Maxentius to cross the Tiber and reach the battleground in force, his field engineers bolted together a string of boats to supplement the narrow stone bridge known as the Milvian Bridge. At a crucial moment in the battle, when Constantine's smaller army seemed to be gaining the advantage over the much larger forces of Maxentius, the rear guard began to fall back across the Tiber. The engineers, panicking at the sight of the pursuing army of Constantine, pulled the bolts and allowed the boats to float away, thus hoping to prevent Constantine's army from crossing the river and reaching the gates of Rome. The unfortunate men on the boats, Maxentius among them, were thrown into the river—and, weighted down by their armor and equipment, they drowned.

To the true believer, of course, even a battlefield accident can be seen as the handiwork of God. Indeed, Eusebius encourages us to see Constantine as a new Moses, and Maxentius as a new pharaoh—he describes how Maxentius and his men "went down in the depths like stone," echoing the words of Exodus and suggesting that the Battle of the Milvian Bridge was the scene of a miracle like the one God had performed at the Red Sea.

A far less pious scene is recorded in the ancient chronicles. The body of Maxentius washed up on the shores of the Tiber. The head of the corpse was hacked from the body, fixed to a lance point, and held aloft as a symbol of the victory that Constantine had won over his rival for the imperial crown. And so it was a grisly kind of *labarum* behind which the army of Constantine marched into the ancient capital of the Roman empire. But a severed head, as it turned out, was a wholly fitting symbol for the new age that was about to begin.

CHAPTER SIX

THE HARLOT IN THE BISHOP'S BED

The War Within the Christian Church
over the Divinity of Christ

From the time that Christianity was invested with the supreme power,
the governors of the church have been no less diligently employed in
displaying the cruelty, than in imitating the conduct,
of their Pagan adversaries.

—Edward Gibbon, *The Decline*
and Fall of the Roman Empire

Constantine had vanquished both Maximian and Maxentius,
his father-in-law and brother-in-law, but he was not yet the
only man in the Roman empire to wear the imperial diadem.
Licinius (c. 265–325) still reigned the east as coemperor, and Constantine was not ready to challenge him. Rather, he adopted the favorite tactic of generals and emperors in ancient Rome—a tactic that
both he and his father had mastered—by brokering a diplomatic
marriage and thus bringing himself into kinship with his rival.

A soldier of peasant stock from Transylvania, Licinius had fought
his way to a generalship. As a comrade in arms and boon companion
of Galerius, he was granted the title of Augustus in 308. According to
the intricate workings of the imperial civil service that Diocletian had
invented, Licinius outranked Constantine. After the victory at the
Milvian Bridge, Constantine sought to make the senior Augustus into
a brother-in-law by offering his half sister, Constantia, in marriage.

Licinius returned the favor by agreeing to recognize Constantine's sovereignty over the western half of the empire, including not only Gaul, where Constantine was the lawful emperor, but also the lands he had "liberated" by force of arms. So it was that Constantine and Licinius both showed up at Mediolanum (Milan) in February 313 to celebrate the arranged marriage and, not incidentally, seal their deal to reign as "brother emperors." The fact that Licinius was a dutiful worshipper of the old gods and goddesses apparently mattered not at all to Constantine.

By now, the imperial edicts that had provided the legal framework for the Great Persecution under Diocletian were a dead letter. Galerius, the arch-persecutor who had once urged Diocletian to engage in mass murder of Christians, formally renounced the anti-Christian decrees on his deathbed in 311. The last of the pagan rigorists to engage in active persecution of Christianity, a rival emperor named Maximinus Daia, was defeated in battle by Licinius and died of cholera in 313. Licinius adopted a policy of grudging toleration toward the Christians under his rule. Constantine himself, like his father, had avoided any participation in the Great Persecution even before he turned from *Sol Invictus* to the Christian god on the eve of the Battle of the Milvian Bridge.

Still, soon after the nuptials of Licinius and Constantia had been celebrated at Milan, Constantine prevailed upon his new brother-in-law to sign the document that formally dismantled the machinery of the Great Persecution. The imperial decree has been enshrined in the history of monotheism as the Edict of Milan, but a close reading reveals it to be an embodiment of the purely pagan virtue of religious toleration.

The Peace of the Church

Strictly speaking, the Edict of Milan was a letter to the governor of Bithynia, a province of the Roman empire in what is now Turkey, that revoked the anti-Christian laws of Diocletian. The missive was issued jointly in the names of Constantine and Licinius, and recites their statesmanlike concern for the promotion of "public well-being and security." No particular deity, pagan or Christian, is mentioned—the brother emperors refer only to "the highest divinity," a phrase that was crafted with care to avoid giving offense to either monotheists or polytheists. Above all, the Edict of Milan restores the status quo of paganism as it existed before the Great Persecution—*all* gods and goddesses may be freely worshipped, and the Christian deity is put in a position of parity with Apollo, Isis, the Great Mother, Mithra and the other gods and goddesses.

"We thought it right that the Christians should be given full liberty to follow the religion of their choice," the emperors explain in the Edict of Milan. "This is why we thought that, with wholesome and just purpose, we should embark upon this policy of not refusing to anyone the opportunity of devoting himself either to the cult of the Christians or to whatever religion he feels is most suited to him, so that the highest divinity, whom we freely worship, may in all things bestow upon us his customary favour and goodwill."[1]

The Christians were to be granted "complete and total freedom . . . to practise their religion"—but, notably, they were granted no special status and no special privileges. Indeed, they were to be treated with precisely the same degree of tolerance that was enjoyed by every other faith in pagan Rome, both foreign and domestic: "[O]pen and free liberty has likewise been extended to others, too, that they should be utterly free to follow whatever cult they choose," the emperors pause to point out in the edict. "We have done this lest we should appear to diminish any worship or any religion."[2]

The theological rationale of the Edict of Milan, in fact, was purely and characteristically pagan. The same anxiety over offending *any* particular god that prompted the erection of altars "to the Unknown Gods" now prompts the emperors to welcome the worship of *all* gods "so all that is divine in the celestial seat may be appeased and propitious towards us and towards those under our authority." For that reason, the edicts and decrees of the Great Persecution strike the two emperors as "unfortunate" and "altogether alien to our clemency"— or, to put it another way, they were more fitting to a rigorous monotheism than an open-minded polytheism—and "should be utterly abolished."[3]

The Edict of Milan was only the first and least of the revolutionary changes that Constantine was prepared to work in the faith and politics of the Roman empire. Constantine and Licinius were seeking to reestablish the "peace of the gods," the old bargain between gods and mortals by which Rome had traded prayer and sacrifice for divine favor. But it is also true that the document put an end, once and for all, to the policy of state terror that had afflicted the Christians in pagan Rome for several centuries. That is why Christian tradition credits the Edict of Milan for establishing the so-called Peace of the Church.

Over the three centuries since the apostles Peter and Paul first came to Rome, the Christian church had grown into an impressive religious institution. Christians still represented only a fraction of the population of the Roman empire, probably no more than 10 percent of the 50 to 60 million people over whom Constantine reigned. Even so, the church possessed an elaborate and extensive hierarchy of bishops, priests and deacons; a collection of sacred writings that included both the Old Testament (that is, the Hebrew Bible) and the Christian scriptures known as the New Testament; a series of sacramental rites such as baptism and communion; an ornate and distinctive liturgy; and a welfare system that even its pagan persecutors admired and envied. But the persecutions that had afflicted the Christians over the three centuries since Nero had forced the church to operate behind closed doors.

Now, thanks to the Edict of Milan, the Christian church was granted the same freedom of religion that pagan cults had long enjoyed. No longer were Christians forced to worship by night and in secret—they could gather openly in churches rather than in the base-ments and back rooms of private houses. Christians were now entitled to publish their writings, to bequeath property to the church, to hold public office. Indeed, Constantine welcomed Christians into his army, his court, even his intimate family circles—Lactantius, the chronicler and church father who is the source of so much firsthand testimony about the reign of Constantine, was hired to tutor the emperor's children in the Christian faith.

Not every Christian, however, regarded the Peace of the Church as an unalloyed blessing. By the greatest irony of all, the freedom of religion that Licinius and Constantine established at Milan was the source of a wholly new kind of terror. For the true believer in monotheism, as we have already seen, the freedom to embrace *any* faith raised the risk that some benighted men and women would embrace the *wrong* faith. For the Christian rigorists, that risk was itself intolerable: "So, in the century opened by the Peace of the Church," explains Ramsay MacMullen, "more Christians died for their faith at the hands of fellow Christians than had died before in all the persecutions."[4] With the Peace of the Church begins a new, remarkable and terrible phenomenon—some Christians hastened to turn themselves from the persecuted to the persecutors.

The Church of the Martyrs

The blessing of official toleration that was bestowed upon the Christians by Constantine raised a new and ugly question. What was to be done about the Christians who had betrayed the faith during the Great Persecution—and who was empowered to decide whether and how they should be punished?

Only a few Christians had been willing to defy the imperial authorities during the Great Persecution, and the greater number managed to avoid martyrdom by going along and getting along. Some succeeded in fooling an inattentive or ignorant official by turning over secular or heretical writings in place of Christian holy books—

and some friendly officials, whether bribed or not, knowingly went along with the charade. Others simply saved their own lives by obeying the command to offer a sacrifice to the pagan gods and goddesses. Still others, as we have seen, bribed a greedy magistrate to leave them unmolested. And some escaped the Great Persecution by moving to towns and villages where the authorities were more easygoing.

"I ran before *that* storm," says one Christian schoolmaster who was accused of being a *traditor* in 320. Remarkably, we have the transcript of his examination by a pair of inquisitors who urge him to save his own life by testifying against a high-ranking bishop who was charged with the same crime. If the schoolmaster affirmed that he had seen the bishop turning over sacred books to the pagan authorities, he would be spared. "Just admit it," urges one of the two inquisitors who questioned him in an early example of good cop/bad cop. "If you will not, you have to be interrogated under torture."[5]

Thus were the lapsed Christians forced to present themselves to the reconstituted authorities of the church: the bishops who had returned from their places of exile, reclaimed their old clerical titles and offices and set themselves to the task of judging and punishing any congregant accused of a crime against the faith. Excommunication was reserved for the worst offenders—the ones who betrayed the faith by betraying their fellow Christians to the pagan authorities—but most of them were required only to perform an act of penance, ranging from almsgiving to fasting to public humiliation, all according to a scale that varied according to the seriousness of the crime against the church. Even those among the laity who sacrificed to the pagan gods or turned over Christian writings might be readmitted to communion after a suitable punishment for their sins.

Some of the highest-ranking clergy, however, were themselves accused of the same misdeeds. The rigorists in the Christian community of Carthage, for example, declared themselves to be scandalized at how readily their own bishop, Mensurius, complied with the decrees of the pagan authorities by surrendering the holy books that had been entrusted to him. To use the vocabulary of church politics, he was a traitor rather than a martyr, a coward who had turned over the Bible for burning rather than confessing his faith and suffering the consequences.

Yet it was Mensurius who now acted on behalf of the church in Carthage in deciding what punishment, if any, the other lapsed Christians must endure in order to reenter the congregation. For those who had suffered the worst tortures—and for those who had suffered no torture at all but who admired the confessors and detested the *traditores*—Bishop Mensurius was compromised beyond redemption by his own betrayal of Christianity. They rejected his claim that the books he had turned over to the authorities were, in fact, not Holy Writ but rather heretical writings that deserved to be burned. In their eyes, the bishop was no better, and arguably worse, than the pagans who had carried out the Great Persecution in the first place.

The recriminations among the Christians only grew sharper when Mensurius died and his archdeacon, Caecilian, was elected as bishop. Caecilian was regarded by the rigorists as an even greater traitor to the faith because of an incident that supposedly took place when Mensurius was in exile and Caecilian was in charge of the Christian community at Carthage. Under the penal system of ancient Rome, prisoners relied on their friends and families to feed them while in confinement. Caecilian, however, was accused of aiding and abetting the pagan authorities by preventing his fellow Christians from bringing food to the prison where a band of confessors had been locked up—he posted guards outside the prison, it was charged, and they used leather whips to drive off the good-hearted Christians. The food they carried was fed to the dogs, and the prisoners died slowly of starvation as their heart-rending pleas were cruelly ignored.

Here is an example of the sparks that are struck whenever zeal and true belief come into conflict with the spirit of compromise and accommodation. Caecilian indignantly denied the charges against him, but he may well have been among the pragmatic churchmen who sought to save the lives of his congregants during the Great Persecution by discouraging them from engaging in acts of provocation. Ultimately, fewer Christians would be tortured or killed if they saw that they could not count on the encouragement and support of their fellow Christians when they decided to defy the pagan authorities—or so a man like Caecilian may have believed.

Such reasoning was appalling to the rigorists of Carthage. Now that no Christian in the Roman empire was at risk of martyrdom, it was all the easier to denounce those who had struggled to survive the Great Persecution and to sentimentalize and celebrate those who had martyred themselves. So the rigorists refused to recognize the spiritual authority of Caecilian or the church over which he presided. They elected a bishop of their own, and they sought to distinguish themselves from their rivals by constituting themselves as a new and separate church—the Church of the Martyrs.

Errors, Schisms and Heresies

The first bishop of the Church of the Martyrs in Carthage was a man called Maiorinus. His successor was Donatus, and so the clerics and congregants of the Church of the Martyrs came to be known as Donatists. The rebellion of the Donatists against the authority of the established Christian church is called the Donatist schism, a bloodless phrase that conceals the zealousness of the true believers on both sides who fought against one another in the name of the Only True God. When Constantine and Licinius issued the Edict of Milan in 313, and thereby established the Peace of the Church, the Donatist schism was already an open wound.

The Christian bishops who sought to crush the Donatists claimed to be acting in the name of the "catholic" and "orthodox" church. According to the literal meanings of these terms, "catholic" means "universal" and "orthodox" means "correct belief"—and they were used by the enemies of Donatists to suggest that the established church was the guardian of the only authentic and authoritative version of Christianity.* By contrast, the Donatists were condemned by the officials of the established church as rebels against their rightful authority.

Ironically, Donatism was only one of the many "errors," "schisms" and "heresies" that plagued the Christian community at precisely that moment in history when Christianity was free to offer itself to the pagan world as the right and proper way to worship the Only True God. By the fourth century, one bishop was able to count a total of 156 false beliefs and practices within the community of Christians, and a whole new vocabulary was required merely to categorize and describe the heretics and schismatics—the Archontici, the Barbelognostics, the Cerinthians, the Encratites, the Menandrians, the Nazarenes, the Ophites, Phibionites, the Quartodecimians, the Stratiotics and the Valentinians were just a few of the sects that came to be harshly condemned and ruthlessly persecuted by the authorities of the Christian church that called itself "catholic" and "orthodox."

Many of the so-called heretics of the fourth century were charismatic preachers and teachers whose rigorism was especially off-putting to some of their fellow Christians. The supposed sins of a Spanish bishop called Priscillian (c. 340–385) included "extravagances in self-discipline"—that is, he forbade his congregants to indulge in carnal pleasure of any kind, including the consumption of meat and wine, out of a conviction that the body was a dungeon in which souls were confined as a salutary punishment for sin.[6] Sex was always a touchy subject, of course, whether it was a matter of too much or too little. Thus, for example, the followers of a man called Carpocrates, who engaged in what one historian calls "sexual communism," were condemned as heretics—and so were the followers of a man called Marcion, who suffered the same fate for insisting that

---

*As the terms are used today, the "Catholic Church" refers to Roman Catholicism, and "Orthodoxy" generally refers to the various churches that constitute Eastern Orthodoxy, including the Greek Orthodox Church, the Russian Orthodox Church, the Armenian Orthodox Church and so on. As used in conventional scholarship on the history of the early Christian church, the "catholic" and "orthodox" church was the established church that set itself against various "heretics" and "schismatics," including the Donatists.

sex even between married couples was equivalent to fornication.[7]

Sexual excess and other exotic practices have always attracted the attention of those who see their mission as maintaining law and order among the men and women over whom they exercise authority. The same anxieties that prompted the Senate of pagan Rome to ban the public celebration of the Bacchanalia in the second century B.C.E. were at work among the church councils of the fourth century that condemned the less conventional varieties of Christianity as heretical.

But the Christian authorities differed from their pagan counterparts in one fundamental way. The pagan senators voted to condemn the Bacchanalia only because they believed it posed the acute risk of anal rape in the streets of Rome—they did not object to the worship of the good-natured god of wine as long as it was conducted in private, and they never even considered the notion of criminalizing mere belief in Bacchus or, for that matter, any other god or goddess, no matter how bizarre. By contrast, the believers in the Only True God concerned themselves with far more than unruly or unseemly public conduct among their fellow Christians. Indeed, the bishops who gathered in great church councils and voted to declare one sect or another to be "anathema"—that is, so hateful to the revealed truth of Christianity that its members merited excommunication from the orthodox church—felt themselves to be empowered and even obliged to dictate not only what a Christian might *do*, whether in public or in private, but also what a Christian might *believe*.

700 Dedicated Virgins

Women, according to the stern fathers of the early church, were at the greatest risk of seduction by teachers of false and dangerous ideas— heresy, as they saw it, was "the besetting sin of the female mind."[8] That is one reason why, starting around 318, the bishop of Alexandria was so unsettled by a strikingly tall, slender and handsome priest

whose sermons seemed to attract a remarkable number of women—
"700 dedicated virgins," according to one ancient source—and set
them aflame with passion.[9] His name was Arius (c. 250–336) and his
teachings prompted a crisis so profound that it shattered the "Peace of
the Church" that Constantine had established only a few years before.

Arius was severe in appearance and solemn in demeanor, and his
gravitas was only deepened by a life of self-denial and self-mortification
so rigorous that it left him pale and emaciated—a quality that the
women in his congregation seemed to find compelling. Then, too, he
was a charismatic speaker who was gifted with the ability to express
complex and subtle ideas in an accessible, even lyrical way. He wrote
a book of theology with the cheerful title *Thalia*—"Happy Thoughts."
He reduced his teachings to simple phrases that his followers chalked
on the walls as graffiti or chanted out loud at public gatherings. He
even set them to catchy tunes so that they could be sung like work
songs or drinking songs. That's why his church in a suburb of Alexandria was always filled with attentive and enthusiastic parishioners,
not only ardent women but also schoolchildren, sailors and steve-
dores who chanted his ditties as they worked on the docks of the
busy port.

The fact that Arius was capable of inspiring such ardor in ordinary men, women and children only served to deepen the distrust
and sharpen the suspicions of the higher clergy, who regarded him as
a dangerous rabble-rouser. What did Arius teach that the bishops
found so appalling? Reduced to its simplest expression—and that is
exactly what Arius himself tried to do—Arianism was based on the
seemingly unremarkable idea that Jesus is the Son of God and not
God himself. After all, that's exactly what the Christian Bible says of
Jesus in perhaps its single most affecting and oft-quoted line of text:
"For God so loved the world that he gave his only begotten Son," goes
the verse in the Gospel of John, "that whosoever believeth in him
should not perish, but have everlasting life."[10]

The whole crisis of the so-called Arian heresy begins with a uniquely Christian innovation in the theology that Christianity inherited from Judaism. The Hebrew Bible is simple and straightforward on the subject of monotheism: "Hear O Israel, the Lord thy God, the Lord is One."[11] But when Paul declares that "for us there is but one God," he does not stop there. Rather, he goes on to distinguish between "one God, the Father" and "one Lord Jesus Christ."[12] Elsewhere, he further complicates the question by acknowledging the existence of the "Holy Spirit, whom God has given to those that obey him."[13] But Arius felt obliged to simplify and humanize the theological complexities of the Trinity by reducing them to words and phrases that ordinary people could understand—Jesus was "more than a mere man, but less than God."[14]

Of course, the Christian belief that God begat a son by causing a woman to conceive was a notion that their fellow monotheists—the Jews—found alien and offensive. Jewish theology held that God might endow a man or woman with the power of prophecy or appoint a king or conqueror to perform wondrous feats as a Messiah or "anointed one," but he simply did not sire children, whether mortal or divine.

Ironically, the same idea was perfectly plausible to the pagans whom the Christians sought to convert to monotheism. Indeed, it is a commonplace in the myth and legend of paganism—gods were both willing and able to impregnate mortal women, according to the pagan way of thinking, although mortal men were believed to be incapable of doing the same with a goddess. Thus, as one of countless examples, Alexander the Great was reputed to be the flesh-and-blood offspring of Zeus-Amon, who was said to have conveniently manifested himself in the form of a snake and engaged in sexual intercourse with Alexander's mother, much to the shock and distress of Alexander's human father.

Then, too, the notion of a father-son relationship between God and Jesus was a convenient way for Christians to explain to the pagan world what the New Testament means when it seems to refer to not one but three divinities: "All power is given to me in heaven and earth," Jesus tells his disciples, instructing them to "teach all nations, baptizing them in the name of the Father, the Son and the Holy Ghost."[15] Once Constantine ascended to the throne—and once Christianity was decriminalized by the Edict of Milan—the churches began to fill with curious pagans who were willing to sit and listen to Christian preachers like Arius, and he expressed himself in words and phrases from the Holy Writ that they would understand.

Those who condemned the way Arius explained the Trinity readily conceded that it was not easy to express or understand "the single divinity of the Father, Son, and Holy Spirit," as one church historian puts it, "within an equal majesty and an orthodox Trinity."[16] That is exactly why the whole idea is referred to as "the *mystery* of Trinity." Even Augustine, who participated in the struggle against Arianism, concedes in *The Confessions* that he has not penetrated the mystery— "the Trinity appears unto me," he writes, "in a glass darkly"—and he doubts that anybody else has a much better grasp. "Which of us comprehendeth the Almighty Trinity?" he shrugs. "Rare is the soul which while it speaks of It, knows what it speaks of."[17]

Still, the enemies of Arius in the church of Alexandria insisted that he was putting a not-so-subtle pagan spin on Christianity. Father, Son and Holy Ghost must be understood as three "attributes" of the Only True God or three "persons" in which the divinity manifests itself. Arius, according to the orthodox critique, was suggesting that Jesus Christ and the Holy Spirit are "secondary gods,"[18] and thus his theology was "nothing but a disguised polytheism."[19] His clever little ditties reduced the solemn mystery of "Unity in Trinity" to a kind of "tri-theism," and reduced Jesus to "a demigod, a sort of inferior deity, tricked out in divine attributes."[20] And for that sin—the sin of false belief—they condemned him as a arch-heretic.

The Harlot in the Bishop's Bed

Arius and his parishioners, according to the Edict of Milan, enjoyed "complete and total freedom" to believe that the Bible means what it says when it calls Jesus the "only begotten son" of God. But Alexander, the bishop of Alexandria, true to the oldest traditions of monotheism, refused to tolerate a theological stance that he regarded as wrong. Alexander summoned a council of his fellow clergy in 321, and they voted to excommunicate Arius and to send him into exile. The Arian heresy, as the teachings of Arius came to be called, was declared to be "anathema"—and so it is still called in histories of the church that was the ultimate victor over Arianism.

Not every Christian, however, was quite so appalled. The teachings of Arius, in fact, were rooted in old and honorable traditions of early Christianity, including such revered figures as Origen and Lucian of Antioch, the martyr under whom Arius himself had studied. For every cleric who sided with Alexander, others of equal or greater stature sided with Arius. Among the churchmen who embraced his ideas were highly influential Christians who served in the court of Constantine, where they counseled the emperor on the intricacies of church politics and tutored his children in the new faith. For that reason, Arius could be denounced by Bishop Alexander as a "heresiarch" and driven from his parish, but—unlike Priscillian and thousands of other Christians only a few decades later—he could not lawfully be put to death by his fellow Christians under the authority of imperial law.

Still, the disputation between Arius and his adversaries resulted in a flood tide of theological propaganda and counterpropaganda, much of it expressed in concepts so airy and language so convoluted that the whole debate sometimes seems like gibberish. At its hottest moments, the argument was reduced to a few simple words and phrases that could be flung back and forth like stones by the contending factions. Was Jesus "begotten," as the Arians insisted with fervor—that is, was he created by God? Or was he "unbegotten," as the anti-Arians insisted with equal fervor—that is, was he one and the same as God? Was Jesus created by God *ex nihilo*—("out of nothing") or had he coexisted eternally with God?

"We are persecuted," Arius complained, summing up the arguments that his enemies made against him, "because we say, 'The Son has a beginning but God is without beginning.' "[21]

Ultimately, the theologians in each camp succeeded in boiling down the whole controversy to a choice between one of two catchwords. One faction insisted on characterizing God and Jesus as *homoousion*, a Greek word that can be translated into plain English as "made of the *same* stuff," that is, God the Father and God the Son were actually one and the same divinity. The other faction insisted on characterizing them as *homoiousion*, that is, "made of *similar* stuff," that is, God the Father could and should be distinguished from God the Son. The two words are spelled the same in Greek with the exception of a single tiny letter, an *iota*, which turns *homoousion* into *homoiousion*. The irony was immortalized by Edward Gibbon, who refers to the crucial Greek letter as "the important diphthong."[22]

"[T]he profane of every age," he writes with sly good humor, "have derided the furious contests which the difference of a single diphthong excited between the Homoousians and the Homoiousians."[23]

Remarkably, the arcane theological debate over Arianism was not confined to theologians. Rather, the struggle between the Arians and their adversaries tapped into the reservoir of fear and loathing that seems to well up whenever two human beings fix their attention on some difference between them, whether it is a matter of race or religion, class or color, age or sex. The question of whether God and Jesus were made of the same stuff or different stuff was and is ultimately unanswerable—indeed, that was what church authorities meant when they characterized the Trinity as a mystery—but that did not stop ordinary men and women throughout the Christian community from literally brawling with one another over an *iota*.

"If you ask a shopkeeper for change, he will argue with you about whether the Son is begotten or unbegotten," wrote theologian Gregory of Nyssa (c. 335–394) at the hottest moment of the crisis within Christianity over Arianism. "If you inquire about the quality of bread, the baker will answer, 'The Father is greater, the Son is less.'

And if you ask the bath attendant to draw your bath, he will tell you that the Son was created *ex nihilo*."[24]

Nor was it merely a war of words. Followers of one faction or the other were willing to take to the streets with rocks and cudgels, burn down each other's churches, lodge false charges against each other with the imperial authorities, and even drag out and string up each other's priests and bishops. To impugn his adversaries, for example, an Arian bishop in Antioch instructed a couple of priests to recruit a prostitute from a local brothel and slip her into the bed of a visiting anti-Arian bishop from Cologne as he lay asleep at an inn—they were to break into his bedchamber at daybreak, reveal him as a whoremonger, and thus cast shame on the enemies of the Arian cause. But the harlot refused to play her role in the plot—once smuggled into the bishop's bed, she raised an alarm and betrayed the plotters. On that day, it was the Arians whose reputation was sullied.

That Stranger God

Nothing in Constantine's upbringing in pagan Rome would have prepared him for the theological viper's nest into which he wandered when he put himself under the patronage of the Christian god. Polytheism, to be sure, was fully as diverse in its beliefs and practices as monotheism; if, as we have already seen, one bishop was able to count 156 heresies in Christianity, a pagan priest of the same era counted 360 gods and goddesses whom he deemed worthy of worship, one for each day of the ancient Egyptian calendar. But there was a crucial difference between the two kinds of diversity—paganism embraced *all* the rival gods and goddesses, and the very idea of "heresy" was something alien and baffling.

What's more, Constantine was distracted by far more urgent and worldly concerns. His coemperor, Licinius, was fully as ambitious as Constantine himself, and each of them aspired to be the one and only Augustus. Licinius, for example, had tried to discourage any new challengers to the imperial status quo by murdering the surviving

blood relations of all the dead emperors of the old Tetrarchy, including the wife and daughter of Diocletian, the son of Severus and the
whole family of Maximian. Licinius was also implicated in an elaborate plot against Constantine himself, an incident that prompted the
two emperors to send their armies into the field against each other
only a year or so after the wedding of Licinius and Constantine's half
sister. After a few early and tentative skirmishes, they backed off from
open civil war, and each of the willful emperors waited for the opportunity to strike a decisive blow against the other.

One sign of Licinius's concern over the ambition of his brother
emperor can be seen in his policy toward the Christian population in
the half of the Roman empire over which he reigned. Although the
Edict of Milan obliged him to refrain from persecution of *any* faith,
Licinius suspected the Christians of sympathies toward Constantine—if the two emperors challenged each other on the battlefield
again, the Christians could be expected to side with Constantine.
Christians had always been regarded as subversives by the pagan emperors of Rome, of course, but the anxieties of Licinius were even
more acute now that his coemperor reigned under the sign of the
cross.

Licinius began to issue a series of decrees that were aimed at de-
terring the perceived threat from the Christians in his realm. Christians were once again forbidden to serve in the palace, the
government and the army in his portion of the Roman empire.
Christian rituals were to be conducted out-of-doors, where the worshippers could be easily watched by imperial agents. And bishops
were forbidden to gather in church councils to consider matters of
theological controversy like the ones provoked by the Donatists and
the Arians. The pagan emperor, of course, was unconcerned whether
one faction or another provided the next man to wear the bishop's
miter in Alexandria or Carthage—rather, he wondered what plots the
Soldiers of Christ were preparing against *his* crown when they met
behind closed doors.

The renewed persecution of Christians in the eastern empire

supplied Constantine with a lofty motive for escalating his rivalry with Licinius into open warfare. "Licinius' growing dislike for the Christians," insists the historian John Holland Smith, "was simply one of the justifications for war found by Constantine's propaganda machine."[25] Indeed, Licinius may have been provoked by Constantine into sending an army into Thrace, which lay on the boundary between the eastern and western portions of the empire, and thus providing Constantine with a plausible excuse for going to war. After seven years of peaceful but troubled coexistence between the coemperors, Constantine once again raised the battle standard called the *labarum* and marched out at the head of an army to do battle against a pagan enemy.

Constantine had already elevated two of his sons, Crispus and Constantine II, to the rank of Caesar, and now he placed Crispus in command of the war fleet that gathered in the Bosphorus. The armies of the rival emperors met in battle at the gates of Adrianople in the summer of 324, and Constantine's victory sent Licinius into retreat toward Byzantium, where he was cut off by the fleet under the command of Crispus and then besieged by Constantine's army. Licinius and a remnant of his army escaped to Chrysopolis, the site of his final and crucial defeat.

Constantine's campaign against Licinius can be seen as a cunning and decisive blow against a rival for supreme political power. But the ancient sources, both Christian and pagan, insist on characterizing it as a holy war, the opening battle of the final struggle between God and the gods. Licinius fought under the aegis of the old pantheon of pagan Rome—his battle standards were decorated with images of the traditional gods and goddesses, and his army included a corps of *magi* who offered blood sacrifices in a desperate effort to enlist them in the battle with Constantine and pored over the entrails of the slaughtered animals to read the auguries of the battle to come. Constantine, by contrast, fought under battle standard that bore the "monogram of Christ," his corps of priests offered prayers to the

Christian god alone and he taught his troops a new war cry: "*Deus summus salvator!*" ("God the Highest, Savior!")[26]

"Constantine is not fighting against us but against the gods," Licinius announced in advance of the decisive battle, according to Constantine's chronicler, Eusebius of Caesarea. "Now we shall see who is wrong. If the gods prove themselves in battle to be true helpers, we shall march against all the godless. But if that stranger god wins, we have sacrificed to our gods in vain. We shall know what to do, for one must follow the conquering god."[27]

Of course, the final victory of Constantine can be measured in purely political terms. A pagan historian called Eutropius insists that the struggle between the emperors was a rivalry for absolute power between two ambitious men: "[O]nce he had decided to rule the whole world," insists Eutropius, Constantine "occasioned a war with Licinius."[28] Indeed, the defeat of Licinius meant that the Roman empire was now ruled by a single all-powerful monarch; for the first time in nearly a half century, only one man held the lawful title of Augustus. A coin issued by Constantine in celebration of his new stature was inscribed with the boastful and self-revealing phrase *Rector totius orbis*—"Ruler of the Whole World"—and now, at least in terms of the vast empire that was the Roman world, the words were literally true.[29]

Then, too, the imperial politics of ancient Rome can be seen as an intimate family affair. The surrender of Licinius was negotiated by his wife, Constantia, the half sister of Constantine, in exchange for a promise to spare the defeated emperor's life. It is a measure of Constantine's ruthlessness that he ultimately repudiated the promise he made to Constantia, his favorite of among all his brothers and sisters. Just as Licinius carried out a purge of potential rivals, Constantine ordered Licinius to be put to death by strangling in 325. Apologists for Constantine insist that he was compelled to murder Licinius for reasons of state—the old intriguer was accused of engaging in a treasonous conspiracy with barbarian tribes of Gaul—but even the ancient

Christian sources concede that the murder of Licinius was carried out "secretly" and "in defiance of civilised custom when oaths have been sworn."[30]

God the Highest

Constantine had favored the Christians within his realm ever since the victory at the Battle of the Milvian Bridge, of course, but even after the defeat of Licinius, the fate of Christianity in pagan Rome was not yet clear. After all, the vast majority of the Roman population, including all but a few members of the imperial household and the ruling class, were still pagans. Would Christianity merely continue to enjoy the generous gifts and personal protection of the man who happened to be the reigning emperor, or would it replace the old imperial cult as the state religion of the empire?

Constantine had put an end to the Great Persecution and secured for Christians the same freedom of religion that the various pagan cults had always enjoyed, but he still served as the *Pontifex Maximus* of the priestly colleges that preserved and practiced the worship of the old pantheon. He had granted Christian clergy the same rights and privileges as those enjoyed by priests of the various pagan cults, but the official coinage of his realm continued to feature the images of Jupiter and Mars, Hercules and *Sol Invictus*, all of them condemned by the Christians not merely as false gods but as devils and demons. At the celebration of his *decennalia*, the tenth anniversary of his reign, he had declined to participate in the customary blood sacrifices, but he had permitted the uttering of prayers of thanksgiving to the pagan deities. Above all, while his official pronouncements had always invoked a supreme deity in words and phrases that *seemed* to refer to the Christian god—"God the Highest," for example, or "The Supreme God"—he had not yet submitted to the fundamental Christian rite of baptism and, for that reason, was not yet a formal convert to Christianity.

With the victory over the last pagan emperor of the old Tetrarchy, however, Constantine was poised to make a decision for Christ that would have world-changing and history-making consequences. Now that he was the one and only emperor of the Roman empire, it was up to Constantine to determine exactly what measure of power and privilege would be bestowed upon the community of Christians whom the emperors who reigned before him had persecuted so cruelly. It was also within his power to decide which of the many contending factions within Christianity was entitled to hold itself out as what we are accustomed to call "*the* Church." For exactly that reason, as we shall see, the bitter struggle within early Christianity over the name and nature of the Only True God turned out to be a battle for the heart and mind of one man—the emperor Constantine.

CHAPTER SEVEN

THE RULER OF THE WHOLE WORLD

The Invention of the Totalitarian State
by the First Christian Emperor of Rome

Begin now to cast aside the causes of that disunity which has existed
among you, for by so doing, you will with one stroke be acting in
the manner most pleasing to the Supreme God, and confer
an extraordinary favor on me.

—Constantine to the bishops
at the Council of Nicaea

Among the legal petitions, military dispatches and diplomatic
notes from all over the ancient world that reached the palace
of the Augustus were two letters that had nothing at all to do
with affairs of state. Each one was signed by an ardent and eloquent
Christian cleric who carefully argued the merits of his case in the arcane theological debate over Arianism that raged within Christianity,
and each appealed to Constantine to act as the final arbiter and decide the case in his favor. Thus did the question of the begottenness
or unbegottenness of Jesus Christ come to the attention of the man
who ruled the Roman empire.

"It were better not to have asked," replied Constantine, "nor to
have answered such questions."[1]

Constantine never fully grasped the finer points of the argument
that he was called upon to decide one way or the other—but he was
quick to understand the dangers of dissent against authority, and he
knew well how to go about suppressing it. Indeed, his preference for
monotheism over polytheism reflected his own ambition to achieve

the same absolute power on earth that the Christian god was believed to exercise in heaven. "The division of the Empire into four sections by Diocletian required four divine patrons for the four rulers," explains historian Andrew Alfoldi. "The restoration of the unity of the Empire, on the other hand, led inevitably to the belief that a single divine power must watch over the single earthly ruler."[2]

"Just as there is only one God, and not two or three or more," affirms Eusebius, "so there is only one Emperor."[3]

Christianity also appealed to Constantine's preference for order over chaos. Polytheism, as we have seen, empowered every person across the Roman empire to seek spiritual truth from whatever source he or she found most appealing, but the church demanded absolute and unquestioning obedience of everyone who had been admitted to communion. "How could Constantine," asks Alfoldi, "fail to see the advantages of this unique organization?"[4] Constantine had been instructed in the dangers of heresy—a wholly new concept for a lifelong pagan—by the Christian priests who were now among his closest advisers, and he had taken the lessons to heart. "We have received from Divine Providence," he said of himself, "the supreme favor of being relieved from all error."[5]

"The First Totalitarian State in History"

As a ruthless campaigner and an expert intriguer, Constantine was perfectly willing and able to search out and punish anyone who challenged his political authority. Among his innovations, for example, was the establishment of the so-called *agentes in rebus*, a corps of imperial couriers who served as fixers, enforcers and informers. These "doers of things," as the Latin phrase is rendered in literal English, functioned as the ancient equivalent of a secret police, and they came to be feared and loathed by the men and women of all ranks and stations on whom they spied. The very existence of such apparatus of state security is what prompts biographer A. N. Wilson to characterize imperial Rome as "the first totalitarian state in history."[6]

The mind-twisting abstractions of theology, of course, were less threatening to Constantine than political intrigue, but he feared that one might encourage the other. Thus, for example, he banned private acts of divination out of concern that the auguries might encourage enemies of the state to conspire against his regime. If a soothsayer predicted the death of the emperor, the prediction might encourage a would-be assassin to make it happen. For the same reason, he continued the ancient practice of consulting the College of Haruspices, the imperial diviners, to interpret the meaning of a lightning strike on the palace or some other public structure. If the Haruspices detected a plot against Constantine, he wanted to know about it. The Christian clerics in his court condemned *all* pagan divination as the work of the devil, but Constantine did not care about the source of intelligence if it resulted in the arrest, torture and death of anyone who conspired against him.

Conflict and dissension within the church had long troubled Constantine, but all his earlier efforts to tame the unruly Christians had been defeated by the ardor with which the various factions battled against one another. The Donatists, for example, stubbornly clung to the Church of the Martyrs despite the escalating series of imperial measures that were designed to bring them back into the orthodox church. When arbitration and conciliation proved futile, Constantine resorted to banishment of Donatist bishops and seizure of their churches. The Donatists, however, still refused to recognize the authority of a church whose high clergy they regarded as cowardly and even traitorous.

Still, notably, Constantine did *not* resort to the threat or use of torture or capital punishment in dealing with the bitter debate over religious belief and practice—he preferred persuasion to coercion when it came to matters of faith. He may have placed himself under the protection of the Christian god, he may have bestowed his own largesse on those who worshiped the Only True God, but he still acted in the spirit of tolerance that was so deeply embedded in the pagan mind. "Let those who still delight in error be assured of the same degree of peace and tranquility as those who already believe," he declares in one of his encyclicals. "It is one thing voluntarily to take up the fight for eternal life; it is quite another to compel others to do so from fear of punishment."[7]

Now that he reigned over a newly unified empire, however, Constantine resolved to use his influence and authority to unify the Christian church, too. As the one and only Augustus, he was ready to recognize the one and only god of the Christians—and he expected the Christians to submit to the sovereignty of one god, one emperor and one church. Christian theology, as we have seen, provided the rationale for absolute monarchy—a single all-powerful deity reigned in heaven, and a single all-powerful monarch reigned on earth. Thus did Constantine claim to be nothing less than "the vice-regent of God,"[8] and his coinage declared him to be "Ruler of the Whole World." As such, Constantine regarded the theological civil war that the Christians were waging among themselves over the nature of the Only True God as both unseemly and unsafe.

On the occasion of his *vicennalia*, the twentieth anniversary of his accession to the throne, Constantine invited all the bishops of the Roman empire, some 300 or more, to gather at the palace at Nicaea. To speed them on their way, he granted them free passage on the imperial mail coaches that crisscrossed the network of Roman roads. As they arrived, he welcomed them with rich gifts, housed them in comfort, provided them with abundant food and drink. But he expected the quarrelsome churchmen to present him with something in return: the restoration of the "Peace of the Church." Constantine sought to impose law and order on the church in the same way that he had successfully imposed law and order on the empire that he ruled as the sole and absolute Augustus.

Constantine and the Confessors

Among the bishops who gathered at the emperor's charming lakeside villa at Nicaea in the spring of 325 were "confessors" who had suffered at the hands of the imperial authorities rather than surrender their Bibles or sacrifice to the pagan gods. Not so long ago, they had placed their own lives at risk by defying the harsh decrees of one Roman emperor, but now they found themselves enjoying the hospitality of another, more benevolent one. For these venerable heroes of the Great Persecution, the opening ceremonies of the so-called Council of Nicaea were tinged with deep and bitter irony.

Constantine, after all, wore the imperial diadem that had once crowned the heads of the emperors who had been their tormentors. The Roman legionnaires who lined the approach to the palace wore the same uniforms as the soldiers who had dragged them into dungeons where they were put to torture. As they walked past the guard of honor and entered the vast hall where Constantine waited to receive them, more than a few of the bishops hobbled on legs that had been sliced or shattered beyond healing. At the most sublime moment, according to one eyewitness account, Constantine himself bent down to kiss the empty eye sockets of a blind old man whose eyes had been gouged out by the imperial torturers during the Great Persecution.

"One might have thought it a foreshadowing of Christ's kingdom," enthuses Eusebius of Caesarea, "and a dream rather than a reality."[9]

Constantine, in fact, pointedly showed his deference to the convocation of bishops. His entourage consisted only of his family and a few of the Christians who served in his court—the bodyguard that always accompanied the emperor had been left outside the hall. He remained standing until one of the bishops granted him permission to be seated on his gilded throne, a reversal of the protocol that usually governed an audience with the Roman emperor. When the bishops celebrated the Christian rite of the Eucharist, he dutifully rose and left the hall—since he had not been baptized, he was not permitted to participate in the Holy Communion.

Yet Constantine was not wholly self-abasing in the presence of the bishops who had answered his call and were now dutifully gathered before him. He was arrayed in a gold and purple mantle, which symbolized his imperial authority, and he was perfectly willing to lecture the churchmen on their duties. When he rose to address the Council of Nicaea, Constantine did not bother to comment on any of the bitter disputes that had prompted him to summon the bishops in the first place. Significantly, he spoke in Latin, the official language of government, rather than Greek, the language of theology and the Christian Bible. And he made it clear that unity within the church was as crucial as unity within the empire.

"I will and wish for all of you peace and unanimity," declared the old warrior whose sword had been washed in the blood of his vanquished enemies, foreign and domestic.[10] "Internal strife within the Church of God is far more evil and dangerous than any kind of war."[11]

The Government of All Earthly Things

The Council of Nicaea was charged by the emperor with the task of curing all of the afflictions that disturbed the Peace of the Church. One of the most vexing problems was the date of Easter, a question that generated much bitterness because one faction relied on the Jewish calendar to determine the date and thus suffered the indignity of consulting the Jewish clergy to find out when to observe the holiest day in the Christian calendar. Another was the making of peace within the Christian community in Egypt; a breakaway faction in Alexandria, the Meletians, just like the Donatists in Carthage, refused to recognize the authority of the orthodox bishops, whom they accused of having been *traditores* during the Great Persecution, and declared their allegiance to the Church of the Martyrs. As for the subtle and corrosive debate between Arius and his adversaries over the proper distinction to be made between God the Father and God the Son—the debate over "the important diphthong"—all that mattered to Constantine was that the question be decided one way or the other and the whole noisy argument be silenced once and for all.

Constantine always claimed to be acting out of lofty Christian motives in addressing churchly matters, but even his most pious utterances betray a certain pragmatic concern that is more characteristic of polytheism than of monotheism. The traditional pagan idea of the "peace of the gods" was based on the sure conviction that a deity must be cosseted in order to win and keep its divine favor. Any offensive words or deeds by the worshiper posed the danger of alienating the god to whom worship was offered. Constantine took the same stance in his dealings with the new deity who had granted him victory over his enemies. The clamor in the church must be quieted so that the Christian god would not be disquieted. What was at stake, as far as Constantine was concerned, was the very survival of his imperial regime.

"I consider it utterly contrary to divine law that we should neglect such quarrels and disputes, by which the Highest Divinity may perhaps be roused to anger not only against the human race but also against me myself, to whose care He has entrusted, by His celestial will, the government of all earthly things," Constantine declared when he first attempted to repair the breach between the orthodox church and the Church of the Martyrs. "For I shall not be able to feel truly and fully secure . . . until I see everyone venerating the Most Holy God in the proper cult of the catholic religion with harmonious brotherhood of worship."[12]

The fact that Constantine mentions himself as often as God or the church reveals the real and urgent concern that prompted him to convene the Council of Nicaea. Indeed, if the Arian controversy interested the emperor at all, it was only out of the anxiety that the god of the Christians, who had entrusted Constantine with "the government of all earthly things," might grow so displeased with Constantine's apparent inability to silence the debate that he would change his mind and choose someone else to govern over the Roman empire.

A Death in the Latrine

Ultimately, the Council of Nicaea failed at every one of the principal tasks assigned to the bishops by Constantine. The Meletians, for example, refused to go along with the compromise that was adopted by the bishops, and the Church of the Martyrs continued to challenge the legitimacy of the orthodox church in Egypt. Indeed, the rivalry sputtered on for years, provoking riots, vandalism, book burnings and one notorious criminal case, in which Bishop Athanasius was charged with complicity in the murder and dismemberment of a Meletian bishop. Athanasius, it was alleged, used the severed hand of the dead bishop in a ritual of black magic. When the defendant was brought before a tribunal, a shriveled hand was offered in evidence against him—but the case ended in acquittal after the alleged victim showed up in court, alive and well and plainly in possession of both hands.

Even the dispute over something as simple and straightforward as the date of Easter was never fully resolved. The conflict, of course, had less to do with calendaring than with the ethnic and regional rivalries that already existed within a church that aspired to universal sovereignty over Christendom. Like so many other schisms and heresies, the Easter controversy cracked open along exactly the same linguistic and geopolitical fault lines that divided the Roman empire into eastern and western halves. Christianity, too, ultimately split into two separate spheres of influence, one Latin and the other Greek, one under the authority of the bishop of Rome and thus called the Roman Catholic Church, the other under the authority of the various churches that constitute Eastern Orthodoxy. And, to this day, Easter is observed on different days in eastern and western churches.

On the hottest point of all, the Arian heresy, the Council of Nicaea showed its greatest impotence. To be sure, the bishops were coerced into adopting a formal confession of faith, the so-called Nicene Creed, which declared God and Jesus to be *homoousion* rather than *homoiousion*—"of the *same* essence" rather than "of *similar* essence"—and thus repudiated the teachings of Arius. But many of the clerics, including one who served as a counselor to Constantine himself, soon renounced their vote and repudiated the Nicene Creed: "We com-

mitted an impious act, O Prince," wrote Bishop Eusebius of Nicomedia* to Constantine, "by subscribing to a blasphemy from fear of
you."[13]

The Arian controversy, in fact, only grew more rancorous as the
moderate bishops who advocated a compromise were outshouted by
the extremists on both sides of the question of whether God and
Jesus were made of the same or different stuff. Constantine, whose
court included both Arians and anti-Arians, was characteristically
mercurial and temperamental, sometimes siding with Arius and
sometimes with his principal adversary, Bishop Athanasius of
Alexandria. Both men endured sporadic periods of exile when one or
the other fell out of imperial favor, depending on who was whisper-
ing into Constantine's ears at any particular moment.

Athanasius, for example, was favored by Hosius of Córdoba, the
influential Spanish priest who had long served as Constantine's principal adviser on Christian matters and, as John Holland Smith puts
it, his "ecclesiastical intelligence officer."[14] Arius, on the other hand,
was favored by Constantia, the emperor's half sister, who had taken
up residence in the imperial palace after the murder of her husband,
the pagan emperor Licinius. Constantine himself cared not at all
about the theological niceties that moved other men and women to
violent words and violent deeds—he sought only to suppress the
whole rancorous debate. That is why, at the urging of his half sister,
he invited Arius to the imperial capital and ordered the orthodox
bishop to admit him to communion.

The bishop who was charged with welcoming Arius back into the
orthodox church was deeply distressed at what Constantine wanted
him to do, and he asked for a sign of divine will—or so the tale comes
down to us. If the belief that Arius held was pleasing to God, he should
be allowed to live, the bishop prayed, and if not, he should be made to

---

*Bishop Eusebius of Nicomedia is to be distinguished from the church historian Bishop Eusebius
of Caesarea, both of whom were Arians, and a third Eusebius, who served Constantine as chief
imperial eunuch.

die. On the day before the service at which he would be offered the Lord's Supper, Arius was seized with a violent spasm of pain as he hastened down the streets of Nicomedia, and he stumbled into a public latrine near the forum to relieve himself. When he squatted down, his bowels literally dropped out of his body in a sudden and massive hemorrhage, and he died then and there. The pious chroniclers insist that the bishop's prayer had been answered and Arius had met the fate that God willed for him. But there is another way to understand the ugly death of Arius.

"Those who press the literal narrative of the death of Arius," Gibbon observes, "must make their opinion between *poison* and *miracle*."[15]

"A Picture of Christ's Kingship"

Arius, as it turned out, won a posthumous victory. His teachings were embraced by Christians across the Roman empire for centuries after his death. Still, even if the Council of Nicaea failed to end the debate over Arianism, it marks a crucial event in the history of monotheism. When the bishops marched into the imperial palace, Christianity could still be seen as a radical and subversive movement that set itself against the power and the glory of Rome. When they marched out again, however, the bishops had "sealed an alliance of throne and altar"[16] and the church could be regarded as "a branch of the Imperial civil service."[17]

The Christian church now functioned as "the Christian 'state-within a state,'"[18] a kind of shadow government that styled itself after the imperial administration that had once sought to persecute Christianity. The word "vicar," for example, is derived from *vicarius*, a title that was first used by the arch-persecutor Diocletian to identify the deputies whom he placed in charge of various provinces, and "diocese" is derived from the term that described the area under their administration. "Basilica" originally described a public building that housed the royal courts and other government offices—the word comes from "*basileus*," the Greek word for "king"—but, significantly, it came to be associated with church architecture after Constantine deeded a basilica to the bishop of Rome for use as a church.

Christians had once been taught to believe that they would witness the end of the world—the final destruction of Rome, the "Whore of Babylon," and the elevation of the faithful to a heavenly kingdom—but now the church was allied with and dependent on the all-powerful Roman emperor who continued to rule here on earth. "The selfsame imperial government which used to make a bonfire of Christian sacred books had them adorned sumptuously with gold and precious stones," writes Jerome in frank amazement, "and, instead of razing church buildings to the ground, pays for the construction of magnificent basilicas with gilded ceilings and marble-encrusted walls."[19]

So the apocalyptic visions of the Book of Revelation were now replaced by *realpolitik*. When the high clergy of the Christian church beheld Constantine wearing the diadem that had once crowned their persecutors, they no longer saw an agent of Satan but rather "the Lord's angel," and they regarded the sight of the Augustus on the imperial throne as "a picture of Christ's kingship."[20]

A Death in the Palace

One measure of Constantine's piety—or, perhaps more to the point, his lack of it—is found in the short, unhappy life of his firstborn son, Crispus. Like Constantine himself, Crispus was the offspring of his father's first consort, a woman who may have been his concubine rather than his wife. Crispus's mother, Minervina, was dismissed when his father married the daughter of the emperor Maximian, but Constantine kept Crispus in his own household, encouraged him to acquire the skills of a soldier and ultimately raised him to the rank of Caesar. Still, Constantine turned out to be not the champion of his eldest son but his betrayer.

Crispus distinguished himself as his father's second in command

in the war against Licinius. Indeed, the young war hero won the adu-
lation of the Roman citizenry for his courage and daring in battle,
but Crispus may have been doomed by his own celebrity: "This dangerous popularity," writes Gibbon, "soon excited the attention of
Constantine, who, both as a father and as a king, was impatient of an
equal."[21] Then, too, Crispus may have fallen afoul of the imperial secret police whom Constantine charged with detecting and destroying
all potential rivals, real or imagined. Some nameless informer may
have whispered the name Crispus to one of the *agentes in rebus* who
were charged with rooting out conspiracies against the crown, and
the accusation of treason, whether true or false, was carried back to
Constantine.

The most lurid tales that reach us from antiquity accuse Crispus
of a sexual rather than a political offense: he is charged with conducting a love affair with his stepmother. Variants of the same story hold
that Fausta tried to seduce her handsome stepson, and when he dutifully rebuffed her advance, she revenged herself by falsely accusing
him of either a failed seduction or a successful rape. Yet another tale
accuses Fausta of dynastic intrigue—perhaps she falsely accused
Constantine's firstborn son of political or sexual treachery in order
to secure his death and thus clear the way for one of her own three
sons to mount the throne on the death of the Augustus.

A crucial role is assigned by some of the ancient sources to Constantine's mother, Helena. She had been "put away" by Constantine's
father, as we have seen, when he was first raised to the rank of Caesar
some thirty years earlier. Now she carried the title of empress and
was an influential figure in her son's court. Helena is said to have denounced her daughter-in-law, perhaps because she knew of Fausta's
sexual misdeeds with Crispus, or perhaps because she had invented
them, and she supposedly demanded that Constantine punish his
faithless wife by putting her to death.

Whatever the real reason for the suspicions that now afflicted
Constantine—and we do not know which of them, if any, were
grounded in fact—he resolved to do something about them while the

imperial entourage was en route from Nicaea to Rome in 326 for the formal celebration of his *vicennalia*. At a stopping place along the way, Crispus was arrested, shackled and charged with some unspecified crime. Constantine himself sat in judgment of his son and pronounced him guilty as charged; Crispus was stripped of the badges of rank that he wore as Caesar and put to death as a common criminal.

Fausta's life ended shortly afterward. One chronicler credits her with taking her own life in order to avoid the indignity of death at the hands of the public executioner. Others insist that she was murdered in the baths of the imperial palace—by drowning, by scalding or by asphyxiation, according to the various tellers of tales—and one especially gruesome version depicts the beautiful young woman dispatched like a stewed lobster after the doors to the baths were barred and the fires stoked to bring her bathwater to the boiling point. No matter how Fausta died, however, the consensus of the ancient sources is that Constantine was complicit in her death.

The death of a third victim of Constantine's purge is devoid of gruesome details but it allows us to see the likeliest reason for all of the carnage. Living under Constantine's protection in the imperial court was his nephew, Licinianus, the son of Licinius. Both Crispus and Licinianus had been granted the rank of Caesar in the happier days when their fathers served as coemperors. Now both of them were dispatched, along with their companions and comrades, on Constantine's orders. Sexual scandal and family politics aside, the simplest explanation is that Constantine was acting with typical ruthlessness to preclude any challenge to his reign.

The sons whom Constantine left alive did not yet pose a threat. The point is made in Constantine's selection of a replacement for Crispus as commander of the Roman garrison in Gaul. The troops who had served under Crispus were charged with pacifying the barbarian tribes along the northern frontier, but surely Constantine recalled how his own troops had once raised him to the purple in defiance of the lawful emperor. When he finally dispatched a new officer to replace the murdered Crispus, he chose one of his and

Fausta's three sons: the boy, who already held the title of Caesar and now assumed the command of the praetorian guard at Augusta Trevorum, was eleven years old.

The City of Constantine

Constantine and his court, now much reduced in size by the murders of his various relations, did not linger at the old imperial capital. Helena promptly set off on a pilgrimage to Palestine, perhaps as an act of contrition for her role in the deaths of Fausta and Crispus, and she embarked on a new career as the world's first and most successful biblical archaeologist. According to pious Christian tradition, she sought and found the sites where Jesus was crucified and entombed, and she is even credited with bringing back the True Cross. Constantine, too, undertook an ambitious new enterprise—he resolved to establish a glorious new capital for the empire that he ruled as the sole and supreme Augustus.

Constantine's city is conventionally depicted as a purely Christian enterprise. Like Akhenaton, we are invited to believe, he set out to build a pristine new capital on virgin soil. Just as the young pharaoh sought to distance himself from the old gods and goddesses of Egypt, the emperor aspired to create a place that would be wholly free of pagan shrines and statuary that adorned the streets of Rome. And so, on November 4, 328, Constantine put his hands on the handles of a plow and cut a furrow in the empty plain that marked the outermost boundaries of the city that he proposed to build, the city he called Constantinople. Another version of the same event depicts him using an implement with which he was surely more familiar—the point of a lance. Either way, Constantinople was the creation of the willful emperor who ultimately named the city after himself.

Constantine claimed to have been divinely inspired to build the city that turned out to be his most enduring monument, and he thus inspired the chroniclers to supply the colorful and evocative details that he neglected to mention. One tale reports that Constantine dreamed of an old crone who changed into a beautiful young woman, "so charming to his eye . . . that he could not refrain from kissing her." The dream supposedly baffled him until the late bishop of Rome, Pope Sylvester I, appeared to him in a second dream and explained that he was being instructed to build a new city: "You should make it famous with your own name," the pope tells the emperor, "and your descendants shall reign here forever." [22]

Another story proposes that as Constantine was marking out the future city limits, one of his courtiers ventured to observe that the site was surely large enough and to ask when the emperor would finally stop. "Not until He who walks before me stops." So Constantine walked on, dragging the spear behind him. Constantine himself was never specific about what deity, if any, he had in mind; it is Christian tradition that supplies the capital H in the word "he," suggesting that the invisible guide was the Only True God. [23]

History tells a rather different story. The city was not built on virgin soil—the site was already occupied by the ancient city of Byzantium, a place that had long figured in pagan myth and legend and, since it marked the place where Europe ends and Asia begins, provided both symbolic and strategic advantages. Nor was Constantine's new city untainted by paganism. The emperor sought the advice of pagan astrologers and augurs in choosing an auspicious day for the ancient pagan ritual of marking the boundaries. The dedication of the completed city, which took place only two years after the groundbreaking, was celebrated with "ancestral rites" of pagan origin that lasted forty days, including public feasts, games and processions. [24] Among the *prominenti* who were invited by Constantine to participate in the festivities were Sopater, a leading practitioner of the mystic pagan philosophy called Neoplatonism, and Praetextatus, a man who was famous for multiplying his various priesthoods, including those of *Sol Invictus*, Isis, Cybele and Mithra.

To symbolize the fact that the city of Constantine was now the "New Rome," wholly replacing the old capital as the seat of the empire, Constantine ordered the statue of the goddess Athena to be seized and carried from Rome to Constantinople. At least two pagan temples were erected in Constantinople while Constantine himself was yet alive—one was dedicated to the demigods Castor and Pollux, patrons of horsemanship in general and cavalry in particular, and another to Fortuna, the goddess who was believed to determine one's fortune, good or ill. A third shrine, dedicated to the spirit of "Holy Peace," was also associated with pagan tradition, and a fourth was devoted to Constantine himself.

"So much for Eusebius' assertion, in his *Life of Constantine*," declares Diana Bowder, "that Constantinople was a wholly Christian city, without a single pagan temple!"[25]

According to Eusebius of Caesarea, Constantine ordered that idols in pagan temples throughout the empire be seized and stripped of their gold and silver shells so that the wooden armatures and straw stuffing would be revealed—the pagans would be confronted with the fact that the idols were not gods at all. But Constantine's real motive in looting the pagan treasures had less to do with Christian idealism than with raising money to pay for the construction of his new city. After all, even the pagan emperors had been willing to melt down statues fashioned out of precious metals in order to pay for armies or palaces. Significantly, Constantine destroyed the pagan statuary that could be melted down into gold or silver ingots while preserving those fashioned out of brass, wood or marble: "For the decoration of his new capital," writes the nineteenth-century historian Jacob Burckhardt, "Constantine was very willing to use images whose material was of no great value."[26]

Even the gargantuan statue of Constantine, fashioned out of gilded bronze and set atop a column of stone, was free of Christian iconography of any kind. He was depicted in a manner that was strongly suggestive of a pagan god—the head was adorned with the radiate crown that was an attribute of *Sol Invictus*, the sun god, and the right hand carried the figure of Victory, one of the most cherished pagan goddesses of ancient Rome. The figure itself, in fact, was a statue of Apollo from the site of ancient Troy whose face was re-worked to resemble Constantine. And the whole elaborate display was artfully designed to invoke the loyalties of both pagans *and* Christians. The installation incorporated the most precious artifact of the pagan world—the statue (or "Palladium") of Athena, reputedly brought from Troy by Aeneas in distant antiquity—and the most precious artifact of the Christian world, a supposed fragment of the True Cross that Helena brought back from her expedition to Palestine.

"The foundation of [Constantinople] was a careful piece of symbolic and spiritual engineering, conducted according to the age-old techniques of Pagan magical technology," insist historians Prudence Jones and Nigel Pennick.[27] But Jacob Burckhardt offers quite another way of understanding Constantine's motives in founding and adorning the city he named after himself: "Here Constantine is neither pagan nor Christian—for he affronted both religions by carrying images of the gods off to Byzantium—but a self-seeking plunderer for the sake of glorifying his own name."[28]

The Tinted Wig

According to a charming tale that is preserved in the ancient sources, Diocletian was invited by Maximian to resume the rank of Augustus at a particularly tumultuous moment in the struggle that followed his retirement. Now living in obscurity at his villa on the Dalmatian coast, Diocletian was offered the opportunity to once again wear the diadem and the purple mantle, to take up residence in the imperial palace and to rule the Roman empire as its lord and master. All these blandishments, however, left the old emperor unmoved.

"He rejected the temptation with a smile of pity," writes Gibbon, "calmly observing that, if he could show Maximian the cabbages which he had planted with his own hands at Salona, he should no longer be urged to relinquish the enjoyment of happiness for the pursuit of power."[29]

No such scene was ever played out in the life of Constantine. He reigned for more than thirty years, and as he aged, he only grew more attached to absolute power and its trappings: "He wore the garb of kings adorned with jewels," reports the ancient historian Zosimus, "and on his head a diadem constantly."[30] Indeed, his harshest critics depict him as a ludicrous and even laughable figure toward the end of his reign, given to wearing tinted wigs in a rainbow of colors and draping himself in garish silks. No longer the handsome, fit and forceful young man who is depicted in the statuary that he left behind, Constantine was now thickset and gone to fat. Zosimus notes that "in common parlance he was called 'Bullneck.' "[31]

Even Eusebius of Caesarea, his mostly worshipful biographer, finds himself forced to concede that the old emperor was an odd sight, although he insists that Constantine was only seeking to please the plebs. "He smiles at his dress," writes Eusebius of the occasion of Constantine's *tricennalia*, "with its embroideries of gold and flowers, and at his imperial purple and diadem, when he sees the crowds staring like children in wonderment."[32]

But, quite unlike the more notorious pagan emperors, Constantine could not be fairly accused of the sins of carnality. "[F]rom his earliest youth to a very advanced season of life," allows Gibbon, "he preserved the vigour of his constitution by a strict adherence to the domestic virtues of chastity and temperance."[33] He was, in fact, "a puritan of sorts," according to John Holland Smith.[34] Among his decrees and edicts were laws that were designed to discourage concubinage, the prostitution of inn-servants and the seduction of slaves, all of which may have been prompted by the fact that his own mother was reputed to have been the victim of one or two of these offenses against public morality.

The crowning moment of his reign was the *tricennalia*, a public celebration of the supreme power that he had achieved by force of arms and preserved by force of will for more than thirty years. Ambassadors from all over the ancient world presented themselves at court to honor the old emperor, including a delegation from Persia, the once and future enemy of the Roman empire. Yet Rome was no less troubled at the end of Constantine's reign than it had been at the beginning, and history would reveal that nothing Constantine had accomplished as the all-powerful Augustus would halt its decline and fall.

The construction of Constantinople had exhausted the royal treasury. The barbarian tribes along the Danube continued to threaten the *Pax Romana*. Plague had broken out in the provinces of Asia Minor, famine in the villages of Syria, bread riots in the streets of Antioch. Now and then, the more militant Jews in Palestine rose up in protest against the Roman occupation of their homeland. A usurper set himself up in Cyprus as a rival for the imperial crown. The emperor of Persia was engaging in provocative acts of persecution against his own Christian population, perhaps as a prelude to war against Rome. By 337, the last year of his long life and reign, Constantine bestirred himself yet again to lead his army into battle—a battle that he would not live to fight.

Was Constantine a Christian?

One question remained unanswered even at the very end of his long reign: Was Constantine an earnest convert to Christianity, or merely a cunning politician who saw in Christianity a tool for his own self-aggrandizement? For the pious chroniclers of Christianity, the *bona fides* of Constantine are beyond dispute—that is why he is hailed as "Constantine the Great" in Catholic tradition and even as "St. Constantine" in Orthodox tradition. "What is really remarkable and astonishing," insists historian Andrew Alfoldi, "is the fact that Constantine succeeded, in one short decade, in shedding his last vestiges of polytheism."[35] But secular historians are a bit more guarded in their judgments about the so-called conversion of Constantine.

Some historians suspect Constantine of being a halfhearted Christian at best, a man who was motivated by political calculation rather than true belief. "His religion, if he had any, would seem to have been purely nominal," argues John Holland Smith. "Constantine neither persecuted Christians nor, apparently, favoured them until it became expedient for him to do so, when he needed them as allies in the war for Rome."[36]

Other historians are willing to credit Constantine with sincerity if not purity of motive in his embrace of Christianity. "It was no cynical calculation that made Constantine a Christian, and at the date of his conversion, Christianity was far too unimportant, especially in the West, to justify an appeal to its adherents," insists Diana Bowder. "It is clear from our sources that Constantine was a deeply religious man, quite incapable of any self-interested pretence in this sphere. . . . [T]o the end of his life, he acted out of his conviction that he had been chosen by the God of the Christians to inaugurate a Christian Roman Empire."[37]

Constantine was surely a visionary and a revolutionary, no less so than Akhenaton or Josiah—"a man of action," according to a modern historian who sums up the testimony of the Christian chronicler Philostorgios, "just as brutal and decided as he is farsighted and intelligent."[38] Like them, Constantine claimed to have been on a divinely ordained mission: "This was my glorious task," he says of himself, "God's gracious gift to me."[39] From the pagan perspective, of course, he was "a wicked innovator and tamperer with the time-hallowed laws," as Julian sees it, "and the sacred ethical traditions of our fathers."[40] But an argument can be made that Constantine remained open-minded on the subject of religion even after he embraced a high god whose name and identity he often neglected to mention, referring instead to a kind of all-purpose deity that he called the "Highest God" or "Supreme God."

"He seems in fact to have been a normal polytheist, and he both permitted and founded shrines to other divinities," insist Jones and Pennick. "What Constantine actually did was to grant freedom of religion to all within the Empire, [and] he was personally inclined to the worship of a supreme and nameless deity, as the philosophers had been before him."[41]

No historian, pious or secular, can dispute the simple and compelling fact that Constantine was not formally admitted to the Christian church until he fell ill in 327 and called a priest to his sickbed to baptize him only hours before his death. Until that moment, he was never more than a "hearer" in the Christian church, a term that was reserved for those who were preparing for conversion, and he had never tasted the wafer or sipped the wine of Holy Communion. At one moment of candor, in fact, he revealed to a council of Christian clergy that he regarded himself as "the bishop of those outside the church."[42]

If Constantine was an early and enthusiastic convert to Christianity, as conventional Christian sources have always claimed, why did he delay his own baptism for so many years? All three of his surviving sons had been baptized and raised as Christians, but Constantine himself never joined them at the baptismal font.[43] The conventional explanation is that deathbed baptism was a common practice in early Christianity—since baptism was believed to cleanse the soul of all sin, some Christians preferred to wait until all opportunity to sin was over. Indeed, Tertullian was distressed at what he called "the cunning postponement of baptism,"[44] and complained that it actually encouraged some men and women to take advantage of the delay by indulging in as much sinning as possible before the baptism.

Some historians speculate that Constantine sought to be baptized, ardently and repeatedly, but he was denied admission into the church by the bishops because of some ghastly but undisclosed moral offense, perhaps the cold-blooded decision to murder his wife and son. The story was plausible to the ancient pagan chroniclers, who insisted that Constantine embraced Christianity only after he was first told by stern and high-minded pagan priests that his crimes could not be forgiven and then turned to a Christian priest "who offered him the free forgiveness of Christ."[45] Indeed, the orthodox bishop who served as Constantine's confessor and counselor, Hosius of Córdovba, may have "used Constantine's guilty conscience," as Diana Bowder puts it, "as a means of tightening [Christianity's] hold upon him."[46]

Still, even if Constantine can be said to have "converted" to Christianity as early as 312, when he was granted a vision (or a dream) of the cross (or the *chi-rho*) on the eve of battle, the fact remains that he was never a rigorist or a true believer. To be sure, he clearly favored the Christian god and those who worshiped him, and he issued a series of decrees that were meant to make it easier to practice the faith. Sunday, the holy day of the Christians, was declared a legal holiday. Crucifixion was abolished, and displays of gladiatorial combat, which had been the occasion for so much carnage against the Christian martyrs, were discouraged if not outrightly prohibited. Christian clergy were granted the same rights and privileges that had long been afforded to the priests of pagan cults, and Christian churches were permitted to receive bequests. Constantine bestowed gifts of money and property on the church, including basilicas, palaces and a shrine of Apollo that was converted into the Church of St. Peter.

Constantine deferred to the church on matters of ritual purity among Christians. Thus, he did not confine himself to a decree that prohibited magistrates from *compelling* a Christian to offer sacrifice to the pagan gods; rather, he went one step further by issuing a second decree that prohibited Christians from *willingly* participating in pagan sacrifice. The same sensitivity was at work when it came to a syncretistic cult that worshiped at a shrine in a grove of trees near Hebron where, according to the Book of Genesis, God and two angels appeared to Abraham and Sarah. The visitation of the three divine figures was regarded as an early manifestation of the Father, the Son and the Holy Spirit, but the whole nasty debate over Arianism cautioned the church against anything that seemed to link the Trinity to the practices of polytheism. So Constantine ordered the altar to be torn down and the figures that decorated its shrine to be burned.

But the fact remains that Constantine never criminalized the beliefs and practices of paganism itself. He may have ordered the closure of one or two pagan temples, but his decrees had more to do with his own sexual puritanism than a policy of antipaganism. One temple of Aphrodite in Lebanon was razed, for example, but only because it was reputedly a gathering place for transvestites and prostitutes of both sexes. At another shrine of Aphrodite in the same distant province, where only female prostitutes plied their trade, the emperor left the temple intact and contented himself with urging the populace to show "greater restraint."[47] And Constantine may have condemned the practice of priestly castration in Egypt, but he did not prohibit the priests from conducting the pagan ceremonies that were thought to ensure the annual flooding of the Nile that was crucial to Rome's food supplies—why take the risk of drought and famine by offending the old gods and goddesses?

Even the city that carried his name was a showplace of pagan art and statuary, much of it seized from shrines and temples around the empire and shipped to Constantinople to adorn the new capital. Eusebius of Caesarea insists that the pagan art works were put on display to show the populace that they were false and detestable things, but the emperor's real motives may have been less pure—Constantine may have hoped that the "magical power" of the gods and goddesses would sanctify his new capital.[48] Thus, for example, Constantine held a gold statuette of Fortuna in his hand on the day of its dedication, and he ordered that an ancient wooden statue of the goddess Cybele, the Great Mother of the Gods, be set up in a portico where she looked out protectively over the city, her hands outstretched in a gesture of prayer.

"Constantine, it has been well said, might have entered on Christianity as a man embarks on marriage," observes Robin Lane Fox, "not realizing at first that it required him to give up his former, disreputable friends."[49]

Still, it is undisputed that Constantine died a Christian. He fell ill on Easter Sunday, 337. Seeking a cure, he visited a hot springs, and then, despairing of a cure, he visited a church, offering prayers for his own healing and vowing to live as an ascetic if his prayers were answered. At last, convinced that death was fast approaching, he summoned the bishops who served him at the imperial court in Constantinople and asked to be baptized. "The moment I have been awaiting for so long has come at last," declared the dying emperor, or so says Eusebius. "Now I, too, may have the blessing of that seal which confers immortality. So be it, then. Let there be no further delay."

On May 22, 337, at the age of sixty-six,[50] after more than thirty years on the throne, Constantine was dead and gone at last. A majority of his subjects were still pagans, and paganism still served as the state religion of Rome. The Christian revolution that he set into motion was only beginning, and its success was far from assured.

CHAPTER EIGHT

THE ORPHANS OF MACELLUM

*The Christian Prince Who Survived a Blood Purge and
Struggled for the Restoration of Paganism*

Only a little more effort and the Devil will be
completely overthrown by your laws.
—Firmicus Maternus, *On the Error
of Profane Religions*

No miracle is required to explain how Constantine continued to reign long after his death. The Chief Eunuch and Master of the Sacred Bedchamber greeted the corpse at dawn and bid it a good night's sleep at nightfall. Ministers and generals kneeled before the body, which was displayed on a golden bed and adorned with the diadem and the purple robe, and offered their customary reports. Petitions were read aloud to him, and edicts were issued in his name. The imperial courtiers who had served the Augustus during his long reign feared the chaos and conspiracy that might ensue if the Roman empire found out that the emperor was gone before his sons had secured the crown for themselves. Not until all three of his surviving sons reached Constantinople in the late summer of 337 did they announce the momentous passing and send the corpse to its final rest in the Church of the Holy Apostles.

The solemn rituals that attended the belated imperial funeral offered a glimpse into a brave new world that Constantine had never seen. Constantine may have distanced himself from some pagan traditions—he discouraged blood sacrifices, as we have seen, and he closed down a few of the most provocative pagan shrines—but he tolerated and even participated in the more sedate rituals of paganism. When selecting men of rank and skill to serve in his army and his imperial administration, Constantine favored Christians but did not exclude pagans. Now, however, an unmistakable sign was given by the new regime that Christianity was to be granted an even more intimate and influential role in the governance of the Roman empire.

A public procession and a military funeral were conducted, and the coffin of the dead emperor was placed atop an ornate catafalque, fashioned of gold, decorated with gemstones and surrounded by the supposed relics of the apostles. The final interment of Constantine's mortal remains was a moment of innovation in Christian history—countless thousands of Christians had been buried in tombs and catacombs throughout the Roman empire according to the prescribed rites of the church, but never before had a Christian emperor been laid to rest.

All pagans, even those of the highest rank, were wholly excluded from the sanctuary when the burial actually took place. The respect and tolerance that Constantine had extended to paganism, if sometimes only grudgingly, was now withdrawn, and only those who had been admitted to communion in the Christian church were permitted to witness the interment. Even so, out of long habit, the pagans of Rome afforded Constantine the same honor that pagan emperors had enjoyed ever since Octavian: they solemnly declared him to be a god.

The Blood Purge

On the death of Constantine, a remarkable document was found in the cold hand of the corpse—the last will and testament of the dead emperor. The will had been entrusted to Bishop Eusebius of Nicomedia, the man who had baptized him on his deathbed, and it was Eusebius who arranged for it to be found in the deathbed. The dying emperor, according to an account provided by the ancient chronicler

Philostorgios, declared in the will that he had been the victim of murder by slow poisoning. He named the culprits as his own half brothers, Dalmatius and Julius Constantius—the sons of his father, Constantius the Pale, and his stepmother, Theodora—and he called on his sons to revenge themselves against his faithless siblings.

The accuracy of the charge against Constantine's half brothers and, indeed, the authenticity of the document in which it was made were called into question even in antiquity. Dalmatius and Julius Constantius almost certainly had nothing to do with Constantine's death; they had both been granted rank and title by Constantine, and they were occasionally entrusted by their half brother with political and diplomatic missions so sensitive that he clearly assumed they were both loyal and discreet.

But the phony will provided both an explanation and an excuse for the blood purge that the sons of Constantine—Constantine II (c. 316–340), Constantius II (317–361) and Constans (c. 323–350)— now carried out. The sons of Constantine were apparently convinced that someone would challenge their claim to rule in their father's place, whether it was an uncle, a cousin or a courtier. When the killing was over, all of the potential rivals for the imperial crown were gone: "The sun of the sons of Constantine rose blood-red," puns the nineteenth-century historian Gerald Henry Rendall, "with the slaughter of their kin."[1]

Dalmatius and Julius Constantius were arrested, hastily tried and convicted, and promptly put to death. Constantine's nephew Hannibalianus, to whom Constantine had granted the lofty title of "King of Kings" and the hand of his daughter, Constantina, in marriage, was seized in his little kingdom on the Black Sea in Asia Minor and murdered without judicial formalities by some of the troops under his command, supposedly on their own initiative but more likely at the instigation of Constantius II. The same fate befell another nephew, also called Dalmatius, who held the rank of Caesar and served on the troubled frontier along the Danube.

Clearly, a family relationship with Constantine and his sons, whether by blood or marriage, offered no security at all. Indeed, the men and women who were closest to the throne seem to have come under the sharpest suspicion. Julius Constantius was both the uncle and father-in-law of Constantius II. A man who had served as praetorian prefect under Constantine was arrested and executed, even though Constans was betrothed to his infant daughter. The husband of Anastasia, Constantine's half sister, suffered the same fate. In sum, two brothers and seven nephews of Constantine were put to death, according to Julian's count, and once the denunciations and executions began, the purge reached far beyond the imperial family.[2]

Constantine's sons, as we shall see, proved to be far less adept than their father at seizing and holding imperial authority, but they followed his example of ruthlessness in their attempts to do so. Ironically, Constantine had supplied them with a memorable display of these qualities when he had arranged for the murder of his firstborn son, Crispus, and his second wife, Fausta.[3] Now they followed his example by arranging for the death of the potential rivals among *their* blood relations. Although all three brothers may have conspired in carrying out the blood purge, Constantius II is generally regarded as its principal author.

Only two other male members of Constantine's intimate family circle survived the slaughter. The eldest of the three sons of Julius Constantius was slain, but the two younger boys were spared. One fanciful story preserved by Christian sources proposes that one or both of them were spirited away by a sympathetic priest through a secret passage in the palace and sheltered from the death squads in a church. A more plausible explanation is that the two young boys, suddenly orphaned by the murder of their father, were so frail and young that neither was regarded as a serious threat—the older child was twelve years old, ailing and expected to die, and the younger was only six years old. Their lives were spared, and they were raised as virtual prisoners of Constantius II, the cousin who had ordered the death of their father. The names of the young wards were Gallus (c. 325–354) and Julian (c. 331–363).[4]

Brothers and Emperors

The same forged will that prompted Constantine's sons to murder their uncles, cousins and in-laws also provided for the division of the Roman empire among the three of them. After some bickering and bargaining, they agreed on how the spoils were to be shared out. The eastern empire went to Constantius II; the western empire was divided between Constantine II and Constans. Following the example of Diocletian rather than that of Constantine, they reigned as co-emperors, each one formally acclaimed by the army and confirmed by the Roman Senate as an Augustus.

None of the three sons of Constantine inspired much admiration among historians, pagan or Christian. Constantine II, they suggest, may have been born out of wedlock to one of his father's imperial concubines. Constans, only fifteen when he ascended the throne, is recalled as a pious hypocrite—he issued a decree that made homosexuality a capital crime, but he recruited his bedmates from among the "handsome barbarian hostages" taken in battle, according to Zosimus, and allowed them "to perpetrate any such misdeeds against his subjects as served him with occasion for sexual depravity."[5] And Constantius II is regarded as a murderous but weak-willed monarch who permitted himself to be manipulated by the men and women in his intimate circle, his wives as well as his courtiers.

"With his chamberlain," cracks the pagan historian Ammianus Marcellinus in a sarcastic aside, "he possessed considerable influence."[6]

The three siblings reigned as fellow Christians and, quite literally, as "brother emperors," but the harmony among them was brief and mostly illusory. Indeed, the purge of imagined enemies within their own family and the division of the empire did nothing to ensure a peaceful reign. While their pagan subjects watched, waited and wondered what life would be like under the rule of three unambiguously Christian monarchs, the brothers went to war against one another.

An Enemy of the People

Perhaps because they had been entrusted in childhood to Christian tutors, the sons of Constantine tended to express their rivalries—both as siblings and as Augusti—in theological terms. On the vexing question of whether Jesus was God himself or only the Son of God, for example, Constantius II sided with the Arians while Constantine II and Constans sided with the orthodox church. Even so, politics and religion were so intertwined in the dealings of the three brothers that they cannot be readily or completely untangled.

Constantius II embraced a watered-down version of the teachings of Arius that came to be known as semi-Arianism—and, tellingly, so did Bishop Eusebius of Nicomedia, the man who came up with the will that bestowed upon Constantius II the richest portion of the Roman empire. By contrast, Constantine II and Constans, who were forced to share sovereignty in the western empire under the terms of the same will, denounced all shades of Arianism as heresy and embraced the orthodox theology of Bishop Athanasius (c. 293–373), the bitter adversary of Arius. Conveniently, and not incidentally, each of the three emperors followed the apparent preferences of the majority of Christians in his realm—Arianism was dominant in the eastern empire where Constantius II reigned, and orthodoxy was dominant in the western empire, where Constantine II and Constans reigned.

One example of how religion mirrored politics under the reign of the three sons of Constantine can be found in the curious fate of Athanasius, bishop of Alexandria, champion of orthodoxy and bitter enemy of the Arians, whom he dismissed as "Ariomaniacs."[7] Over his long and troubled tenure, Athanasius was sent into exile on five separate occasions by various emperors. But Constantine II befriended

Athanasius, sheltered him at his court in Gaul, and even purported to authorize his return to Alexandria, all in defiance of both the political authority and religious affiliation of his brother and fellow emperor.

Constans, who shared Constantine II's commitment to orthodoxy, joined in championing the cause of Athanasius. He sent letters of entreaty to Constantius II in an earnest and even frantic effort to persuade him to permit Athanasius and other orthodox bishops to return to their old sees. When letters were unavailing, Constans sent emissaries, and when the emissaries failed in their mission, he threatened to send an army and a fleet against his Arian brother in the name of orthodoxy. And yet his faith ultimately mattered less than his ambition—when Constans eventually took up arms, it was against his orthodox brother, Constantine II, rather than his Arian brother, Constantius II.

Indeed, the conflict between Constantine II and Constans had nothing to do with matters of theology. As orthodox believers, they both professed that God and Jesus were *homoousion*—made of the same stuff—and they both sided with Bishop Athanasius against the Arian "heretics" who held that God and Jesus were made of similar stuff. But they were also both aggrieved over their respective shares of the western empire. "[T]hey were incapable of contenting themselves," notes Edward Gibbon, "with the dominions which they were unqualified to govern."[8]

In 340, Constantine II crossed the Alps at the head of an army in an effort to take Italy away from Constans. Young Constans did more than merely defend the territory that had been awarded to him on the death of their father: an advance guard of Constans's army lured Constantine II into a fatal ambush, the battered body of the dead emperor was dumped into the Alsa River, and the whole of his realm passed under the sovereignty of Constans. The common faith of the two brothers did nothing to soften the heart of the victorious Constans— he declared his fellow believer in orthodoxy to have been an enemy of the people, annulled his decrees and edicts, and seized his holdings. At seventeen, Constans was the sole emperor of the western empire.

Ironically, the two sons of Constantine who both embraced orthodox Christianity fell out with each other, and yet Constans managed to live in concord with his Arian brother, Constantius II, for a full decade. When Constans met an early and violent death, the blow was struck by an ambitious pagan general who saw an opportunity to claim the imperial crown and restore the old gods and goddesses to the place of honor they had so long enjoyed in Rome.

The Insanity of the Sacrifices

Constantine, as we have seen, may have favored Christianity but he never dared to openly persecute paganism, the colorful array of rituals and beliefs that were still practiced by a vast majority of his subjects. Indeed, by a profound and telling irony, the only faith that was *not* generally if grudgingly tolerated during the reign of the first Christian emperors was Christianity—or, at least, those strains of Christianity that were condemned by one faction or another as heresy and schism. "[V]enerable confessors were tortured into heresy upon the rack," writes Gerald Henry Rendall. "[P]relates or clergy were exiled, starved, strangled, or beheaded."[9]

The sons of Constantine, however, escalated the war of God against the gods by issuing the first recorded edict that criminalized the rites and rituals of paganism. Although they claimed to be re-enacting a law of Constantine, the fact is that no such earlier decree has been found. "Let superstition come to an end, and the insanity of sacrifices be abolished," goes one imperial decree issued in 341,[10] and a second decree ordered that "the temples be immediately shut, and carefully guarded." The death sentence was threatened for anyone who defied the decree: "Let him feel the sword of vengeance."[11]

Here ends the era of official toleration that commenced with the Edict of Milan, and here begins the formal persecution of paganism in ancient Rome. The declaration of open war thrilled the Christian rigorists who had long denounced the pagan gods and goddesses as not merely false but demonic. "Paganism, most holy emperors, must be utterly destroyed and blotted out, and disciplined by the severest enactments of your edicts, lest the deadly delusion of that presumption continue to stain the Roman world," urged Firmicus Maternus, a pagan convert who reinvented himself as a relentless enemy of his former faith. "How fortunate you are that God, whose agents you are, has reserved for you the destruction of idolatry and the ruin of profane temples."[12]

At first, the persecution of paganism was a halfhearted, mostly symbolic undertaking. The oft-quoted decree against sacrifices, according to Pierre Chuvin, was aimed only at the practice of examining the viscera of sacrificed animals, and the other rites and rituals of paganism were still tolerated. Gibbon insists that "this formidable edict was either composed without being published, or published without being executed."[13] A law of 342 specifically prohibited the destruction of the pagan temples that stood just outside the walls of Rome—the traditional sites of spectacles, circuses and games—so that the people of Rome might still enjoy "their ancient entertainments."[14] And Constantius II, like his father, retained the old title of *Pontifex Maximus*, thus serving as high priest of the pagan cults that still functioned, strictly speaking, as the state religion of Rome.

"That emperor suffered the privileges of the Vestal Virgins to remain inviolate," insists the pagan orator Symmachus, "and, though he had embraced a different religion, he never attempted to deprive the empire of the sacred worship of antiquity."[15]

A state of cold war between monotheism and polytheism prevailed for a few more years. Just as many provincial magistrates had declined to enforce the anti-Christian decrees of the Great Persecution, the antipagan decrees were now "largely shipwrecked on the passive resistance of pagan governors," according to Diana Bowder.[16] Among the pagans who converted to Christianity, some did so only as a kind of protective coloration in an effort to promote their careers in public service. As a result, many Romans went to their graves "with Charon's penny on their tongues"—a gesture that honored the ferryman of pagan myth who was thought to carry dead souls across the Styx—"and a cross in their hands," as John Holland Smith puts it.[17]

But even the first tentative measures of repression fired the spirit of opposition among the pagans who had accommodated themselves to the Christian idiosyncrasies of the all-powerful Constantine. The disgruntled and embattled pagans were eventually offered an opportunity for open rebellion in the person of an ambitious officer called Magnentius (d. 353), a soldier of German stock who had risen to noble rank and command of the elite legions of the Roman army. The target of his coup d'état was not the accommodating Christian emperor in the east, Constantius II, but his zealous younger brother, Constans, who ruled in the west. So began the pagan counterrevolution, a conflict in which not only the imperial crown but the whole edifice of classical paganism were at stake.

At Midnight

In 350, Magnentius was feasting with his fellow officers in the winter quarters of the imperial legions under his command, according to the tale as told by Zosimus, when the table talk turned to the excesses of Constans and the notorious young barbarians with whom he surrounded himself. Here is an example of pagan morality at work: pagans were apparently no less scandalized than Christians by the sexual adventures of the young emperor. At midnight, Magnentius excused himself "as if to answer a call of nature,"[18] and when he returned, he had taken off his military uniform and now wore the garb of the Augustus, the purple mantle and the diadem, a wordless but unmistakable claim on the imperial crown.

Constans and the young barbarians who were his intimate companions, in the meantime, were absent from the imperial court, engaging in the pleasures of the hunt—or, perhaps, as Gibbon proposes, "some pleasures of a more private and criminal nature."[19] When Constans learned that the army had rallied behind the pagan usurper, he literally ran for his life. The young emperor reached what he thought was a safe refuge in a fortification at the foot of the Pyrenees—one ancient source suggests that, ironically, the ardent Christian sheltered himself in a temple—but he was betrayed to his pursuers, dragged from his hiding place and slaughtered with no more courtesy or ceremony than he had afforded to his own brother a few years earlier.

The sudden and surprising success of the pagan coup inspired a few other usurpers to make their own claims on the crown, but Magnentius was the one who ultimately prevailed as the champion of resurgent paganism. Six weeks after the fateful midnight feast, Magnentius and his rebel army reached Rome, which lay within the realm of the emperor Constans, and he was acclaimed by the local pagan aristocracy as prefect. By the end of the year, he replaced Constans as emperor of the western empire, ordered the reopening of pagan shrines and temples that had been closed during the reign of the Christian emperors and invited his fellow pagans to resume the solemn sacrifices to the gods and goddesses that had been regarded with such horror by the Christians.

Constantius II was campaigning on the Persian frontier when the first reports of Magnentius's pagan counterrevolution reached him. He withdrew from the front and retreated to the imperial capital, pondering all the while how to battle the threat that he faced from Magnentius and the other challengers, Christian and pagan alike. Both his brothers were now dead, of course, and so were the uncles, cousins and in-laws whom he had ordered to be killed during the purge that followed the death of Constantine. Constantius II himself was married but remained childless. When he cast about for allies and confidants, he was thus forced to consider the only blood relations who had survived the slaughter: the young sons of the dead uncle who had been among the principal victims of the blood purge.

The Orphans of Macellum

Whether or not young Gallus and his half brother, Julian, witnessed the murder of their father is not recorded in the ancient sources, although Rendall imagines that they "listened in hushed terror to the tramp of soldiers and cries of bloodshed" from the hiding place where they had been taken by a kindly priest.[20] After the purge, they were placed under the equivalent of house arrest by Constantius II, and they spent their early years in separate confinement, Gallus in Ephesus and Julian in Constantinople, until they were finally reunited in 344 at Macellum, an imperial estate in a backwater of Asia Minor.

Gallus, born in what is now Tuscany in 325 or 326, was the son of Julius Constantius's first wife, Galla. Julian, born in Constantinople in 331 or 332, was the son of his second wife, Basilina. Both women, however, were already dead by the time that their sons' father was murdered. So the orphans were raised by a series of surrogates— slaves, eunuchs, priests and tutors—who were charged with the task of turning them into good Christians and loyal subjects while monitoring their state of mind and reporting back to their cousin and captor, the emperor Constantius II.

Macellum was an opulent but remote place surrounded by high mountains and forests full of wild beasts. Indeed, the palace had been used as a kind of hunting lodge until it was converted into a place of confinement for Gallus and Julius. Here the orphaned brothers were both sent on the order of Constantius II, whose anxieties had been sharpened by the death of Constantine II and the ascension of Constans to the rank of sole Augustus in the western empire. Constantius II fretted that the boys might find sponsors among his enemies or grow up to make claims of their own on the imperial crown—and so he resolved to put them in a place where they would remain under constant scrutiny of spies and watchers and far beyond the reach of potential conspirators. Julian himself records the experiences of a lonely and fearful childhood.

"How shall I describe the six years we spent there?" muses Julian in *Letter to the Athenians*. "For we lived as though on the estate of a stranger, and were watched as though we were in some Persian garrison, since not one of our old friends was allowed to visit us; so that we lived in glittering servitude, and shared the exercises of our own slaves as though they were comrades."[21]

Constantius II had deprived them not only of their father and their freedom but their patrimony, too. "Of my father's estate nothing came to me," complains Julian, "not the smallest clod of earth, not a slave, not a house."[22] Still, the boys were encouraged by their guardians to regard Constantius II as a benefactor, and the purge in which their father died was prettied up. "[T]hey kept telling us and tried to convince us that Constantius had acted thus," Julian writes, "partly because he was deceived, and partly because he yielded to the violence and tumult of an undisciplined and mutinous army."[23] Constantius II declared himself to be "stung with remorse" over the role he had played in the death of their father, or so went "the gossip of the court," as Julian puts it. "He thinks that his unhappy state of childlessness is due to those deeds, and his ill success in the Persian war he also ascribes to that cause."

Constantius II himself visited Macellum in 347, perhaps to do some hunting in the surrounding woods and, at the same time, to satisfy himself that his prisoners were not nursing a dangerous grudge against him. Three years later, when he was seeking someone to serve as his second in command in the struggle against Magnentius, he was forced to consider the orphans of Macellum. Gallus, after all, was not only his cousin but his brother-in-law—Constantius II's first wife had been Gallus's sister. With so pitifully few candidates available to the emperor, and so many enemies arrayed against him, Gallus must have seemed a chance worth taking.

Gallus, now in his midtwenties, is depicted by the ancient sources as a striking figure, blond and handsome, but also a man with a cold and cruel nature. Julian himself insisted that the years at Macellum, where they were denied the care of their own parents or the companionship of boys their own age, so distressed Gallus that he blamed Constantius II for the character flaws that his older brother would later display. "[W]hatever cruelty or harshness was revealed in his disposition was increased by his having been brought up among those mountains," writes Julian. "It is therefore I think only just that the Emperor should bear the blame for this also."[24]

Gallus himself, as we shall see, proved himself to be far more dutiful than Constantius II had any right or reason to expect. An imperial messenger appeared at Macellum in 351 with a wholly unexpected summons—Gallus was ordered to present himself at the imperial court in Constantinople and put himself in service to his cousin. When he arrived at court, he found himself suddenly and unpredictably elevated from the "splendid slavery" of Macellum, as the nineteenth century historian Augustus Neander puts it, to the very highest circles of power and privilege.[25]

The former prisoner of state was now advanced to the rank of Caesar. He was presented with a wife—Constantina, the eldest daughter of Constantine the Great, thus making him a brother-in-law of Constantius II for a second time. He was also placed in command of an army and charged with the crucial task of securing the eastern frontier of the Roman empire while Constantius II marched off to do battle with Magnentius and the other rebellious pagans. In fact, Gallus discharged his new duties so well that Constantius II was able to devote his attention to the crushing pagan counterrevolution in the west. By 353, only three years after Magnentius had replaced Constans as western emperor, the pagan had been defeated and driven to suicide—he took his own life when the last of his troops proposed to surrender him to the Christian emperor—and Constantius II now reigned as the sole Augustus of the whole of the Roman empire.

"Bloody Adventures"

Gallus is not warmly recalled by the more pious historians, ancient or modern. "His private life was frivolous, completely taken up with gladiatorial shows and games in the circus," insists Abbot Guiseppe Ricciotti, a biographer of Julian. "[He] wandered about Antioch at

night in search of bloody adventures."[26] And yet Gallus displayed a
surprising aptitude for the role of Caesar—he succeeded in keeping
the Persians at bay, crushing one of the Jewish insurrections that still
flared up in Palestine, suppressing the bandits and barbarians who
threatened the peace of his realm, foiling an assassination attempt organized by Magnentius and even coping with a crisis in the supply of
grain at Antioch, the ancient city in Asia Minor that served as the seat
of his imperial government, all with a degree of brutality that
shocked even the chroniclers who otherwise admired the results.

"Through the murders of many thousands of men—even those
too young to pose a threat—Gallus suppressed the Jews," writes
Jerome, "and he put to the torch their cities Diocaesarea, Tiberias,
and Diospolis and many towns."[27]

Constantius II, in fact, apparently decided that he had chosen *too*
well in Gallus. "The moment that Constantius had invested him with
the purple," insists Julian, "he at once began to be jealous of him."[28]
His anxieties were stoked by the agents and informers who told the
emperor that Gallus aspired to not merely serve but replace him.
When Gallus invited his younger brother to join him at the theater
during a visit to Nicomedia—how the two of them must have mar-
veled at their remarkable new circumstances!—the rendezvous was
regarded as suspicious and even subversive by the watchful Constantius. Only three years after releasing Gallus from confinement and
raising him to the purple, the ruthless and remorseless emperor resolved to correct the mistake that he believed he had made in letting
Gallus live.

Now, once again, Constantius issued a summons to his cousin,
inviting Gallus and Constantina to join him at his winter quarters in
Milan. Constantina, an active and expert intriguer, surely understood
that her brother's intentions were not benign, and the couple did not
make haste to answer the call. Indeed, when Constantina fell ill of a
fever and died en route, Gallus tarried at Antioch, fearful of what
might happen at court without his wife, the emperor's sister, to speak
in his defense. Constantius II urged Gallus on his way with an

encouraging letter that suggested he intended to grant Gallus the title of Augustus and make him coemperor. Gallus dutifully if reluctantly resumed his journey toward the imperial court—but he never arrived.

As he neared Milan, Gallus and his entourage stopped for the night at a palace. When he awoke the next morning, he found himself surrounded by a death squad under the command of one of the dreaded *agentes in rebus* in service to Constantius II. Gallus was seized, stripped of his imperial robes and taken under guard to Pola, the very same place where Constantine the Great had arranged for the arrest and murder of Constantius's half brother so many years before: "The blood of Crispus," writes Rendall, "still cried from its prison walls."[29] With hands bound and head forced down for the convenience of the executioner, Gallus was beheaded and the body was discarded without the simple decency of a Christian burial. And so the extermination of Constantine's brothers and nephews that had begun on his death was nearly complete. Julian was now the sole survivor.

"Let the Curiosity to Know the Future Be Silenced Forever"

The pagan majority that had taken hope in the short-lived reign of Magnentius now confronted a Christian emperor whose authority was unchecked. Constantius II adopted the title "His Eternity" in place of "His Majesty,"[30] and his belief in the Only True God seemed to burn hotter in him than it had in his father. "What I will," announced Constantius, "should be the law of the Church."[31] Starting in 353, the year of Magentius's suicide, the emperor issued a series of imperial decrees that enforced and expanded the formal persecution of paganism. The pagan restoration appeared to be stillborn, and the victory of God against the gods was assured—or so it seemed at this moment in history when the Roman empire still teetered between monotheism and polytheism.

First, the rituals of sacrifice carried out by night—and later *all* sacrifices—were formally banned. According to a decree issued in

354, the pagan temples were to be closed and, two years later, the use of pagan statuary in rituals of worship was condemned. All the practitioners of divination were proscribed—soothsayers and seers, astrologers and augurs, sorcerers and "readers of entrails"—and even the most distinguished of pagan philosophers might be tortured on suspicion of having practiced black magic. "Let the curiosity to know the future," decreed Constantius II, "be silenced forever."[32] At last, the death penalty was officially adopted as the punishment for what was now the crime of paganism. "For if anyone consulted with a soothsayer about the squeaking of a shrew-mouse," complains the pagan Ammianus, "or a meeting with a weasel or a similar omen, or applied an old wife's charm to soothe pain—which even medical authority permits—he was indicted from an unknown source, dragged into court, and suffered the death penalty."[33]

By 357, when Constantius paid a state visit to the old imperial capital at Rome, the citizenry witnessed a display that seemed to symbolize the abandonment of the oldest, most cherished traditions of Roman paganism: the Christian emperor demanded that the altar to the goddess of Victory be hauled out of the chambers of the Roman Senate. By long tradition, the pagan aristocrats who served in the Senate had paused before the statue and sprinkled a pinch of incense on the altar fire, thus making the offering to the goddess who was believed to preserve the *Pax Deorum* and the *Pax Romana*.

Yet, significantly, a statue of the goddess herself was permitted to remain on display, and the removal of the altar was only temporary— Christians and pagans would still be fighting over the same issue a half century later. Constantius II himself may have issued decrees that appealed to the Christian rigorists who were his ardent supporters— and the laws may have been enforced in Constantinople and the eastern empire—but they were still mostly a dead letter in the more distant provinces and Rome itself, the seat of classical paganism. On the same visit to Rome in 357, for example, Constantius II still found it convenient and appropriate to perform his duties as *Pontifex Maximus*, visiting pagan temples and making appointments to the pagan priesthoods, both of which continued to enjoy the support of the imperial treasury.

Christianity itself, in fact, was tugged and torqued in so many directions by its various contending rigorists, each one condemning the others as apostates and blasphemers, that none of them could plausibly claim to act with the authority of the "orthodox" and "catholic" church. "It is a thing equally deplorable and dangerous," warned Bishop Hilary of Poitiers, "that there are as many creeds as opinions among men."[34] Indeed, the same zeal that had sustained Christian true believers during the persecutions of the pagan emperors inspired the dissidents who were now persecuted by the Christian emperor.

At Alexandria, the churches where orthodox clergy still presided were put under siege by the legions of the Arian emperor: "Many were killed who may deserve the name of martyrs," reports Gibbon. "Bishops and presbyters were treated with cruel ignominy; consecrated virgins were stripped naked, scourged and violated."[35] At Rome, rival candidates for the papacy were championed by rival mobs, and the Christian rioters spilled one another's blood "in the streets, in the public places, in the baths, and even in the churches."[36] And, at Constantinople, more than 3000 Christians lost their lives in the battle for the bishopric of the imperial capital: "One of the ecclesiastical historians has observed, as a real fact, not as a figure of rhetoric," Gibbon points out, "that the well before the church overflowed with a stream of blood."[37]

The most fanatical of the Donatists in North Africa, known as Circumcellions ("vagabonds"), rose up in open insurrection in defense of their rigorous strain of Christianity. Armed only with crude weaponry, the poor folk who rallied to the Church of the Martyrs carried out attacks on orthodox clergy and pagan priests alike. Significantly, they used the term "Israelite" to identify the stout wooden clubs that they carried, thus invoking the example of the original holy warriors of the Hebrew Bible. When routed by the imperial cavalry, the Circumcellions were known to seek assistance in achieving martyrdom by stopping passersby on the highway and offering to pay them to deliver a coup de grâce—and to kill them if they refused the offer.

"The great Christian commonwealth seemed drifting into helpless anarchy," writes Gerald Henry Rendall. "Bishops had become so many centres of confusion and ringleaders of heresy."[38]

Even after the practice of paganism had been formally criminalized by Constantius II, in fact, the politics of religion in the Roman empire remained so unsettled that some pagans still hoped—and expected—that the Christian revolution would be defeated by its own true believers, so numerous and so fiercely at odds with one another. "No wild beasts are so hostile to mankind," Ammianus famously remarked, "as are most of the Christians in their savagery toward one another."[39] Magnentius may have failed in his effort to restore the worship of the old gods and goddesses, but the pagans consoled themselves with the simple fact that paganism was still the preferred faith of the majority of Romans. What they did not yet suspect was that the man who was determined to succeed where Magnentius had failed was not some disgruntled pagan general but the last surviving orphan of Macellum, the young Christian prince called Julian.

CHAPTER NINE

THE SECRET PAGAN

Gods, Empresses, and Julian's Unlikely Rise to the Imperial Throne

And shall I write about things not to be spoken of and divulge what
ought not to be divulged? Shall I utter the unutterable?

—Julian, *Hymn to the Mother of the Gods*

Julian, too, was summoned to the imperial court at Milan by
Constantius II. On the way, the ship that was carrying him back
to Italy called at a port near Ilion, the site of ancient Troy, and he
took advantage of the opportunity to visit the shrines that celebrated the gods and heroes who would have been deeply familiar to
any educated Roman, pagan or Christian. But an incident that took
place during his brief sojourn at Ilion offers us an early and intriguing glimpse of the dark and dangerous secret that Julian was still
guarding from all but his closest confidants.

Julian was welcomed to Ilion by the local bishop, a man called Pegasius, who escorted him to the pagan temples that remained open in
apparent defiance of the imperial decree that all such structures be
destroyed. Unlike his more rigorous brethren in the church, who carried out the decree with pleasure and even ardor, Pegasius had made
only a gesture of compliance by removing a few blocks of stone from
the exterior façades—he sought to fool the Christian rigorists into
thinking that the temples had been emptied and defaced. Now the
bishop boldly conducted the emperor's cousin into the shrines of

Athena and Hector and Achilles, where Julian noticed that the altar fires were still burning and the statuary were still anointed with oil.

"What does this mean?" Julian asked the bishop. "Do the people of Ilion offer sacrifices?"

"Is it not natural that they should worship a brave man who was their own citizen," replied Pegasius, "just as we worship the martyrs?"[1]

Julian's ulterior motive, as he later discloses in his own writings, was to take the temperature of Bishop Pegasius. Was he one of the Christian zealots who condemned paganism as nothing more than devil worship? Or did he secretly harbor somewhat warmer feelings for Athena and Achilles? Such questions could not be safely asked aloud, but Julian was watchful for some sign of the bishop's unspoken attitude toward paganism.

The telling fact, as Julian carefully noted, was something that the bishop did *not* do. The most zealous Christians, as Julian knew, displayed their fear and contempt by making certain unmistakable gestures when confronted with pagan artifacts, which they regarded as demon-infested. "For this is the height of their theology," Julian writes in his account of the incident, "to hiss at demons and to make the sign of the cross upon their foreheads."[2] But the bishop, like Julian himself, was perfectly at ease in the pagan shrines and, in fact, eager to show him "all the statues in perfect preservation"[3]—and so the two men may well have recognized in each other a kindred spirit.

At that moment, Julian may appear to us as a highly civilized Christian who was still able to appreciate the literary and historical resonance of what he beheld in the pagan shrines. But the fact is that he had already renounced the Only True God and embraced the old god and goddesses whom the Christians regarded as demons and devils. He was already at risk for purely political reasons—Gallus, a Christian, was only the latest example of Constantius II's willingness to kill his cousins—but the open avowal of paganism would have put him at even deadlier peril. For now, but not for long, Julian's new faith remained unspoken.

The Purified and the Perfected

We do not know exactly when, where or how Julian made the fateful decision for paganism. Both Julian and Gallus had been raised as Christians during their years of confinement—they were duly baptized and granted communion, instructed in theology and the Bible, raised through the ranks of Christian initiation from "the purified" to "the illuminated" to "the perfected"[4] and eventually admitted to the lower rank of the clergy as "lectors," an office whose duties included reading aloud from the Bible to fellow congregants at church services. As an exercise in Christian piety, the young princes even built a martyrium, a shrine that marked the grave where the mortal remains of a local martyr called Mama were buried and where the suffering of the martyr was recalled and honored.

"[Julian and Gallus] were cultured and educated in a manner corresponding to the dignity of their birth," reports the fifth-century church historian Sozomen. "Their habits and actions indicated no dereliction from piety. They respected the clergy and other good people and persons zealous for doctrine; they repaired regularly to church and rendered due homage to the tombs of the martyrs."[5]

Among Julian's first instructors in the fundamentals of Christianity was Eusebius of Nicomedia, the Arian bishop who had baptized Constantine on his deathbed and, as it happens, a distant relation of Julian's dead mother. Eusebius, of course, tutored Julian in the theology of Arius, which was not regarded as heresy in the imperial household of Constantius II. When Eusebius was ultimately raised to the rank of bishop of Constantinople, other attentive priests took his place as the royal tutor. "From the poison of Paganism," insists historian Gerald Henry Rendall, Julian "was to be guarded inviolate."[6]

What Julian came to regard as toxic, however, was Christianity itself. "What he knew from personal observation of Christianity, what he witnessed of its moral power, was not encouraging," Rendall frankly concedes. After all, the murderer of his father was a pious Christian, and so were most of the men and women who acted as his

jailors. "The man he most hated for his crimes," writes Rendall, referring to Constantius II, "was the man most loud in his Christian pro-
fession."[7] Of all his many caregivers, in fact, the only one who seemed
to earn his trust and affection was an aging eunuch called Mardonius, whom Julian describes as "a barbarian, by the gods and goddesses"[8] and who may well have been, as the historian (and abbot)
Giuseppe Ricciotti puts it, "an honest pagan."[9]

Blood and Outrage

Mardonius was a family slave who was assigned to serve as peda-
gogue to the seven-year-old Julian, first at Nicomedia and possibly
later at Macellum, the same function he had performed years before
for his mother, Basilina: "He was my mother's guide," as Julian puts
it, "through the poems of Homer and Hesiod."[10] Julian describes him
as a "curmudgeon"—"boorishness he called dignity, lack of taste he
called sobriety"[11]—but he does not conceal the affection he feels for
the old man who represented his only living link to his family of origin: "Among so many memories of blood and outrage," writes Ricciotti, "only that of Mardonius came to [Julian's] mind like a beam of
light shining in the darkness."[12]

Julian recalls Mardonius as a strict, even puritanical schoolmaster, teaching him to walk with his eyes cast down to avoid even a
glimpse of the forbidden pleasures that were on display in the streets
of Nicomedia—"the pantomime, the dance, the horse-race," as Rendall writes, "everything that to a Roman boy savoured at all of fun or
excitement."[13] Julian attests that, thanks to his watchful tutor, he
never attended the theater until "I had more hair on my chin than on
my head."[14] Fatefully, Mardonius used the poetry of Homer to pound
Julian into the mold of a civilized man.

"Have you a passion for horse races?" he asks his young charge.
"There is one in Homer, very cleverly described. Take the book and
study it."[15]

Constantius II issued an order that Julian was not to be instructed in the tales of the gods and goddesses that were the core texts of classical paganism. At least one of his tutors gamely attempted to comply, or so the ancient sources insist, but it turned out to be impossible. Any Roman of the higher classes, whether Christian or pagan, would have studied the same pagan writings, which were regarded even in late antiquity as classics and still provided the curriculum of the basic course of study called *paideia*. Mardonius, in any event, plainly paid no attention to the imperial decree in choosing the books that he assigned Julian to read. And Julian, like his mother, read them not just dutifully but joyfully.

"Some men have a passion for horses, others for birds, others for savage animals," writes Julian of himself, "but I for books."[16] And he credits his cherished teacher for opening his eyes to the improving truth to be found in such pagan poets as Homer and Hesiod, such pagan philosophers as Plato and Socrates, Aristotle and Theophrastus: "This old man convinced me that if I should emulate those famous men in all things," he recalls, "I should become better than my former self."[17]

By his "former self," Julian can be understood to mean his Christian self, although he is guarded about the source of his pagan instruction or the time and place of his formal conversion to paganism. He refers to the years he spent as a professing Christian as the time "when I wandered, as it were, in darkness."[18] But he openly declares that the pagan philosophers served as a buffer against the "cruelty" and "harshness" of the strange and tragic childhood that Constantius II imposed on him: "The gods, by means of philosophy, caused me to remain untouched by it and unharmed by it," recalls Julian.[19] And he claims to have been inspired by King Helios—the same solar god that Constantius the Pale and Constantine the Great worshiped as *Sol Invictus*—"from my earliest years."[20]

"This at least I am permitted to say without sacrilege," reveals Julian, scrupulously guarding the secrets of the mystery religions to which he was later admitted, "that from my childhood an extraordinary longing for the rays of the god penetrated deep into my soul."[21]

Later, the ancient Christian historians looked for clues of Julian's pagan tendencies in the otherwise unremarkable events of his childhood. Gallus and Julian practiced their rhetorical skills by engaging in mock debates over the relative merits of monotheism and polytheism—Julian, they insist, always preferred to argue on behalf of the pagan cause and did so with a fervor that betrayed his real feelings on the subject. When the boys set to work on building the martyrium, they report, the portion erected by Gallus was sturdy and strong, but Julian's handiwork fell under its own weight, "as if the earth refused to accept the labors of the future apostate."[22] And they insist on blaming Julian's ultimate apostasy on the defects in his early Christian instruction—the priests and bishops who were his first teachers, after all, had been Arians: "They were not themselves," observes Augustus Neander, "thoroughly imbued with the true spirit of Christianity."[23]

Still, the fact remains that Julian himself revealed none of his pagan interests or inclinations during his years as an inmate at Macellum. "He was by nature a wistful dreamy child," writes Rendall, "full of strange reveries." Yet he was also an alert and aloof child, and necessarily so: "A remarkably beautiful character was strangely marred," Rendall observes. "Hard experiences made him day by day increasingly and sadly worldly-wise: reserve, distrust, dissimulation became a second nature to him."[24] No one yet suspected what visions he beheld in his own imagination or what powerful passions were building up inside the young man as he dutifully read aloud from the Bible in the chapel at Macellum.

The Bridge That Cannot Be Recrossed

When Gallus was called to the capital and raised to the rank of Caesar in 351, Julian, too, was released from captivity. By now, however, he was already so accomplished at grammar and rhetoric that his new tutors at Constantinople recommended to Constantius II that Julian be permitted to pursue his studies at a place where he would find scholars who were able to teach him something he did not already know. Such praise only stoked the anxieties of Constantius II—if Julian were regarded so highly in the imperial capital, might he not attract the attention of conspirators in search of a candidate for yet another coup d'état?

So Constantius II sent Julian from Constantinople to Nicomedia, a place where he would be less likely to attract attention to himself. But first the young man was required to swear an oath that he would not attend the lectures of Libanius, a pagan Sophist whose discourses were so popular that they rivaled the race course and the theater as venues for public entertainment, or so Libanius himself boasted. Julian gave the promise of good behavior that his cousin demanded— and then he promptly engaged one of Libanius's student to take notes of what the famous orator had to say and bring them to Julian after every lecture.

The promise that Constantius II extracted from Julian is doubly significant—we are reminded that pagans were still influential public figures even if paganism was already being persecuted, and that Constantius II was still concerned about the influence that a charismatic pagan might exert over a prince of the blood. And his anxiety, as it turns out, was justified. Julian, at liberty in the cities where Hellenism had flowered—first Nicomedia and later Ephesus, Pergamum and Athens—sought out the practitioners of the arcane and mystical pagan philosophy called Neoplatonism. Now a man in his early twenties, he was eager to be formally (but secretly) admitted into the mystery religions that were still the lively rivals of Christianity.

"I was initiated by those guides, in the first place by a philosopher who trained me in the preparatory discipline," Julian reveals in an oration composed shortly before his death, "and next by that most perfect philosopher who revealed to me the entrance to philosophy."[25]

The Greek word that Julian uses to describe his "initiation" is a technical term that refers to the rites by which the deepest secrets of a mystery religion were formally revealed to an acolyte,[26] including the "red baptism" of the taurobolium as used in the cults of both Mithra and the Great Mother. Elsewhere in his writings, Julian suggests that he made the decision to embrace paganism when he was still living in captivity at Macellum. "Julian was no Paul on the road to Damascus," writes biographer Robert Browning. "It was rather the climax of months, or maybe years, of moral and intellectual struggle in the sinister solitude of his idyllic palace in the arid heart of Asia Minor."[27] But it was at Ephesus that Julian was conducted into a pagan shrine, not as a Christian sightseer but as an ardent convert to paganism.

Several candidates have been proposed to identify the unnamed "guides" who initiated Julian into the pagan mysteries. Mardonius, his childhood tutor, may have been one of them. Later, at Pergamum, Julian studied under several of the disciples of the late Iamblichus (c. 250–c. 325), a prominent Neoplatonist whose eerie rituals of sacrifice once attracted crowds of credulous pilgrims and who was said to "emit a golden glow and float at knee-height or more above the ground."[28] Julian himself describes Iamblichus as "god-like"[29] and he sent a series of rich gifts to one of his followers, Aidesios, in an effort to persuade the old man to grant him instruction and initiation. What Julian sought in Neoplatonism were the ecstasy and mystery that attracted so many other earnest seekers to the mystery religions that competed with Christianity in ancient Rome.

"If you are initiated into our mysteries," promised Aidesios to a tantalized Julian, "you will be ashamed to have been born a man."[30]

But the man who actually administered the rites of initiation to Julian during his student years was probably Maximus of Ephesus (d. 370), a relative of Aidesios and an accomplished magus whose feats of legerdemain included making a torch in the hand of a statue of Hecate, goddess of sorcery, burst into flame and the goddess herself break into a smile and even laugh out loud.[31] Indeed, he was regarded by his own ardent followers as a master of theurgy, the term used to describe the blend of high mysticism and stage magic as practiced by the Neoplatonists. "He seems to have been the kind of half-charlatan," observes Browning, "who deceived himself before he deceives others."[32] Maximus consented to introduce Julian to the mystery of the Great Mother of the Gods and escorted him into the crypt where the ritual was conducted and the secrets were disclosed. At last, the forbidden knowledge that Julian had so long sought was revealed.

"This initiation, with its words and music and incense and light filling the senses and charging the emotions, was a key experience in Julian's life," explains Browning. "He now belonged to the elect, of whom more was demanded than of ordinary men, and to whose souls was promised a rebirth in the higher order of being. He had crossed a bridge that could never be recrossed."[33]

Like all authentic pagans, young Julian did not confine himself to a single god or a single set of rituals. He was soon initiated into the cult of Mithra, the Persian deity who was now fully conflated with the solar god called King Helios or *Sol Invictus*, and "the great and unspeakable mysteries" of Eleusis,[34] where the goddess Demeter and her daughter, Persephone, were worshipped. According to ancient Christian historians, Julian "sought by the Taurobolium and other expiatory rites to wash away from his body the traces of baptism, and especially from his hands the sacred touch of the Eucharist."[35] Yet Julian himself, otherwise candid and even chatty, always honored the strict vows of secrecy that were required of initiates into the mystery religions: "He trembles," writes Edward Gibbon, "lest he should betray too much of these holy mysteries."[36]

All these daring new experiences were thrilling and fulfilling to the ardent young man—Maximus, it is said, told Julian that he "housed within himself the soul of Alexander the Great" and "was destined to equal and even to surpass Alexander's deeds"[37]—but they all represented a terrible risk. Julian may have been granted the freedom to travel and study, but he was always accompanied by an imperial entourage that surely included a few watchers who reported back to the emperor. The sacrificial offerings and nocturnal rites in which Julian participated were now criminal offenses, and *his* presence at such ceremonies would have been treated as high treason precisely because he was a prince of the blood. "Predictions had been widely spread that Christianity was soon about to fall," explains Augustus Neander, "and that a restorer of the ancient religion should rule over the Roman empire."[38] Constantius II would have acted swiftly to prevent Julian from serving, wittingly or not, as the figurehead of a pagan counterrevolution.[39]

Although Julian may not have avoided suspicion, he certainly avoided detection. To conceal his new faith from the spies in his entourage, Julian put on a show of Christian piety, going to church on Sundays and feast days and making pilgrimages to the shrines of martyrs. That is why, when he visited the shrines of Athena and Achilles in the company of Bishop Pegasius, he masqueraded as a Christian sightseer and concealed the fact that he had already been welcomed into more than one pagan cult. Still, as he embarked from Ilion and resumed his journey toward the court of Constantius II, Julian dreamed of the headless body of his half brother, and he must have wondered if what awaited him in Milan was the same fate that had already befallen Gallus—arrest, trial and execution.

"The Beautiful and Virtuous Eusebia"

Julian's anxieties were only aggravated upon his arrival in Milan. Constantius II declined to grant him an audience, and he remained in the quarters assigned to him, once again under close surveillance and living as a virtual prisoner of state. The only friendly words came from Eusebia, the young second wife of Constantius II, who became his self-appointed benefactress. She began to send welcoming and ingratiating letters to the young Julian by means of the palace eunuchs, and she prevailed upon her husband to receive him at court. At last, the emperor consented to see his cousin and, remarkably, Julian found himself in polite if not exactly friendly discourse with the man who was, after all, the murderer of both his father and his half brother.

Eusebia, like Constantius II's first wife, had failed at her principal duty as empress—she had given no sons (or daughters, for that matter) to the emperor. She refused to resign herself to childlessness, and she continued to sip the vile concoctions that various healers offered as a cure for infertility until the day of her death. Indeed, she was apparently not born a Christian, and she remained deeply superstitious even after her conversion. But she was a canny and cagey observer of imperial politics, and she decided that Julian, as Constantius II's closest surviving blood relation, should serve as a surrogate son and heir if she remained unable to bear children. So she took it upon herself to put Julian forward as a replacement for the son she had failed to produce.

Thanks to her willingness to whisper words of encouragement to the emperor, Julian was given permission to take up residence in a modest villa in Bithynia that had belonged to his mother. (Because Constantius II had seized the whole of his father's estate, as Julian acidly notes, it was the only private property that Julian owned.) Still later, she succeeded in persuading the emperor to allow Julian to resume his travels and studies, first at Como in Italy and then in Athens, the seat of classical paganism and a place where Julian was able to participate in pagan worship at somewhat less risk than in Milan or Constantinople.

Julian never failed to acknowledge the role that Eusebia played in saving and enriching his life. Among Julian's writings, for example, are panegyrics to both Constantius II and Eusebia. When praising the emperor, Julian's words are so ornate and overblown that, in retrospect, they strike us as not merely ironic but openly sarcastic: "The Emperor was kind to me almost from my infancy," he writes, "and he surpassed all generosity, for he snatched me from dangers so great that not even 'a man in the strength of his youth' could easily have escaped them."[40] But when Julian credits "the beautiful and virtuous Eusebia" for saving his life by persuading the emperor not to murder him as he had murdered Gallus, his words are plainspoken and utterly earnest: Eusebia was "zealous in my behalf," Julian puts it. "I could not have escaped from his hands myself.[41]

Still, Julian gradually awoke to the danger of drawing *too* close to the wife of the reigning emperor. "She bade me write confidently about whatever I desired," recalls Julian, who promptly composed a letter in which he begged the empress to seek permission for him to leave the court and return to his studies. But he began to worry about the accusations that might be whispered against both of them when his letter was delivered to the palace. "I entreated the gods to inform me during the night if I should send the letter," writes Julian—and, while he slept, he was granted the divine instruction that he sought: "They warned me that if I sent it, I would incur a most shameful death."[42] So Julian did not send the fateful letter, but Eusebia was nevertheless inspired to do his bidding, and he succeeded in reaching safe refuge in Athens.

His sojourn at Athens lasted only a few months. Julian was summoned back to Milan, but under wholly new and extraordinary circumstances. Constantius II was troubled by new rumors of conspiracy and new threats of a coup d'état, and he had been persuaded by Eusebia to regard Julian as his best (and perhaps only) ally in the campaign that would be required to keep his crown. Then, too, the Roman empire was troubled anew by the barbarians along the Danube and by the Persians on the eastern frontier—Constantius II sought someone to secure his western flank while he campaigned against these renewed threats to the *Pax Romana*. Just as he had once recruited Gallus to perform the same function, he now resolved to call Julian to serve as his second in command and to watch his back while he went to war against his enemies.

A Comical Soldier

The young man who presented himself at the court of Constantius II in 355 must have struck the emperor and his courtiers as an odd choice to command an army. Julian was "of medium height, with a beard that ended in a point, and endowed with bright eyes of striking beauty," according to the pagan historian Ammianus Marcellinus. "He had elegant eyebrows, a perfectly straight nose, a rather large mouth with a loose lower lip, a neck somewhat bent, and large, broad shoulders."[43] But he disdained the "soft and delicate way of living" and the "effeminate dispositions" favored by the Roman aristocracy,[44] and he pointedly affected the shabby robe, careless grooming and shambling gait of the kind of wandering philosopher who might have been seen in the marketplace with a staff and a beggar bowl— thus did he later earn the nickname Cercops, a reference to a mythical race of human beings who had been turned into apes by Jupiter.[45]

"For though nature did not make [my face] any too handsome, I myself out of sheer perversity have added to it this long beard of mine, to punish it, as it would seem, for this very crime of not being handsome by nature," Julian later writes of himself in a satirical work titled *Mispogon* ("Beard Hater"). "For the same reason, I put up with the lice that scamper about in it as though it were a thicket for wild beasts. As though the mere length of my beard were not enough, my head is dishevelled besides, and I seldom have my hair cut or my nails, while my fingers are nearly always black from using a pen."[46]

Julian is made to seem almost freakish by a Christian contemporary who claimed to detect his future apostasy in his appearance: "There seemed to me to be no evidence of sound character in his unsteady neck, his twitching and hunched shoulders, his wandering eye with its crazy look, his uncertain and swaying walk, his proud and haughty nose, the ridiculous expressions of his countenance, his uncontrolled and hysterical laughter, the way he jerked his head up and down for no reason, his halting and panting speech," declares Gregory of Nazianzus, a Christian bishop who knew Julian when they were both students in Athens.[47] "As soon as I saw these signs, I exclaimed, 'What an evil the Roman world is breeding!' "[48]

And yet Julian is hardly kinder to himself in his own writings. Indeed, he delights in listing the disdainful and dismissive nicknames that he attracted: " 'Nanny-goat,' 'a talkative mole,' 'an ape dressed in purple,' 'a Greekish pedant,' and 'a lazy, timid, shady character, tricking out his actions with fine words.' "[49] On a note of characteristic irony, he admits in *Mispogon* that he finds himself unable to exhaust his shortcomings: "What a small fraction of my offenses have I described!"[50]

So Julian was an exceedingly unlikely candidate for Caesarship, and not only because of his intentionally eccentric appearance and manners. And yet, as Julian now discovered, he had been summoned by the emperor precisely because his cousin was now ready to raise him to the rank only recently held by his slain brother. He was turned over to the army of body servants in the imperial palace who went to work at transforming him from a Greek philosopher into a Roman general: "They set up a mock barber's shop, cut off my beard, threw a military cloak around me," recalls Julian, "and turned me—as they obviously thought—into a rather comical soldier."[51]

Julian, the secret initiate into the mysteries of Mithra and the Great Mother, was now given a very different and far more public form of initiation. As the emperor Constantius II and the empress Eusebia watched, one surely less gratified than the other, Julian mounted the high tribunal around which the imperial legions were gathered *en masse* beneath the eagle standards of ancient Rome. Constantius II himself bestowed the purple robe on Julian—"At the instigation of God in heaven," he intoned, "I put upon his shoulders the mantle of empire"[52]—and the soldiers signaled their approval by the traditional gesture of striking their shields against their knee armor.

To seal the new alliance between them, Julian was presented with a relation of the Augustus to be his wife—the bride was Helena, daughter of Constantine the Great and the sister of Constantius II, a woman at least five or six years older than Julian. "We shall sustain one another with strong and unshakeable affection," declared Constantius II to Julian, "we shall fight side by side, and we shall rule with equal moderation and sense of responsibility a world to which—God grant our prayer—we have brought peace."[53] Against every expectation, and still only in his early twenties, the young man who had twice avoided death at the hands of Constantius II was now his brother-in-law as well as his brother emperor.

"Purple death and mighty destiny gathered him in," muttered Julian to himself, quoting a line from his beloved Homer that summed up his own misgivings at his sudden change of fortune.[54]

As yet, the new rank carried no real power. Constantius II was now, if anything, even more watchful of Julian: "The slavery that ensued and the fear for my very life that hung over me every day, Heracles, how great it was, and how terrible!" Julian later recalls. "My doors locked, warders to guard them, the hands of my servants searched lest one of them should convey to me the most trifling letter from my friends!"[55] All but a few of the servants who attended the new Caesar had been assigned to him by the imperial chamberlain and, for that reason, Julian had to assume that his household was salted with spies. Of the four servants that Julian had been permitted to bring with him from Athens, only a single one was entrusted with knowledge of Julian's allegiance to the pagan gods and goddesses— "and, as far as he was able," reveals Julian, this man "secretly joined me in their worship."[56]

Nothing in Julian's upbringing, temperament or experience, of course, predicted that he would rise to the rank of Caesar or that, once there, he would have the faintest idea of what to do. Of the two brothers, as we have seen, Gallus was the man of action, impulsive and often brutal, while Julian was the man of letters, given to dreams and reveries. Nevertheless, Julian was not lacking in the stuff that was required to survive and succeed in the imperial family of ancient Rome. Both of them, after all, were grandsons of Constantius the Pale, the rough soldier who had fought and intrigued from the Roman legions to the rank of Caesar. Julian, still a secret pagan, would show that he was capable of doing the same.

"I Engaged the Enemy Not Ingloriously"

When Julian was dispatched to the troubled province of Gaul in the winter of 355, he was given command of a detachment of only 360 legionnaires. The men were so lacking in the both the skill and the spirit of soldiery that, as Julian himself famously puts it, "they knew only how to pray."[57] The sorry state of his miniature army was just the first clue that Julian was a Caesar in name only; the emperor had also provided Julian with a set of handwritten orders that specified exactly how much money he was allowed to spend, and even what kind of food he should eat. The generals who commanded the embattled Roman garrisons in Gaul, Julian understood, outranked him in authority if not in title. "For letters had been sent and orders given that they were to watch me as vigilantly as they did the enemy," he writes, "for fear I should attempt to cause a revolt."[58]

On his arrival in Gaul, Julian was surprised to find himself warmly welcomed by the citizenry of Vienne, a town on the banks of the Rhone River that would serve as his first seat of government. The narrow streets were hung with festive banners and filled with a cheering crowd—the very first taste of public acclaim, and an especially sweet one, for the young man who had been a prisoner of state for most of his life. One old blind woman, according to a tale that came to be preserved in the ancient chronicles, asked the name of the newcomer. When told that he was Julian, the new Caesar, a cousin of Constantius II, the old woman offered a solemn and surprising prophesy—he is the one, she insisted, who would restore the old pagan temples that the Christian emperor had destroyed.

The tale may be purely apocryphal. When he first arrived in Gaul, Julian was still a public Christian, and he enjoyed only such scraps of authority as Constantius II was willing to share with him. For example, Constantius II extended Julian the honor of cosigning a few of the imperial decrees that were formally issued in the names of both the Augustus and the Caesar. As a result, Julian is recorded as the co-author of a law issued in 356 that imposed a sentence of death on any malefactor who dared to sacrifice or even utter a prayer to pagan idols. He put his signature to the decree, according to Ricciotti, "only a few hours after he had himself performed secret acts of pagan worship."[59]

Yet the "comical soldier" now discovered and displayed a genius for command that no one suspected to exist, least of all himself. In fact, the bookish Julian delighted in military life. He insisted on participating in drills and exercises alongside the rank and file, and he pointedly ate the same rations, "sometimes while standing like a common soldier."[60] At the same time, he set himself to the study of the Roman province over which he was as yet only the nominal ruler. Julian understood that a knowledge of the history and geography of Gaul, its fortifications and lines of defense, would be essential if he intended to actually lead his army into battle. Significantly, he also mastered the Latin tongue—Greek was the language in which he discoursed with pagan philosophers in Athens and Ephesus, but Latin was what he needed to address the troops in Gaul.

Julian's first opportunity to put his newly acquired skills to use in combat came during the spring of 356, when Constantius II ordered a general campaign against the Germanic tribes that threatened the frontier, both the Alemanni and the Franks. Constantius II and his army attacked through the Black Forest, and the Roman legions in Gaul marched toward the Rhine. Julian was not even told of the campaign until shortly before it was set to begin, and he was given only a small force of cavalry to command. But when he rode off to join the main body of the Roman legions, Julian chose a perilous route that, he hoped, would bring him into contact with the enemy. By the time he reached the Roman encampment, he had already won his first victory against a band of barbarian marauders and taken the first prisoners.

"I engaged the enemy not ingloriously," recalls Julian,[61] modestly enough, but the fact is that he was victorious over the next three campaigning seasons, driving the barbarians back across the Rhine and restoring Roman sovereignty in Gaul. The generals whom Constantius II sent to Gaul were rarely helpful to Julian—a few may have been under orders from the Augustus to make sure that he was never *too* successful in battle—and, more than once, Julian was forced to face a superior enemy with only his own troops after Roman armies failed to arrive or abandoned the field before the fighting was over.

Julian also insisted on leading his men into battle himself, plainly demonstrating both his newfound genius for command and his own physical courage. "The sight of Julian, conspicuous by the purple dragon pennant at the point of his long lance, shamed some of the officers into rallying their men," writes Robert Browning of one such engagement. "Julian was everywhere, in the thick of the fight, shouting orders, encouraging the timid, restraining the foolhardy, oblivious of personal danger."[62]

Julian did not hesitate to adopt the ruthless tactics favored by the Roman legions, including the taking of hostages and the pillaging and burning of villages, to terrorize the barbarians into submission. On one occasion, he offered a gold coin to every soldier who brought back the head of an enemy warrior, and they soon provided him with a mound of severed heads. But he was also mindful of the need to restore peace and prosperity, to rebuild the cities and resettle the lands, to restore the supply of grain, to lighten the burden of taxation, to feed, house and clothe the men, women and children of Gaul, all of which amounted to a practical expression of pagan morality or, as Browning puts it, "that *philanthropia*—love of one's fellow men— which was part of the heritage of ancient ethical thought."[63]

"One who is just, kind, human, and easily moved to pity" is how Julian defined the ideal ruler, "devising means of protection for the weaker and simpler citizens, and for the poor against those who are strong, dishonest, wicked and so elated by their wealth that they violate and contemn justice."[64]

Julian's surprising success in both war and peace, however, stoked the anxiety and enmity of Constantius II. No longer "a comical solider," Julian had won the affection and loyalty of both the soldiers he commanded and the civilians over whom he reigned as Caesar. "At [first] I provoked their laughter," Julian writes of his remarkable ascent, "but a little later their suspicions, and then their envy was kindled to the utmost."[65] Then, too, Julian was already regarded in some pagan circles as a likely champion of Hellenism in its life-and-death

struggle with Christian rigorism. He still concealed his commitment
to paganism, but he was obviously *not* a Christian zealot. When Julian retired to his winter quarters at Paris in 359, he was very much
on the mind of his cousin back at Constantinople "This billy-goat,"
one fawning courtier told Constantius II, referring to the beard that
Julian wore so proudly and so defiantly, "is becoming a bore with his
victories."[66]

The Poisoned Cup

Helena, sister of Constantius II and wife of Julian, had accompanied
the new Caesar to Gaul, but she did not seem to inspire much passion
in her otherwise highly passionate husband. Julian, for example, is
moved to lavish praise of Eusebia for giving him a small collection of
books on philosophy and history to replace the cherished library that
he had been forced to leave behind in Athens: "She made [Gaul] and
the country of the Celts," he writes, "resemble a Greek temple of the
Muses."[67] He also named a city after his mother, whom he had not
known at all, and he cherished the baubles that she left behind on her
death. But he hardly mentions his own wife, and he says nothing at all
about the fact that she gave him a son in the winter of 356—or that
the infant died only a few days later.

Even if Julian himself is silent on his arranged marriage, both Helena and Eusebia—like so many of the crucial women in the lives of
Constantine the Great and his sons—attracted plenty of attention
from gossipmongers in the court and the camp. Perhaps, they specu-
lated, the childless Eusebia was so jealous of Helena that she arranged
for the midwife to strangle Julian's newborn son "so that this most
valiant man should have no offspring."[68] Just as Fausta, second wife
of Constantine and mother of both Constantius II and Helena, was
accused of adultery with stable boys and even her own stepson, Eusebia was denounced for engaging in sexual adventures with Julian at
the imperial palace in Milan. When Eusebia fell ill and died in 359, it

was suggested that she had been the victim of a plot by the jealous Helena, who was accused of introducing a slow poison into the concoctions that Eusebia was known to drink in a desperate effort to promote her own fertility. Two years later, when Helena herself died, Julian was charged by the rumormongers with using his mother's jewels to bribe her physician to poison her.

The rumors may never have reached Julian, and he certainly said and did nothing to encourage such speculation. "Now when first I came into her presence," he writes of Eusebia, "it seemed to me as though I beheld a statute of Modesty set up in some temple."[69] As for Helena, the only detail of their domestic life that he deemed appropriate to reveal is that his letters to his wife were so restrained and so respectful they could be read aloud without embarrassment. All the lurid tales told about Julian and the women who loved him are dismissed by Ricciotti as "a complete fiction maliciously spun out of the calumnies circulating among the courtiers."[70]

Julian sent Helena's remains to Rome for interment in the eternal company of her sister, Constantina, who had been his brother's wife. Julian never married again, and no mention is made in his own writings or those of the ancient chroniclers about any further sexual entanglements of any kind. "Except in the short interval of a marriage, which was the effect of policy rather than love," writes Gibbon, "the chaste Julian never shared his bed with a female companion."[71] Ammianus affirms that "even his most confidential servants never accused him of any suspicion of lustfulness, as so often happens."[72] Like Constantine, in fact, Julian was apparently a prude and a puritan. Julian himself later acknowledges that his critics taunted him for his chaste ways: "You complain: 'You always sleep alone at night, [but] there is plenty else to be enjoyed, men and lovely boys, and lots of dancing girls.'"[73]

To be sure, Julian was capable of remarkable passion, but only in service of the gods and goddesses whom he continued to worship in secret.

The Sign of Zeus

If the death of Eusebia in 359 saddened Julian, it also further and fatally estranged him from Constantius II. The emperor's wife, who had been responsible for his sudden elevation from prisoner to Caesar, was no longer there to soothe her husband's fear and envy of Julian. Julian himself was emboldened by the ever widening gap—physical, political, religious and familial—that separated the cousins and co-emperors. "Another moral link binding Julian to the emperor," explains Ricciotti, "was broken."[74]

The final breaking point came in January 360, when an emissary sent by Constantius II arrived in Paris with an ominous and unsettling order: the emperor required four of Julian's strongest regiments, as well as 300 men to be drawn from each of the remaining regiments; these soldiers were to be sent to the eastern empire to serve in a new campaign that Constantius II was undertaking against the Persians. Nor was Constantius II content with drawing off the most accomplished and experienced soldiers in Julian's army—he also showed his contempt for the Caesar by addressing the order not to Julian himself but to the generals under his command.

The order was actually occasioned by a new and urgent military concern. The Romans had suffered a catastrophic defeat in the war against the Persians in Mesopotamia, and the emperor sought to replace the six legions that he had lost. But the ulterior motive was unmistakable, and Julian resolved to frustrate the whole effort by playing on the morale of the soldiers who were now being asked to fight on the dangerous and far-distant Persian front. Many of them were local men—or married to local women—and not a few had enlisted in the Roman army on the promise that they would not be sent beyond the Alps. Julian moved among the rank and file and then invited the officers to a banquet. As they dined together, he expressed his sympathy with their plight and his frustration at his inability to do anything about it—he was, after all, only Caesar and not Augustus!

Later the same night, as Julian rested with Helena in her private apartment on the upper floor of the palace, he was alerted by his courtiers to the approach of a crowd of soldiers. At that moment, he did not yet know whether they intended to make him a scapegoat for his cousin's order or make him emperor in his cousin's place. Roman history, as Julian knew well, provided examples of both. Soon enough, however, he was able to make out the fateful words that they were shouting: "*Iuliianus Augustus!*" (Emperor Julian!)

According to his own account of the incident, Julian was not yet sure whether to resist or submit to the will of the mob. So he offered a hasty but earnest prayer for guidance to the high god Zeus. When he happened to glance out the window, he spotted the planet Jupiter in the night sky over Paris. "A man who needs a sign from heaven usually gets one," quips Browning, "and Julian got his, whatever it was."[75] Julian promptly decided that the sight of Jupiter, the Roman counterpart of Zeus, ought to be understood as confirmation from on high that the crown now belonged to him: "Surely it was my duty," writes Julian, "to trust in the god after he had shown me the sign." [76]

Thus resolved, Julian descended from his wife's apartment and addressed the army. "Very well, go back to your quarters and you will not set foot beyond the Alps, since such is your desire," declares Julian, choosing his words with both precision and guile. "I will explain this to the emperor, who is a reasonable and prudent man, and I am sure that I will convince him."[77]

The scene was expertly played by Julian, who granted the army exactly what it sought from him while deftly avoiding an open claim on the crown. Now the soldiers took the initiative, which is exactly what Julian was calculating they would do—Constantine the Great, after all, had been acclaimed as Augustus by his army at York, and Julian expected that his own troops would do the same for him at Paris. And the soldiers obliged.

The impromptu nature of Julian's coronation is confirmed in the surviving account of the antics that preceded the ceremony. Julian was already supplied with the requisite purple robe—Constantius II had bestowed it upon him in advancing him to the rank of Caesar— but he lacked the imperial diadem. Someone suggested prevailing upon Helena for a tiara, but Julian demurred; a bauble filched from his wife's jewel box was hardly an auspicious way to inaugurate his reign as Augustus. Someone else proposed using a chain from one of the harnesses on the cavalry horses, but it was pointed out that a horse was even less appropriate than a woman as the donor of a crown. Finally, Julian accepted the offer of a brass collar that served as a standard bearer's insignia of rank.

An honor guard then approached Julian with a shield, and they raised him to shoulder height, so the rest of the men could plainly see the ceremony that they were intent on carrying out. They swore a solemn oath to Julian and raised their swords to their own throats in a gesture of loyalty that signified their willingness to die for him. The purple cloak was draped over his shoulders, the brass collar was perched atop his head and one of the officers recited the traditional formula for making a man into an Augustus: "Julian, our Emperor, Caesar, Lord, and always our Augustus."[78]

CHAPTER TEN

"BEHOLD, THE RIVERS ARE RUNNING BACKWARDS"

The Pagan Counterrevolution of the Emperor Julian

And he bowed down his hopeless head
In the drift of the wild world's tide,
And dying, *Thou hast conquered*, he said,
Galilean; he said it, and died.
—Algernon Charles Swinburne,
"The Last Oracle"

Julian was not eager to fight Constantius II over the imperial crown, but neither was he willing to conceal his intimate grievances against his cousin. He sent a letter to Constantius II at his field headquarters in Cappadocia with a proposal to put in place the old power-sharing arrangement that had begun under the pagan emperors—Constantius II would continue to reign in the eastern empire, Julian would reign in the western empire, and they would both bear the title of Augustus. When Constantius II, however, sent an emissary to Paris to put Julian in his place and scold him for his ingratitude—had Julian forgotten, the emissary asked, the generosity that his cousin had shown to him when he was a poor and friendless orphan?—Julian did not confine himself to oblique and ironic cracks.

"Orphan!" retorted Julian. "Does my father's murderer reproach me with being an orphan?"[1]

Still, Julian soon saw an opportunity to honor the old gods and goddesses while advancing his own political agenda. At a ceremony in celebration of his *quinquennalia*, the fifth anniversary of his elevation to imperial rank, Julian was ready to make a public demonstration of his authority. He replaced the humble brass collar with a proper diadem fashioned of gold and richly embellished with precious stones. The legions paraded in his honor, and he handed out the traditional gift of gold and silver to the troops. And he chose that moment to issue a remarkable decree: an edict of toleration that annulled the legislation issued by his Christian cousins and thus decriminalized the worship of the old gods and goddesses.[2]

Propaganda and Psychological Warfare

The standoff between the rival emperors continued through the spring of 361. But Julian's spies began to report that Constantius II was preparing an army to march against him. Now Julian was forced to decide whether to wait for Constantius II to attack him in Gaul and thus fight a defensive war on friendly ground, or to cross the Alps and strike first. So he prayed again for a sign from the gods, and he was granted not merely a sign but a vision—a divine apparition manifested itself in plain sight and directed him to a passage in Homer that seemed to predict the death of Constantius II. To prepare himself for the coming battle, Julian again sought out the secret rite of the taurobolium, bathing himself in the blood of a slaughtered bull and imploring the divine favor of the Roman goddess of war, Bellona.

Thus blessed and emboldened, Julian and his army set off in the direction of Constantinople. Along the way, Julian asserted his authority in each province through which he passed, and he sought to win the sympathy and support of the major cities that lay ahead on his line of march—Rome, Sparta, Corinth and Athens—by composing and sending a series of public letters that arrived in advance of his army. Only one of these extraordinary exercises in propaganda and psychological warfare, Letter to the Athenians, survives intact from antiquity, but it reveals how boldly Julian condemned his Christian cousin and how close he was coming to an open declaration of his own pagan faith.

"Close kinsmen as we were," declares Julian with his characteristic sarcasm, "how this most humane Emperor treated us!"

> Six of my cousins and his, and my father who was his uncle and also another uncle, and my eldest brother, he put to death without trial. As for me and my other brother [Gallus], he intended to put us to death but finally inflicted exile upon us; and from that exile he released me, but [Gallus] he stripped of the title of Caesar just before he murdered him.[3]

Julian pointedly refrains from invoking the Christian god in his letter to the Athenians. Rather, he declares that he was spared from death at the hands of his murderous cousin only "by the help of the gods."[4] And, when he recalls the prayers that he offered at the moment when he was called by Constantius II from Athens to Milan to accept the Caesarship, Julian makes a remarkable and even startling confession of faith.

> What floods of tears I shed and what laments I uttered when I was summoned, stretching out my hands to your Acropolis and imploring Athene to save her suppliant and not abandon me, many of you who were eyewitnesses can attest, and the goddess herself, above all others, is my witness that I even begged for death at her hands in Athens rather than my journey to the Emperor.[5]

The argument has been made that Julian was not yet revealing and affirming his own paganism—rather, he was merely employing the conventions of language that would have been familiar and endearing to the gentry of Athens. And, in fact, Julian did not engage in a single public act of unambiguous pagan worship so long as Constantius II remained alive. But the Christians who were his political adversaries, not least of all his cousin, surely understood that his words amounted to a declaration of war not only on Constantius II but on the Only True God, too.

"That goddess did not betray her suppliant or abandon him," Julian says of Athena, a goddess in the eyes of classical paganism and a demoness in the eyes of Christian rigorism. "For everywhere she was my guide, and on all sides she set a watch near me, bringing me guardian angels from Helios and Selene."[6]

On the Knife-Edge

Whether we attribute it to God or the gods, the fact is that Julian was spared the necessity of defeating Constantius II on the field of battle. After Julian and his army reached Naissus in the Balkans in November 361, emissaries arrived on horseback from the court of Constantius II. The emperor, they reported, was dead of a sudden fever at the age of forty-four. To spare the empire from civil war, or so it was later said, the dying man had named Julian to reign in his place, and the armies of the eastern empire promptly declared their allegiance to Julian as the sole Augustus of the Roman empire. At these words, Julian wept, surely as much out of relief as triumph.

"For it seemed almost like a dream that a young man, in the flower of his age, slight in stature but famous for great exploits," writes the pagan historian Ammianus Marcellinus, "had now finally received imperial power by divine will without any injury to the state."[7]

Now that the gods and goddesses had answered his prayers, so clearly and so directly—and now that Constantius II was safely dead—Julian did not bother to conceal his paganism any longer. On the march from Naissus to Constantinople, he paused to offer a blood sacrifice to his divine benefactors, the very first such public ceremony in which he participated. "We worship the gods openly," declares Julian, who wielded the sacrificial blade with his own hands. "I have offered many hecatombs to the gods in gratitude for what they have done for me."[8]

Julian entered Constantinople, the place of his birth, not as a conqueror or a usurper but as the lawful if wholly unexpected successor of the man after whom it was named. Ironically, he was the first emperor to be born in the city that was meant to replace pagan Rome and thus symbolize the triumph of the Only True God in the Roman empire—and yet he promptly set out to restore the reign of the old gods and goddesses throughout the empire. To symbolize the restoration of the cherished old traditions that the Christian emperors had sought to destroy, Julian ordered that the altar of Victory, which Constantius II had removed from the Roman Senate, be restored to its former place of honor.

To the pagans, Julian was the long awaited pagan messiah whose coming had been predicted by the old blind woman at Vienne: "He laid bare the secrets of his heart," writes Ammianus, "and, with plain and final decrees, ordered the temples to be opened, victims to be brought to the altars, and the worship of the gods restored."[9]

The Christians, of course, saw Julian in a darker light: "Sorcerer and blackguard that he was, he had at first pretended to profess the Christian faith," complains John Chrysostom, the fiery Christian sermonizer. "But as soon as his benefactor died, Julian cast aside his mask and barefacedly flaunted for the world to see all those impious superstitions which he had previously concealed."[10]

At precisely this moment, the Roman empire—and, in a real sense, the whole of the Western world—was balanced on a knife-edge between two very different but equally plausible destinies. One possible future was defined by the Christian revolution that Constantine and his sons had set in motion, a world in which all men and women would be compelled to worship the Only True God. The other possible future was defined by the pagan counterrevolution that Julian was now posed to carry out, a world in which all men and women would be free to worship any or all of the gods and goddesses or none at all.

Julian aspired to restore and refurbish the traditions of classical paganism, a set of beliefs and practices that were deeply rooted in Greco-Roman civilization and embodied its highest moral and ethical aspirations. Classical civilization, as we have seen, *was* pagan civilization, and no one could claim to be well read or well educated without a command of pagan philosophy or pagan literature. Nor was classical paganism restricted to the aristocracy or the intelligentsia—the majority of the Roman population across the empire embraced paganism in one form or another. At the core of Julian's vision, then, was the profoundly conservative notion of restoring the old and idealized world that he glimpsed in the pages of Homer and Plato and, even more powerfully, in the secret rites and rituals of Mithra and the Great Mother.

"Behold, the rivers are running backwards,"[11] quips Julian in one letter, quoting an old proverb that is meant to describe the world turned upside down. He is even more plainspoken in another letter: "Innovation I abominate above all things, especially as concerns the gods."[12]

The Christian revolution that Julian proposed to dismantle was still something very new. The reign of the Christian emperors had so far lasted less than a half century. His predecessors may have ordered the closing of the pagan temples and criminalized the worship of the pagan gods, but the thousand-year-old traditions of paganism were not so easily suppressed. "The monuments which are still extant of brass and marble," writes Gibbon, "continue to prove the public exercise of the Pagan worship during the whole reign of the sons of Constantine."[13] Promptly upon the death of Constantius II, for example, the Senate of Constantinople, sitting in a city and acting on behalf of a government that were supposed to be pure expressions of Christianity, voted to grant him the same posthumous honor that was traditionally afforded to all dead emperors: Constantius II, like his father, was formally declared to be a god, a gesture that Julian later satirized as "fashioning gods as others fashion puppets."[14]

Christianity itself had shattered into countless sects and schisms, and no single faction was yet so commanding that it could wield authority as the "catholic"—that is, the universal—church. Obviously, nothing about the Only True God was self-evidently true—the followers of Arius were no less convinced of the truth of their teachings than the followers of Athanasius; the bishops of the Church of the Martyrs asserted their authority with as much zeal as the high clergy of the "orthodox" church; and each faction condemned the others as apostates, blasphemers and heretics.

For all of these reasons, nothing that Julian beheld from the high throne made the triumph of monotheism over polytheism seem inevitable. The Christians could not agree among themselves on the right way to worship the Only True God. Even with the legal and financial support of the greatest superpower in the ancient world, they had not yet managed to put an end to paganism. How would the Christians fare in the struggle for the hearts and minds of the Roman empire if they were denied access to the public treasury, the public courts and the services of soldiers, torturers and executioners?

Julian now resolved to publicly affirm his own pagan faith, to withdraw from Christianity the imperial favor it had enjoyed since the reign of Constantine and to restore official toleration to *all* expressions of religious belief and practice. At his most visionary moments, he dreamed of establishing a pagan "church" that would be as "catholic" as the Christian church claimed to be. Just as Constantine the Great credited the Christian god with his victory at the Battle of Milvian Bridge, Julian saw his bloodless triumph over Constantius II as a sign that he had been blessed by the gods and goddesses. And surely Julian was comforted by the thought that time, too, was on his side. After all, he was barely thirty years old, and his reign as the pagan emperor of Rome had just begun.

A Gift of Purple Slippers

The new Augustus, his head uncovered and dressed in mourning, greeted the cortege that brought the body of his cousin back to Constantinople and participated in the ceremonies by which his remains were interred alongside those of Constantine the Great in the Church of the Holy Apostles. As soon as the tomb was sealed, however, Julian set about the task of remaking the Roman empire in his own image.

Julian promptly set up a military tribunal to purge the imperial administration of the officers and courtiers who had agitated against him and arranged for the murder of his brother during the reign of Constantius II. The eunuch Eusebius, who had played a powerful role in imperial politics as chamberlain to both Constantine and Constantius II, was beheaded. The two men whom Constantius II had put in charge of domestic espionage were tried, condemned and buried alive. The apparatus of state terror was dismantled and the number of *agentes in rebus* was reduced to fewer than a dozen. A greater number of the accused, however, were given mild sentences, including fines, house arrest and banishment.

Julian replaced the purged officers and courtiers with men whom he regarded as both more capable and, crucially, more likely to serve him loyally. Among them were men who shared Julian's passion for paganism, including those who had known him when he was still a secret pagan. Libanius, the pagan orator whose lectures young Julian had been forbidden to attend, was invited to serve as an imperial counselor. So was Maximus of Ephesus, the theurgist who had formally initiated Julian into the mysteries of paganism. Praetextatus, the pagan who so famously collected pagan priesthoods and initiations into the mystery cults, was appointed to serve as governor of the Roman province of Greece. Salutius, a soldier who had served under Julian in Gaul, was now appointed praetorian prefect in the eastern empire. These men had once worshiped with Julian in secrecy and at great risk, but now they participated openly in the rituals of sacrifice over which the emperor presided.

"There came from every corner of the world a whole host of magicians and enchanters, diviners, augurs and mendicant priests, a workshop of every sort of trickery," sputters John Chrysostom in his condemnation of Julian's pagan revival. "Even the imperial palace was bursting at the seams with fugitives from justice and men of infamy!"[15]

Then, too, Julian seemed to delight in the opportunity to rid the palace of the opulence and decadence that so offended his ascetic sensibilities. An emblematic story, often retold, recalls how Julian, soon after he took up residence at the imperial palace, decided that his shaggy locks were all too shaggy and summoned a barber for a quick trim. The man who answered the call was so richly attired that Julian mistook him for a minister of state—"It is a barber that I want," said Julian, "not a receiver-general of the finances."[16] When the man insisted that he was, in fact, the imperial barber, Julian asked how he managed to dress so well on a barber's pay. The barber admitted that he enjoyed not only a generous salary but also a budget sufficient to feed twenty men and twenty horses, and he supplemented his earnings by taking a coin or two in payment for the service of presenting petitions at court.

Such excesses inspired Julian to purge the household staff as he had purged the highest ranks of the army and the government. He dismissed all of the eunuchs who had served as a veritable shadow government, wryly noting that he no longer needed the services for which they were so uniquely equipped because his wife was dead and he did not intend to acquire a new one. He summoned the cook who had prepared the lavish meals that were presented to Constantius II and his courtiers—a man as well appointed as the imperial barber—and stood him side by side with the field cook who had been attached to Julian's army. When the emperor asked his courtiers which one more closely resembled a cook, the man in the fancy dress found himself without a job.

Julian was always proud of his own discipline and self-denial, and the wealth and power that he now enjoyed did nothing to seduce or soften him. He ate only sparingly, often confining himself to meals "of the vegetable kind," as Gibbon puts it.[17] Unlike other Roman aristocrats, who famously gorged themselves at the banquet table and then retreated to the *vomitorium* so they could return to the table and gorge again, Julian boasts that he vomited only once since becoming Caesar and, even then, "by accident and not due to over-eating."[18] At the circus, he lingered for only five or six of the twenty-four races, all the while distracted by the correspondence and documents that he brought with him. Indeed, he worked around the clock, pausing only for hasty meals and brief intervals of sleep, and he was attended at all hours by secretaries and servitors. "He could employ his hand to write, his ear to listen, and his voice to dictate," writes Gibbon, "and pursue at once three trains of ideas without hesitation and without error."[19]

Still, Julian was no mere drudge, and a certain charm and whimsy can be also seen in his reign as a philosopher king. When, for example, a Roman citizen was accused of treason because he had dared to acquire a purple robe, a garment that only a monarch could lawfully own and wear, Julian satisfied himself that it was a matter of vanity rather than ambition. So he sent the informer back to the accused man with a gift—"a pair of purple slippers to complete the magnificence of his Imperial habit."[20]

On another occasion, Julian presumed to engage in the formal ceremony of manumission, the freeing of a slave, while attending the games of the circus. When it was pointed out to him that Roman law reserved the ceremony to the consul who was also in attendance at the games, Julian solemnly put himself on trial and judged himself to be guilty of "trespassing on the jurisdiction of another magistrate." He imposed on himself a fine of ten pounds of gold, thus making the point that no one, not even the emperor, was above the law.[21]

The Gentle Persecutor

Julian is charged by pious Christian historians with embarking upon yet another persecution of Christianity, but the fact is that he was the gentlest of persecutors. "I declare by the gods that I do not want the [Christians] to be put to death," insists Julian, "or unjustly beaten, or to suffer anything else."[22] Even if Julian had been inclined to threaten the Christians with torture and death—and nothing in his nature suggests that he would have or could have—he realized that these were the wrong weapons to use against religious zealots. Indeed, he flatly refused to provide the Christians with a fresh supply of martyrs. Rather, he attacked Christian rigorism by resorting to the oldest pagan tradition of all: religious tolerance.

The edict of toleration that Julian issued in 360 is lost to us, but the document can be understood as a mirror image of the Edict of Milan issued by Constantine almost a half century earlier. Constantine had extended the pagan principle of religious toleration to the persecuted Christians. Under his sons and successors, that principle was abandoned, and it was the Christians who came to persecute the pagans as well as each other. Now Julian restored the status quo as it had existed under Constantine and throughout most of pagan antiquity.

Julian issued a series of decrees that were intended to injure the Christian cause, but only through the mildest of measures. The cross and the *chi-rho* were removed from the imperial standard. Property that had been seized from pagan temples by the Christian emperor was to be returned to its owners. Bequests to the church were no longer permitted, the tax exemptions enjoyed by churches and clergy were ended and the stipends that had been paid to Christian clergy out of the public treasury were cut off. All public rituals of worship were to be tolerated, pagan as well as Christian. Thus, Julian's imperial proclamations can be understood as evenhanded and open-minded: he may have favored paganism, but he acted only to put *all* faiths on a equal footing.

Still, Julian was clever enough to recognize how to cause his Christian adversaries the greatest possible aggravation—he issued an order for the recall of all Christian bishops and other clergy who had been exiled from their places of residence on charges of heresy or schism, including Arians, Donatists and even the famous Bishop Athanasius. Indeed, the Christians regarded religious liberty as a form of persecution: "He began with re-establishing Paganism by law and granting a full liberty to the Christians," explains the eighteenth century historian William Warburton, an Anglican bishop. "He put on this mask of moderation and equity for no other purpose than to inflame the dissensions of the Church."[23]

At a moment of exquisite irony, for example, Julian convened an assembly of Christian clerics, forcing Arians to sit side by side with Athanasians, and he echoed the words of Constantine the Great when he scolded them for fighting so bitterly among themselves. But the pagan emperor insisted that he was entitled to a far greater measure of gratitude from the Christians than his late cousin, the Christian emperor. "For under him, most of them were sent into exile, prosecuted and imprisoned, and many of them were butchered, whereas under me, the opposite has occurred," Julian writes with characteristic sarcasm. "Under my laws, the exiled have been restored and the dispossessed repossessed of everything. I do not permit a single one of them to be dragged to the altars against his will."[24]

Now and then, to be sure, Julian was willing to use his imperial authority to punish his Christian adversaries. At Antioch, for example, Julian was told that Apollo was refusing to communicate through the oracles because his shrine in the suburb of Daphne was polluted by the presence of dead bodies—a church had been built next to the temple of Apollo during the reign of his half brother, Gallus, and the remains of a martyred bishop had been buried there. When Julian ordered that the corpse be moved elsewhere, a crowd of Christians followed the burial party and sang psalms that were intended (and taken) as an insult to the pagan emperor: "Confounded be all they that serve graven images, that boast themselves of idols."[25]

Julian set his fellow pagan and comrade in arms, Salutius, to the task of arresting a few of the Christians and putting them to torture—he wanted to identify the agitators who had organized the demonstration. But the prisoners refused to name names, and the rumor spread through Antioch that one of the victims had been sustained through his agony by the physical presence of an unseen angel. Salutius understood that the whole investigation was likely to spark yet more trouble in the streets. Julian relented and allowed the prisoners to be released. When the temple of Apollo burned to the ground a few days later, he suspected the Christians of arson but did nothing to seek out the culprits, contenting himself with a gesture of tit for tat—he ordered the closing of a church at Antioch that Constantine had built.

Over the centuries that followed his reign, Julian came to be charged with meaner and uglier deeds. One tale, for example, holds that he ordered blood from sacrificed animals and libations from the pagan temples to be sprinkled over the food on sale in the public markets so that Christians would be tricked into partaking of the offerings to the gods—a practice of earlier Roman emperors that was attributed to Julian himself.

Another tale, set down some four centuries after the reign of Julian, imagines the torture and death of a martyr falsely accused of torching the temple of Apollo at Daphne—Julian orders the martyr to be crushed between the two halves of an immense rock that has been cleft in two by stonecutters, but the doughty martyr emerges miraculously alive.

"He was a horrifying sight and a strange example of the human condition: a man naked, his bones shattered, his eyes out of their sockets, yet he walked about and spoke back to the tyrant," goes the martyrology. "Pronounce whatever sentence you like on me, whatever Satan who dwells in your soul inspires you," the martyr himself is made to say to Julian. "Along with your gods, you too will be given to the everlasting and unquenchable fire, to be punished for all time, because you trampled on the Son of God."[26]

Julian has been generally acquitted of these charges by historians, religious and secular. "He was a persecutor of the Christian religion," concedes the ancient pagan historian Eutropius, a contemporary of Julian, "but one who held back from shedding blood."[27] Only a few men and women who were put to death during the reign of Julian are nowadays recognized as authentic martyrs. Some of them were zealots who actively sought out martyrdom by carrying out provocative attacks on pagan shrines, and a couple more are members of Julian's palace guard who suffered the death penalty after they tried to assassinate the emperor. More often, however, Julian resorted to a weapon that drew no blood but one that he wielded with both pleasure and expertise—a pen dipped in the acid ink of satire.

Against the Galileans

The sharpest instrument that Julian brought to bear against Christianity was a purely verbal one—he engaged in open and sustained ridicule of their most cherished beliefs and practices. He employs a contemptuous term, "the Galilean," to identify Jesus—the Galilee was a backwater of the unruly province of Palestine and a notorious hotbed of banditry, as any reader of Josephus would have known. He refers to Christianity as "the cult of the Galilean" when he does not flatly condemn it as "atheism."[28] He disdains the veneration of martyrs and, especially, the enshrinement of their body parts as sacred relics—he describes relics as "corpse-pieces"[29] and the churches where they were piously displayed as "tombs."[30]

The decree that best expresses Julian's own passion and prejudice is one that prohibited Christian teachers from teaching their students about the works of pagan authors—Homer and Hesiod, Herodotus and Thucydides. "Did [they] not receive all their learning from the gods? I think it absurd that men who explain the works of these writers should dishonor the gods whom they honored," writes Julian.[31] "If [Christians] feel that they have gone astray concerning the gods, then let them go to the churches of the Galileans, and expound Matthew and Luke."[32] Since the pagan classics formed the basic curriculum of the course of instruction called *paideia*, the law functioned to keep Christian pedagogues out of the schools. But it was also Julian's way of reclaiming the culture of classical paganism in the same way that he had reclaimed the crown of pagan Rome from the Christian emperors who had worn it for the last fifty years.

"If the reading of your scriptures is sufficient for you, why do you make such a fuss about the learning of the Hellenes?" writes Julian in *Against the Galileans*, a work that is both a tract against Christianity and a manifesto of paganism. "Now, this would give you clear proof—select children from among you and educate them in your scriptures, and if when they come to manhood they prove to have nobler qualities than slaves, you may believe that I am talking nonsense."[33]

At the heart of Julian's case against Christianity is the old grievance that had afflicted him since early childhood: the willingness of Constantine and his sons to murder their kin in order to protect the imperial crown. Christian baptism, he argues, "does not take away the spots of leprosy, nor the gout, nor the dysentery, nor any defect of the body," he writes in *Against the Galileans*, "but it can take away adultery, rapine, and all the crimes of the soul."[34] Julian makes the same point in an elaborate satire titled *The Caesars*, a work in which he imagines that all of the dead Roman emperors are invited to a heavenly banquet by the gods and goddesses of Olympus. The guest list begins with Julius Caesar and ends with Constantine the Great, who is asked to reveal to the gods what his ambition in life had been.

"To amass great wealth," Constantine replies, "and then to spend it liberally so as to gratify my own desires."

"If it was a banker you wanted to be," replies one of the gods, "how did you so far forget yourself as to lead the life of a pastry-cook and hairdresser?"

Thus did Julian indict Constantine for his greed, his gluttony and his garish wigs, all at once. But the more serious charge is yet to come. Each of the emperors is invited to choose a god to serve as "his own guardian and guide," and Constantine runs to the goddess of pleasure. "Dressing him in raiment of many colours and otherwise making him beautiful," she passes him along to the goddess of incontinence.

There too he found Jesus, who had taken up his abode with her and cried aloud to all comers: "He that is a seducer, he that is a murderer, he that is sacrilegious and infamous, let him approach without fear! For with this water will I wash him and will straightway make him clean. And though he should be guilty of those same sins a second time, let him but smite his breast and beat his head and I will make him clean again."

Here we have a haunting and even heartbreaking suggestion that Julian cared rather less about Christianity in general than he did about one or two particular Christians: Constantine, who had murdered his own wife and son, and Constantius II, who had murdered Julian's father and half brother. At the very end of *The Caesars*, Constantine and his sons go "gladly" to Jesus and avail themselves of his offer of easy salvation from sin. "But the avenging deities none the less punished both him and them for their impiety," Julian writes, "and exacted the penalty for the shedding of the blood of their kindred."[35]

The Priest and His Goose

Perhaps the most poignant of the many tales that have come down from antiquity about Julian is the one told about his visit to an ancient temple of Apollo. Here was one of those "uncanny places" where pagans had long gathered to worship—a grove of trees, a waterfall and a shrine where sacred songs were sung, incense was burned, libations were poured and a hecatomb was slain and burned on the altar fire in honor of the high god. Once Julian had restored the right to openly worship the gods, he made a pilgrimage to the shrine on the day of the sacred festival when all of these solemn but joyous festivities were to take place. A whole lifetime of reading and dreaming, starting in the library at Macellum and continuing through his secret initiation into the mystery cults at Ephesus, had prepared him for this glorious day.

"I pictured to myself the procession, as if seeing visions in a dream," Julian writes, "sacrificial victims and libations and choruses in honour of the god, and incense, and the youths of the city gathered round the shrine, their souls arrayed with all holiness and they themselves decked out in white and splendid raiment."[36]

On his arrival, however, Julian was disappointed at what he saw—

or, rather, what he didn't see. A hecatomb required a hundred oxen, but he saw not a single one. No fire burned on the altar, no incense wafted through the shrine, and no cakes or libations had been prepared. No beautiful young women or handsome young men were waiting at the shrine. The whole desolate place was empty but for a single priest and, remarkably, a single forlorn goose.

"When I began to enquire what sacrifice the city intended to make in celebration of the annual festival in honour of the god," Julian relates, "the priest said, 'I have brought with me from my house a goose as an offering to the god, but the city has made no preparations.' "[37]

Julian was disappointed, but he should not have been surprised. Classical paganism as it is enshrined in the pages of Homer, as we have seen, was already in decline when Christianity first arrived in Rome. The official cults had long been reduced to formulaic prayers and hollow ceremonies. All of the exotic mystery religions into which Julian had been initiated—the cults of Mithra and the Great Mother of the Gods as well as the mystical and magical rites of the Neoplatonists—flowered in Rome precisely because Apollo and the other gods and goddesses of the Greco-Roman pantheon no longer seemed to provide their worshippers with a sense of wonder. To turn back the river of monotheism, Julian understood, he would have to restore the faded glory of polytheism that was now found only in the brittle pages of Homer.

Julian found ways to satisfy his own spiritual longings. He personally presided over the offering of hecatombs, drawing the sacrificial blade across the throats of the oxen and hacking them into quarters with a sacred axe. "He was called a slaughterer rather than a priest by many who ridiculed the number of his victims," admits the pagan orator Libanius, now one of Julian's intimate friends.[38] "Men said that if he returned victorious over Persia," writes Robert Browning, "there would soon be a shortage of cattle."[39] And, according to the pagan historian Ammianus, "Julian presumptuously delighted in carrying the sacred emblems instead of the priests and in being attended by a band of women,"[40] a sight that inspired only shock and disgust in his former

schoolmate from Athens, Gregory of Nazianzus. "Julian was habitu-
ally followed by a train of prostitutes, libertines, and perverts," insists
the bitter and ever critical Gregory, "who assiduously assisted at his
functions."[41]

Julian installed a Mithraeum, a shrine for the worship of Mithra,
in his palace on the shores of the Sea of Marmara, and there he submitted again to the ritual of the taurobolium. He made pilgrimages
to pagan shrines, including the temple of Zeus on Mount Casios. He
sent to Egypt for an Apis bull that was regarded as sacred to the god
Osiris. He composed a tribute to King Helios—"May Hermes, the
god of eloquence, stand by my side"[42]—and another one to the Great
Mother of the Gods: "I am well aware that some over-wise persons
will call it an old wives' tale," he concedes. "But for my part I would
rather trust the traditions than those too clever people, whose puny
souls are keen-sighted enough, but never do see [anything] that is
sound."[43]

In fact, Julian suggests in his own writings that he was granted
more than one divine vision, and Libanius is willing to affirm that
these suggestions are more than merely rhetorical or metaphorical:
"You alone have seen the shapes of the gods, a blessed observer of the
blessed ones," writes Libanius. "You alone have heard the voice of the
gods and addressed them in the words of Sophocles, 'O voice of
Athene' or 'O voice of Zeus.' "[44]

The Church of the Gods and Goddesses

Julian was an authentic and earnest pagan, and he embraced the core
value of polytheism—the willingness to recognize and respect the divinity of *all* gods and goddesses. Thus, even though he practiced a
kind of "pagan monotheism,"[45] as Browning puts it—that is, he believed that King Helios was the greatest of all the gods, if not the one
and only god—he offered worship to all the traditional deities of the
Greco-Roman pantheon as well as to such imports as Mithra and the

Great Mother. But it is also true that Julian had learned a lesson from his Christian upbringing—he admired and envied the superior organizational skills that the Christians brought to bear in setting up and running their churches. To overcome the advantage that they enjoyed, Julian proposed to copy what the Christians did best and apply it to the pagan restoration that was now in progress.

Julian envisioned, and promptly invented, something that had never before existed—a pagan "church" with its own all-encompassing theology and its own unified clerical hierarchy.[46] He commissioned the composition of a work titled *On the Gods and the Universe*, a "manual of pagan theology."[47] He established a unified pagan priesthood—one of his first appointments was Pegasius, the former Christian bishop who had conducted him on a tour of the pagan temples of Ilion—and he even adopted the same title of office, *archiereus*, that was used to identify Christian clergy of comparable rank. He encouraged the Hellenes, the term he uses to describe what Christians called "pagans," to follow the Christian example in both chastity and philanthropy. Pagan priests were to avoid the excesses of the tavern, the distractions of the theater and the seductions of erotic literature, and they must shun the company of actors, jockeys and dancers. He even prescribed a set of dietary laws that he extracted from the cult of the Great Mother—root vegetables, pomegranates and pork were forbidden, and fish was to be eaten only when prescribed.

Julian sought to impose order on the chaos of paganism. All of the gods and goddesses who were worshipped across the vast stretches of the Roman empire—some of them stately and solemn, some of them wild and raucous—were to be accommodated in the new pantheon, but all of them would be subservient to the most high god whom Constantine had once worshipped, the solar deity variously called Apollo, *Sol Invictus* and King Helios. "There exists no man who does not stretch out his hands toward the heavens when he prays," writes Julian, "and whether he swears by one god or several, if he has any notion at all of the divine, he turns heavenward."[48] In that sense, the unified and orderly pagan church that Julian envisioned was the perfect counterpart to the orderly Christian church that Constantine tried to create at the Council of Nicaea.

Yet the very notion of a pagan church is a contradiction in terms. The "spongy mass of tolerance and tradition" could not be so readily molded into a single set of approved beliefs and practices. Julian's experiment in "pagan monotheism," scholars have argued, was doomed to failure because it violated the core value of polytheism: the freedom of every man and woman to choose among any, all or none of the gods. Indeed, by a strange irony, Julian's vision of a pagan church betrays how deeply he had been imprinted with the most dangerous features of monotheism—the idea that there is one god who must be regarded as the best of all gods, and the impulse to impose the Only True God on everyone else.

The Skulls in the Crypt

Julian's pagan counterrevolution was intended to be a nonviolent one, but the emperor in Constantinople found that he could do nothing to suppress the religious extremists, both Christians and pagans, who continued to battle one another in the streets of cities across the Roman empire. Shortly after Julian came to the throne, for example, the Christian bishop of Phoenicia was denounced for his role in the destruction of a pagan temple. Bishop Marcus, it was said, was the same man who had rescued young Julian from the blood purge that ended his father's life so many years before. Now, perhaps out of gratitude, Julian imposed a punishment that was mild enough by comparison with Roman criminal justice—the old man was ordered to rebuild the temple.

Like the confessors of the Great Persecution, however, Bishop Marcus stubbornly refused to put his hand on what he regarded as the demon-tainted stones of a pagan shrine. That act of Christian zeal was enough to rouse the pagan mob to vengeance. First, they dragged him into the street, plucked out his beard, hair by hair, and turned him over to "the refined cruelty of schoolboys, who amused themselves by piercing him with their [pens]," according to Giuseppe Ricciotti, an abbot as well as a biographer of Julian.[49] At last, they smeared his body with honey and left him to be stung to death by insects.

The pagan equivalent of zealotry was also at work in the death of George of Cappadocia. Constantius II had appointed George, an Arian bishop, to serve in place of the exiled Athanasius in the see at Alexandria, and he had turned over an abandoned Mithraeum to George for use as a church. When workers broke into the crypt of the old temple, they found an accumulation of human skulls—and the discovery was the flash point of a clash between Christian and pagan rigorists.

To Bishop George, the skulls were evidence that the site had once been used for rituals of human sacrifice. To the pious pagans, they were the sanctified remains of men and women who had been properly buried there—and they saw the conversion of the Mithraeum into a church as an act of desecration. George only managed to make matters worse for himself when he was overheard making a dismissive remark about the temple of Agathos Daimon, the tutelary god of Alexandria: "How long will *that* tomb continue to stand?"[50]

When Constantius II died and Julian declared the pagan restoration, the pagans of Alexandria felt themselves at liberty to seize George and throw him in jail. On December 25, 361—by pagan tradition, the birthday of *Sol Invictus*—a mob broke into the public cells, dragged out several Christian prisoners, including George, and lynched them. The corpse of Bishop George was tied to a camel, and the others were dragged along behind, all to the amusement of the mob. At last, the bodies were burned—as a precaution against supplying the Christians with yet more "corpse-pieces"—and the ashes were dumped into the sea.

Julian, as it turned out, had known George in early childhood.

During his years of confinement at Macellum, long before George was appointed to the see at Alexandria, Julian had been permitted to visit the library that George maintained in his quarters in nearby Caesarea. The young man admired the works of philosophy and rhetoric that he found there, and the bishop allowed him to borrow them for reading and copying, although Julian later wrote contemptuously of the books that were concerned with "the teachings of the impious Galileans, which I would like to see entirely destroyed."[51]

Julian did not instigate the pagan riot that ended in the murder of Bishop George, but neither did he do much about it. He contented himself with a mild scolding of the citizenry of Alexandria. "Perhaps your anger and rage led you astray," writes Julian in a public letter. "I administer to you the very mildest remedy, namely admonition and arguments."[52] Then he turned to what he found to be a much more compelling aspect of the whole ugly incident. The bishop had brought his books with him to Alexandria, but his library had been broken up and dispersed. Now the emperor wrote to his agent in Alexandria and instructed him to gather up as many of the volumes from the dead bishop's library as he could recover and send them back to Constantinople.

Julian was plainly guilty of indifference to the sufferings of the Christian victims of the mob violence that erupted during the pagan restoration. "I might even admit," he writes of George, "that he deserved even worse and more cruel treatment." From the Christian perspective, however, he was an accomplice to murder. The pagan rioters in Phoenicia and Alexandria, as the Christian sources see it, were Julian's unwitting agents in a subtle campaign of terror against the Christian minority. "Julian shrank from a death penalty," concedes Ricciotti, but only because to do otherwise "would have removed the disguise from his system of veiled persecution."[53] Whenever the mob took to the streets, he insists, they were doing the emperor's dirty work: "Churches were sacked, priests tortured, consecrated virgins violated, stomachs of victims were slit open and barley thrown into them to feed the pigs," reports Ricciotti. "Local governors, knowing the attitude of the emperor, tolerated such crimes."[54]

"One Stone Upon Another"

Far more often, however, Julian's torment of the Christians was characterized by the wry and whimsical, if also slightly devilish, quality that sparkles in the letters and orations that were his best-loved pastime. But nowhere is Julian's fanciful nature more richly on display than in the single most grandiose of all his undertakings—the restoration of the temple in Jerusalem where the God of Israel had been worshipped until the end of the Jewish War in 70 C.E., when one of his less gentle predecessors on the throne pulled it down. Julian intended to honor the ancient faith of the Jews by permitting them to return to their homeland and rebuild their temple, or so he vowed. He also delighted in vexing the Christians by bestowing imperial favor on the original monotheists—whom, ironically, they now regarded as their worst enemies.

So Julian addressed a remarkable public letter to the Jewish community of the Roman empire in which he vows that they, too, would enjoy the blessings of pagan toleration. Julian promises that the punitive taxes that had been imposed on them by his predecessors— "by far the most burdensome thing in the yoke of your slavery"—will be lifted. The various accusations and denunciations by Christians against Jews "that were stored in my desk," he assures them, "I threw into the fire." He declares that "everywhere, during my reign, you may have security of mind," and he implores them to "offer more fervid prayers for my reign to the Most High God, the Creator, who has deigned to crown me with his own immaculate right hand."[55]

Then he makes a vow that reveals not only his expert knowledge of monotheism, not only his pagan commitment to religious toleration, but—above all—his guile and his sly gamesmanship. Julian knew from his own reading that the Jews once sacrificed to the God of Israel at the Temple of Solomon in Jerusalem, the only place where sacrifice had been permitted since the days of King Josiah. And he saw a striking commonality between the worship of Yahweh as it was actually described in the Bible and the worship of the gods and goddesses of paganism. The Jews, of course, offered worship to one god only, and the pagans offered worship to many gods. "We have all else in common—temples, sacred precincts, altars for sacrifice, and purifications," writes Julian, "in all of which we differ not at all from one another."[56] But he also understood that Judaism had been cut off from the old rituals of worship to the God of Israel after the Roman legions marched into Jerusalem and razed the Temple.

Julian understood, too, that the events of the Jewish War figured crucially in Christian theology and, especially, the Christian denunciation of Judaism. Jesus is shown to prophesy the destruction of the Temple in the Christian Bible: "Verily I say unto you, there shall not be left here one stone upon another."[57] The new temple that Jesus promises to raise up in its place is not a physical structure but rather "the temple of his body."[58] The fact that the Roman army left the Temple in ruins at the end of the Jewish War was seen by Christians as incontrovertible physical proof that the prophecy of Jesus had been fully realized and, therefore, Jewish monotheism had been repudiated and superseded by Christianity.

So Julian decided to strike a blow against Christianity by the simple if astounding feat of rebuilding the Temple and thus permitting the Jews to resume the rituals of animal sacrifice to the God of Israel that had been abandoned nearly 300 years before. Jesus had destroyed the old Temple, but now Julian would build a new one. "The high priest of the Hellenes would embarrass the God of the Galileans on His own terrain," as Abbot Ricciotti puts it, "making Him out to be a charlatan."[59] What more eloquent way to repudiate the Christians, Julian calculated, than to befriend the Jews and, especially, to prove the cherished scriptures of the Only True God to be wrong?

Julian acted with characteristic energy and resolve to set his audacious plan into motion. He allotted funds from the imperial treasury, and he dispatched one of his trusted courtiers, a man called Alypius, from Antioch to Jerusalem to oversee the project. Encouraged by the remarkable decree, Jews from both the Roman empire and Persia began to make their way to Jerusalem, a place from which they had been excluded by imperial decree. Some of the rabbis, who had replaced the old priesthood after the destruction of the Temple, saw the remarkable promise of Julian as a sure sign that the Messiah was on his way.

A synagogue was opened in one of the Roman colonnades that had been built over the site of the former Temple. Rubble and ruins were removed from the site by an ardent and inspired workforce that included both Jewish men and women who rejoiced at the opportunity to rebuild the sacred structure. Stonemasons started cutting and dressing the first of the massive stones that would be needed for the new temple; by pious tradition, their tools were fashioned out of silver rather than iron, all in compliance with the dictates of the Bible. An inscription carved into one of the surviving stones of the Western Wall—"When you see this, your heart shall rejoice"—may be the handiwork of one of those masons.[60]

The work on the temple was interrupted, according to the ancient chronicles, by a series of ominous mishaps. First came torrential rains; then an earthquake caused the stonework to tumble and crush several of the workers. "Frightful balls of flame kept bursting forth near the foundations of the temple and made it impossible for the workmen to approach the place," writes Ammianus, "and some were even burned to death."[61] The flames reached storerooms where the building materials were stored. Secular historians are willing to entertain the idea that these were unremarkable natural phenomena, and one Jewish historian proposes that the damage was the result of vandalism and arson by Christian zealots who resented the whole undertaking, just as Julian himself had intended.[62] Christians, of course, saw the tremors and fireballs as nothing less than the wrath of the Only True God. Whatever the cause of the calamities, construction of the new temple came to a halt.

Julian himself recognized that the task would not be completed until he had attended to the urgent task that now faced him: the defeat of the Persian armies that were once again threatening the *Pax Romana* on the eastern frontier of the empire. Indeed, he would have to put aside *all* his visionary undertakings in order to devote himself to the campaign against the Persians. He implored the Jews to address "their supplaint prayers on behalf of my imperial office to Mighty God" at this moment of greatest peril to his life and reign.

"This you ought to do," he concludes, "in order that, when I have successfully concluded the war with Persia, I may rebuild by my own efforts the sacred city of Jerusalem, which for so many years you have longed to see inhabited, and may bring settlers there and, together with you, may glorify the Most High God therein."[63]

To the Persian Front

Julian rode out of Constantinople at the head of an army to engage the Persian enemy in the summer of 362. The Roman road on which Julian traveled was now put to its original and essential use—a military highway intended to permit the rapid deployment of the legions to the farthest stretches of the empire. On his way, he paused at the ancient temple of Cybele, the Great Mother of the Gods, and he passed the site where Alexander the Great had fought and beaten the Persian army seven centuries before—Julian, it was said, believed himself to be the reincarnation of the original philosopher king and the founder of Hellenism. At last, he reached Antioch, where the army would rest and resupply while he awaited the campaigning season to come the following spring.

The sojourn at Antioch lasted eight months. Julian found an opportunity to pore over the books that had formerly belonged to Bishop George, which caught up with him there, and he dutifully presided over public sacrifices to the old gods in the company of his old comrades and confidants, including Maximus of Ephesus and Priscus, his former tutors in the Neoplatonist mysteries, and his personal physician, Oribasius, all of whom had known him when he was still a secret pagan. The largely Christian citizenry of Antioch, however, treated the young emperor with coldness and contempt.

The local Christians resented his pagan piety. They bridled at the decrees he enacted to address the problem of grain shortages and price inflation and they even scorned the new currency that he had introduced, both for its pagan motifs and for the fact that the emperor was depicted with a beard in defiance of long tradition. Julian, in an utterly characteristic gesture, responded in the self-revelatory and bitterly sarcastic *Misopogon* ("Beard Hater"). He ordered the work to be posted on the palace wall, where all could read his account of his own flaws and eccentricities. "For criticising myself," writes the Augustus in a startling exercise of *lèse-majesté*, "I have countless reasons."[64]

Julian contented himself with the company of his fellow pagans, and he busied himself with preparations for the campaign on which he would soon embark. He also found encouragement in a series of good omens that seemed to confirm that he enjoyed the favor of the gods, if not the citizenry of Antioch. A swan, the bird whose form the high god Zeus had once taken, was caught along the nearby banks of the Orontes. And when Julian offered a blood sacrifice in the temple of Zeus, the swan rose in flight and headed toward the east, a sure sign that he was destined to vanquish the Persians.

A Willing Sacrifice

On March 5, 363, Julian and his army resumed the march toward the Persian frontier. Along the way, he paused to sacrifice a white bull, a particularly auspicious offering, and later he celebrated the festival of Cybele by ritually immersing an image of the Great Mother of the Gods in the waters of the Euphrates. Soon the whole of Julian's army was across the Euphrates and then the Tigris, and he began to encounter mounted patrols of Persian cavalry on reconnaissance missions.

On the day before he crossed into Persian territory, Julian

addressed the soldiers under his command with words that were recorded by an eyewitness, the pagan historian Ammianus. "Angered by the fate of captured cities and defeated armies, I am resolved to make our territory safe and strong," he declared. "Should I be killed in battle, it will be as a willing sacrifice for my country."[65]

Now that his army was on Persian soil, Julian found himself under attack by units of Persian archers and cavalry that were testing his strength and harrying his progress. The terrain was broken up by irrigation canals and tributaries of the bigger rivers, and the Persians flooded the line of march. The Roman army moved with difficulty into its first major operations, besieging a series of fortified Persian cities that ultimately fell to Julian's catapults and battering rams, and suffering a series of stinging attacks as the legions slogged off in search of the Persian army. By May 29, Julian's army caught up with the enemy and Julian himself marched into battle as he had once done in Gaul, personally directing his men in close combat. When the sun set, some 2500 Persians lay dead against a Roman death toll of only 70. The auguries, it seemed, had been accurate, and the gods seemed to be on Julian's side.

Julian was utterly serious and characteristically single-minded about the campaign. Booty taken from the Persian towns and cities along the line of march was distributed among the soldiers, according to Ammianus, but Julian took for himself only "three gold coins and a young deaf-mute who expressed himself gracefully with his hands."[66] And the chaste and ascetic young emperor, who may have believed that he was the bearer of the soul of Alexander the Great, followed the famous example of the philosopher king: Julian refused to lay eyes, much less hands, on the beautiful young women who were taken as prizes of war.

"Thou Hast Conquered, Galilean"

The next day, however, the omens went suddenly sour. Ten bulls had been brought along to serve as offerings along the way—nine of them dropped dead before they could be slaughtered, and the last one escaped altogether. "The skeptical historian may hazard the guess that someone had poisoned the sacrificial animals," offers Browning, "for reasons of his own."[67] The exertion and privation of a long march over rugged terrain supplies an equally plausible explanation. Whatever the actual cause, Julian himself was alarmed and unsettled—he was, after all, the most pious of pagans.

Still, the army now resumed its march in the direction of the Persian capital, Ctesiphon. Again, the Persians resorted to harrying tactics—they burned the crops and the grassland that stood along Julian's line of march; they fired stones and spears from catapults; and they sent small detachments of cavalry to ride down on the long columns, strike a sharp blow and then ride off again. At last, a new and terrifying sight presented itself on the far horizon to Julian and his comrades in arms—the cloud of dust and the occasional glint and sparkle of light on polished armor that revealed the presence of a sizable fighting force. On the next morning, as the sun rose, the Romans could plainly see the army of Shapur II, the emperor of Persia, arrayed for battle.

Julian fought again—and he won again. The soldiers who had once refused to cross the Alps at the command of Constantius II had done so at the command of Julian, and they now followed him into battle against the archers, cavalry and battle elephants of the Persian emperor. They drove off the Persian army but they did not succeed in destroying it. His tactical victory presented Julian with a new crisis—he was deep in enemy territory, far from any source of reinforcement or resupply, his provisions were depleted, his men were underfed and tired and he was at risk of yet another attack by a fresh Persian army.

Alone in his tent, Julian comforted himself in the same way he had done as a frightened child at Macellum—he opened a book and read by lantern light. But the book failed to work its old magic. He lay awake, anxious and fretful, and he wondered what he might have done to displease the gods and goddesses who had so far favored him so richly. At his darkest moment, he imagined that he saw a spectral

figure cross the floor of the tent and exit into the darkness outside—
the tutelary god of the Roman people who had once championed the
pagan emperor but was now abandoning him to his fate.

Julian promptly summoned the band of seers who were formally
attached to his army, and he demanded that they perform the ancient
ritual of divination by which the gods might reveal their will. The
Haruspices consulted their sacred texts and reported that all signs
were against him—Julian must not engage in battle on that day. But
Julian, a seasoned soldier as well as a pious pagan, apparently decided
that the risk of a new Persian attack outweighed the risk of defying
the auguries. At his order, the army marched at first light—and, just
as he had feared, the Persian horse and elephant cavalry promptly
began to strike the Roman formations here and there along the
whole line of march.

Julian, like Josiah and Constantine before him, was not only a king
but also a fearless general who insisted on showing himself where the
fighting was fiercest. When word reached him that the Persians were
striking his left flank and his men were falling back, he abruptly
turned toward the skirmish. Julian moved in such haste that he forgot
or neglected to strap on the breastplate that his armor bearer carried,
and he moved so fast that his bodyguard lost sight of him in the
clamor and chaos of the fighting. And so there was nothing—and no
one—to stop the soldier who charged the emperor, thrust a long spear
into his side and left it there, the spear point lodging between his ribs
and piercing his liver.

Suddenly and grievously wounded, Julian struggled to pull the
spear out of his body but succeeded only in wounding his hand on its
sharp edge. When his comrades in arms finally reached him, they
drove off the Persian cavalry and sought out Oribasius to care for the
fallen Augustus. Maximus and Priscus, too, were summoned to comfort their old friend during his final agony. Julian bravely called for
his weapons so he could resume the fighting, but his bandaged
wound broke open and began to bleed again. "He delighted in his
wound," insists Libanius, "gazing joyfully upon it, asking those who

were weeping if his lot was not preferable to growing old."[68] At last, Julian called for cold water, swallowed it with difficulty, and died without uttering another word.

Who delivered the fatal spear thrust? His fellow pagans suggested it was not one of the Persian cavalrymen but rather a treasonous and treacherous Christian zealot serving in the ranks of the Roman army, "an idea that was not displeasing to some Christians," according to Pierre Chuvin.[69] Whether it was a Roman or a Persian, a Christian or a pagan, however, the Christian true believers welcomed his death as a miracle and a blessing. Indeed, one Christian chronicler, writing a century or so after the fact, imagines that Julian conceded defeat to the Christian god at the moment of his death, collecting the blood from his battle wound in his cupped hand and casting it toward the heavens as he cried: "Thou hast conquered, Gaililean!"[70]

The tales are purely legendary. But surely, as he lay dying, Julian must have wondered—and so can we—what he might have been able to accomplish if he had reigned, like Constantine the Great, for thirty years. Would he have fulfilled the promise of religious toleration that is implicit in polytheism, or reverted to the uglier practices of religious persecution that both Christians and pagans had more recently embraced? All we know for a fact, however, is that when Julian died on June 26, 363, he was barely thirty-two years old, and only eighteen months had passed since the day when he replaced the Christian emperor on the imperial throne and the pagan restoration had begun.

THE HANDLESS SCRIBE

The Price of Victory of the Only True God

What should be said of us, who are forced to live piously,
not by devotion but by terror?

—Maximus of Turin

S ometime around the year 1000, an artful but curious reliquary
was put on display in a village church in southern France—a
near-life-sized statue that was used to preserve the relics of a
martyr known as St. Fides. In life, she was famous for having resur-
rected a dead mule and, after her death, her body parts were believed
to possess the same miraculous power. The face is fashioned out of
gold, and the figure is richly embellished with precious stones. She is
a martyr, not a monarch, but she sits on a throne. This simple fact reveals something remarkable about the origins of the image. "The de-
vout had somewhere found the image of an emperor of Julian's time
or thereabouts," explains Ramsay MacMullen, "and used it to make a
reliquary."[1]

The reliquary of St. Fides is doubly ironic. An image of the man
whom Christianity condemns as Julian the Apostate may have been
recycled into the resting place for the bones of a revered Christian
martyr. Yet Julian himself, as we have seen, detested the Christian
adoration of "corpse-pieces." Nonetheless, the reliquary is a wholly
appropriate symbol of what happened after the death of the last
pagan emperor of Rome. The whole of the Roman imperial government, in fact, was put in service of the Christian church in the

crusade to exterminate both paganism and what the orthodox church regarded as Christian heresy. Within a generation after Julian's death on a battlefield in Persia, the Roman empire was once against a Christian realm.

Christian tradition salutes Constantine as "the Great" and condemns Julian as "the Apostate." According to Bishop Gregory of Nazianzus, who knew Julian when they were both students in Athens, Julian "concealed his evil character under a mask of goodness," and Constantius II stopped too soon when he set out to murder his uncles and cousins: "He did not realise he was training up an enemy of Christ," writes Gregory in *Against Julian*. "In this one thing he did not do well, in showing kindness, saving the life and giving rule to him who was saved and crowned for evil."[2] Edward Gibbon, by contrast, saluted Julian as a man of impressive and even exalted qualities: "The throne of Julian was the seat of reason, of virtue," insists Gibbon, and "the apostate Julian deserved the empire of the world."[3] For later historians, he presents "a baffling problem in psychology," as historian Edward J. Martin wrote in the early twentieth-century.[4] But, whether we admire Julian or detest him, Bishop Athanasius correctly predicted that he was "only a little cloud that would soon pass."[5]

"Behold, the rivers are running backwards," writes Julian—but the nineteenth-century historian August-Arthur Beugnot insists that "Julian's life was an accident, and at his death events reverted to their natural channel."[6]

Both the pagan restoration and the dynasty of Constantine the Great died with Julian. The Roman officer who was elected by the army to take Julian's place on the throne, Jovian, was unrelated to him by blood. Donning the purple robe that had belonged to Julian, Jovian promptly sued for peace with the Persian king. When the treaty was signed, he hastened back to Rome, carrying the embalmed body of Julian to his birthplace, Constantinople, where it would lay in state before it was interred among the graves of his mother's family. An old monk approached the corpse, pierced in the side with its

Christ-like wound, and composed a hymn to celebrate the triumph
of the Only True God over "the unclean one."

> I stood over him and mocked his heathendom
> and I said, "Is this the one who raised himself
> against the living name and forgot that he is dust?"[7]

Jovian reigned as a Christian emperor, but he did not promptly
reenact the antipagan decrees of Constantius II. Indeed, he issued an
edict of toleration of his own, promising that no one would be persecuted for the practice of any religion, pagan or Christian, with the
exception of magic workers and fortune-tellers. The pagans who had
enjoyed imperial favor under Julian sought to hide themselves in fear
of the expected purge—but it did not come. Or, at least, it did not
come quite as soon as they expected.

Men in Black

Even if the first of Julian's successors stayed his hand against paganism, however, a new kind of Christian zealot took up the banner of
the Only True God with a righteous wrath that was now charged with
a taste for revenge. The monks who had taken vows of poverty and
chastity in imitation of Christ—"men in black," as Libanius, the
fourth-century Sophist, describes them[8]—had first appeared early in
the fourth century in Syria and Egypt as anchorites and hermits.
"They train to live like angels," as the preacher John Chrysostom puts
it,[9] and they refrained from all pleasures of the flesh. Indeed, the
monastics were rigorists in the purest sense—pious men and women
who sought the isolation of the wilderness to punish their bodies and
nurture their souls. Thus did one scholar quip that Julian "was probably as proud of the lice in his beard as any monk in Egypt."[10]

At first, the monks did violence only to themselves. The hermit
monk called Anthony (c. 251–c. 356) banished himself to a tomb in the
wilderness, where he was famously afflicted by demonic apparitions:

"The walls opened, and the daimones appeared as serpents, lions, bulls, wolves, scorpions, leopards, and bears."[11] The sufferings of Hilarion (c. 291–c. 371), who confined himself to a stone cell only five feet high, were even more lurid—his vows of abstinence were sorely tested by visions of naked and lascivious women, as well as banquet tables richly laden with delicacies. So famous were some of these hermits that they did not remain alone for long—Hilarion, for example, looked out of his cell one day to see a man and a camel, both perfectly real and both a bit cranky. He was called upon by the man to exorcise the evil spirit that had obviously possessed the camel.

Now, however, the monks boiled up out of the wilderness *en masse* and descended upon town and countryside as self-appointed "shock troops" in the holy war against paganism. Urged on by the most militant of the bishops, they took it upon themselves to search for and destroy any expression of paganism that they could find. They delighted in pulling down altars, smashing statuary and ruining shrines and temples. They helped themselves to the treasures of the temples they destroyed, and they set upon any unfortunate man or woman whom they suspected of engaging in pagan rituals of worship. So thorough were the monks that their path of destruction can be traced by archaeological evidence of the pagan shrines that they ruined.

"Men in black, who eat more than elephants and exhaust themselves with the number of cups they drain, who have drink served to them in the middle of their psalm-singing, rush upon the temples," writes Libanius in a tract titled *In Defense of the Temples*. "Roofs are knocked off, walls undermined, shrines thrown down, altars totally destroyed. And as for the priests: they can choose between silence and death."[12]

The riotous monks, as it turned out, were the advance guard of a renewed and reinvigorated Christian revolution, and they set an example that would be followed by revolutionaries who came along many centuries later. "As France long ago had its revolutionary mobs and China more recently its Red Guards," explains historian John

Holland Smith, "so too the empire in the closing years of the fourth Christian century had its propaganda-directed gangs of rioters who went from place to place smashing, burning, looting and destroying in defiance of the laws and defence of their own cultural revolution."[13]

The monks were so unruly, in fact, that an imperial decree was issued in 390 in a vain effort to compel them to return to the wilderness from whence they had come. But the zeal of the monks eventually came to infect the Christian emperors who followed the benign Jovian to the throne, and the era of religious toleration finally came to an end. Once again, the machinery of the Roman state—the prison, the torture chamber, the gallows and the executioner's block—was used to punish anyone who refused to confine his or her worship to the Only True God, as well as anyone who worshiped the Only True God in a manner that the orthodox church regarded as heretical.

"In the long truce between the hostile camps, the pagan, the sceptic, even the formal, lukewarm Christian, may have come to dream of a mutual toleration which would leave the ancient forms undisturbed," writes historian Samuel Dill. "But such men, living in a world of literary and antiquarian illusions, know little of the inner forces of the new Christian movement."[14]

Julian has been blamed for the escalation of the war on paganism that was conducted by the Christian emperors who reigned at the end of the fourth century and thereafter. "It was only after the near-catastrophe of Julian's reversion to paganism that the Christian emperors systematically legislated against paganism so as to destroy it," explains Jewish historian and theologian Jacob Neusner. "His brief reign brought in its wake a ferocious counterrevolution, with the Christian state now suppressing the institutions of paganism, and Christian men in the streets acting on their own against those institutions."[15] Church, state and mob were now fused into a single instrument of terror that was brought down on *all* expression of religious diversity, both pagan and Christian.

With the reign of Theodosius I (c. 346–395), a fierce and even fanatical Christian true believer who ascended to the throne in 379, the war of God against the gods entered its final and decisive phase. The Spanish-born emperor, according to historian Hugh Trevor-Roper, deserves to be regarded as "the first of the Spanish Inquisitors."[16] He was the first emperor to formally elevate Christianity to the legal status of the state religion of Rome. As a faithful member of the "orthodox" and "catholic" church, he condemned Arianism and other Christian beliefs and practices that the orthodox church regarded as apostasies and heresies. And he issued a series of decrees that criminalized the practice of paganism: pagan ritual and sacrifice were prohibited, pagan temples were closed and the property of the pagan cults was confiscated. Not only blood sacrifice, but any ritual use of fire, wine, incense, trees or garlands, was now a public offense. The punishment for violation of the new decrees was death.

"It is Our will that all the peoples who are ruled by our Clemency shall practice that religion which the divine Peter the Apostle transmitted to the Romans," decreed Theodosius I in 380. "We command that those persons who follow this rule shall embrace the name of Catholic Christians. The rest, however, whom We adjudge demented and insane... shall be smitten first by divine vengeance and secondly by the retribution of Our own initiative."[17]

In 385, the Christian rigorist Priscillian was put on trial by a Roman magistrate on charges of heresy, tortured to extract a confession of doctrinal error and then executed—the first time a public court enforced Christian doctrine. In 386, the bishop of Apamea in Syria was provided with legionnaires and gladiators by the praetorian prefect to demolish the temple of Zeus. Even the Roman emperor might find himself outranked (or, at least, outflanked) by a cleric. When a band of monks destroyed a synagogue in Callinicum, a town on the Euphrates, in 388, for example, Theodosius I ordered the local bishop to pay reparations to the Jewish community; the bishop defied the order and announced that he would no longer celebrate the Eucharist until it was withdrawn. The emperor ultimately yielded to the bishop.

"I have now learned the difference," Theodosius later remarked, "between a Prince and a Bishop!"[18]

Akhenaton and Josiah, as we have seen, were monarchs who tried but failed to impose monotheism on their subjects—they were true believers, but they did not possess the terrible power of the totalitarian state. Constantine and Julian were the first monarchs in recorded history to command the whole arsenal of totalitarianism, but neither of them was willing to put it to use in service of true belief. Each of them, to a lesser or greater degree, was willing to tolerate a certain degree of diversity in religious belief and practice. But Theodosius I was not so kind or gentle, and he used what he called "the thousand terrors of the laws" to achieve the final victory of monotheism over polytheism.[19]

"Theodosius appears on history's stage like a Roman Cromwell, Napoleon, or Stalin," explains Richard E. Rubenstein in *When Jesus Became God*, "an authoritarian figure whose mission was to consolidate the Christian revolution by conservatizing it, adapting it to existing social realities, and incorporating it into the structure of state power."[20]

Plutarch describes how the passengers on a becalmed ship off the coast of Italy once heard a mysterious voice that cried out in despair: "The great god Pan is dead." Ironically, the incident supposedly took place during the reign of Tiberius (14–37 C.E.), the same period during which, by tradition, Jesus of Nazareth met his own death on a cross in Palestine. Three centuries later, under the reign of Theodosius I, the plaintive cry of the unseen spirit could be understood in retrospect as an augury of things to come: "The rustic god who for centuries had inhabited the mountain slopes and who typified the simpler and frailer spirit of paganism," explains Edward Alexander Parsons, "was as the symbol [for] the death of *all* the gods."[21]

The Death of Hypatia

The pagan tradition of religious liberty may have outlasted the last pagan emperor, but only for a few decades—history provides us with a series of benchmarks that signify the final and total victory of monotheism in the war of God against the gods.

In 390, for example, a mob of Christian zealots attacked the ancient library of Alexandria, a place where works of the greatest rarity and antiquity had been collected. Here were preserved the oldest manuscripts of the Bible and other writings of Jewish and Christian origin, far older than the Dead Sea Scrolls, and the pagan texts were even more ancient and even more abundant, some 700,000 volumes and scrolls in all. The whole collection of parchment and papyri was torched, the library itself was pulled down, and the loss to Western civilization is beyond calculation or even imagination.

The next year, Theodosius I ordered the destruction of the Serapeum, a magnificent temple that served as the principal shrine of Isis and Serapis and "the most important monument in the Empire after the Capitol in Rome."[22] The order was carried out with ardor by the Christian patriarch of Alexandria—his name was Theophilus, and he is memorably described by Gibbon as "a bold, bad man, whose hands were alternately polluted with gold and with blood."[23] Pagan diehards fortified the shrine, but they were overwhelmed by the Christian attackers, and the Serapeum was left in ruins. The heartbroken defenders consoled themselves with the idea that the gods had abandoned the shrine "and gone back to the heavens."[24] Meanwhile, the Christians delighted when they broke up a wooden statue of Serapis and discovered that it was infested with vermin.

"The Egyptians' god had become an apartment-block for mice!" exults the ancient Christian historian Theodoret. "So they broke him into pieces and fed them to the flames. But the head they dragged through the whole city, so that his worshippers could see it, and with it the impotence of the gods they had prayed to."[25]

The most poignant incident of all, however, took place in 415. A pagan woman called Hypatia, who is recalled as both beautiful and brilliant, succeeded in scandalizing the Christians of Alexandria, not only because of her faith but also because of her gender. She participated in the study of the old pagan texts on astronomy, mathematics and philosophy, and she did so alongside the otherwise male faculty and student body. She even insisted on wearing a short tunic that was regarded as something both grotesque and immodest on a woman. But Hypatia, like Julian, was a pagan ascetic who was said to regard the human body, including her own, as "a pile of garbage," and she once sought to discourage one of her love-smitten students by displaying one of her blood-soaked menstrual pads.

"That, young man, is what you have fallen in love with," she admonished him, "and there is nothing beautiful about it."[26]

Such eccentricity might have been regarded as charming and endearing by a man like Julian, who boasted of the lice in his beard. And Palladas, among the last of the pagan poets of ancient Rome, hails her as the "[u]nsullied Star of true philosophy."[27] But Hypatia inspired only contempt and disgust in the zealous Archbishop Cyril of Alexandria, a nephew of Theophilus, and he prevailed on the "men in black" to do something about the vile woman. So it was that a "wild black army," as the English novelist E. M. Forster describes the mob, followed her carriage as she headed toward the hall where her students were waiting—they dragged her out, carried her into the convenient darkness of a nearby church, stripped her naked, tortured her with broken shards of pottery and finally hacked her body into pieces. Then they put her butchered body parts on public display and, finally, tossed her remains on a bonfire.

"With her the Greece that is a spirit expired," writes Forster in his own tribute to Alexandria and its pagan heritage, "the Greece that tried to discover truth and create beauty."[28]

The Handless Scribe

The embers of paganism, of course, continued to glow even after the torching of the library, the destruction of the Serapeum and the butchering of Hypatia. "For the majority of the rural population, down to the eighth century (and often much later still)," writes historian J. N. Hillgarth, "some form of ancestral paganism was at least as attractive as Christianity."[29] The last academy where the texts of the pagan philosophers had been taught without interruption since the era of Julian was not closed down until the eleventh century. Yet the brutal death of Hypatia remains an enduring symbol, heart shaking and haunting, of the fate that befell men and women whose only crime was a belief in the many gods rather than the Only True God.

No longer was zealotry a matter of rigorist bishops and riotous mobs. Church and state now acted together to purge the Roman empire of religious diversity and dissent. "The triumph of Catholic Christianity over Roman paganism, heretical Arianism [and] pagan barbarism," argues Hillgarth, "was certainly due in large part to the support it received, first from the declining Roman State and later from the barbarian monarchies"—that is, the kingdoms of western Europe whose tribal armies conquered imperial Rome in the fifth century.[30]

Nor were human beings the only victims of the new Christian state. Tragically, Rome under the Christian emperors set out to destroy its own rich patrimony—the writings of the pagan poets, philosophers and historians, which were among the highest achievements of classical civilization. Scribes were forbidden to copy out the old pagan texts on pain of death or, perhaps worse, the amputation of the scribe's writing hand. Existing texts were seized and burned or, sometimes, literally erased—because vellum was both expensive and reusable, the old pagan writings were often rubbed off the page so that a pious Christian text could be put there in its place.

"Our sole copy of the sole work about political good sense by the person arguably best able to deliver it to us from classical antiquity,

Cicero," writes Ramsay MacMullen, "was sponged out from the vellum to make room for our hundredth copy of Augustine's meditations of the Psalms."[31]

Ironically, many of the pagan writings that survive from antiquity were preserved by pious Christian tract-writers who quoted their pagan adversaries in order to repudiate them. The only fragments of Julian's fiery anti-Christian manifesto *Against the Galileans* that survived Christian censorship, for example, appear in a refutation that was composed by Bishop Cyril of Alexandria in the fifth century. The original text, consisting of three books, is lost to us, and we are forced to rely on Cyril—"a hostile witness," as Robert Browning points out[32]—for a glimpse of what Julian actually wrote.

Similarly, some pagan traditions were rescued from the bonfires because they were expropriated for use in Christian ritual. Christmas is celebrated on December 25, the traditional birthday of *Sol Invictus*, because the early bishops realized that the pagans whom they sought to convert to Christianity were accustomed to celebrating *something* on that date. The depiction of Horus at the breast of Isis in the pagan art of Egypt, insists James Frazer in *The Golden Bough*, "is so like that of the Madonna and child that it has sometimes received the adoration of ignorant Christians."[33]

Even those "uncanny places" that served as venues for the worship of pagan gods and goddesses—caverns, grottoes, crags and glens— were recycled into sites for the construction of Christian chapels, shrines and martyriums: "Let altars be built and relics be placed there," decrees Pope Gregory the Great (c. 540–604) "so that [the pagans] have to change from the worship of the *daemones* to that of the true God."[34] And thus did a bejeweled statue of Julian the Apostate take on a new life as the reliquary of a Christian martyr.

"God Is Great! Truth Has Come! Falsehood Is Vanquished!"

Ultimately, the legacy of classical culture was too rich to be repudiated merely because it was also the legacy of pagan culture. "Early

Christian writers composed diatribes 'against the Pagans,' by which they meant philosophers and theologians such as Plato, Porphyry, Plutarch, Celsus and other predecessors or contemporaries," write Prudence Jones and Nigel Pennick.[35] But the art, science, philosophy and literature of the ancient pagans were preserved in the remote stretches of the former Roman empire that came to embrace Islam, the third and last of the great monotheisms, in the seventh century and afterward.

The prophet Mohammed was no less a rigorist than his Jewish and Christian counterparts when it came to polytheism and idolatry. In 620, for example, he led an army of 10,000 devoted followers into Mecca, where he used his own staff to shatter the 360 pagan idols that had long been displayed in the Ka'bah, the shrine that came to serve as the focal point of the annual pilgrimage known as the *Hajj*. "God is great!" he cried. "Truth has come! Falsehood is vanquished!"[36] Nevertheless, the Islamic civilization that came to power after the death of Mohammed was willing to spare the pagan writings that the Christian civilization of medieval Europe was so quick to burn. For example, the scientific writings of Aristotle were preserved in Arabic long after the original Greek texts had been destroyed.

Ironically, Christian Europe reconnected with its pagan roots when the Crusaders embarked upon a campaign to take back Jerusalem and the Holy Land from the Muslims during the eleventh, twelfth and thirteenth centuries. Of course, these latest Soldiers of Christ did not hesitate to spill the blood of *all* their fellow monotheists—Jews, Byzantine Christians and Muslims were murdered in horrific numbers during the Crusades. But the Crusaders were exposed to the remnants of classical Greece and Rome that had been preserved under Islam, and they returned to Europe as the bearers of a lost civilization. From the very moment that the West reconnected with the traditions of classical paganism, the so-called Dark Ages—an era of obscurantism, stagnation, and terror in the service of true belief—slowly began to recede. "[S]ome Christians were learning from Arabs and Jews instead of slaughtering them in the name of God," explains Karen Armstrong in

Holy War, "and from this fruitful and positive cooperation a new intellectual life was born in Europe."[37]

Still, the restoration of religious liberty and religious diversity was a long, painful and halting process. Pope Innocent III sent a crusade into southern France to exterminate a sect of Christian rigorists known as the Cathars ("Pure Ones") in 1208, for example, and the Cathars were the very first target of the Inquisition, which was organized in 1233 and continued to prey upon Christians, Muslims and Jews for the next six hundred years. Women accused of witchcraft were being tried in public courts and hanged in the American colonies as late as the seventeenth century. And Jews were being executed on utterly false charges of murdering children to obtain blood for religious rituals well into the twentieth century.

In fact, the impulse to seek out and punish anyone who did not embrace an approved set of beliefs and practices turned out to be an enduring legacy of monotheism. Long after the coming of the "Age of Reason," when the modern nations of Western Europe prided themselves on embracing the ideal of universal human rights, new and ever more terrible instruments of persecution were still being invented. As much ingenuity as the ancients showed in devising ways to maim and kill, they were far outclassed by the totalitarians of the twentieth century. And, as we know only too well, torture and murder have been put to use in the name of various kinds of true belief in our own benighted world on a scale that the ancients simply could not have imagined.

When power of true belief is alloyed with the power of the totalitarian state—a phenomenon that began in ancient Egypt under the pharaoh Akhenaton, reappeared in biblical Israel under King Josiah and reached its fullest expression in Rome under the Christian emperors—anyone and everyone who does not embrace the approved beliefs and practices, or does not embrace them with sufficient ardor, is at risk of death. The same rigorism and zeal that characterized the war of God against the gods can be found in *all* totalitarianism, and nowhere more terribly than in such modern and

supposedly secular phenomena as Nazism and Communism. Eusebius of Caesarea came to the conclusion that the Only True God had
appointed a single man as "the Ruler of the Whole World"—the emperor Constantine—and, in their own way, the followers of more recent autocrats did the same.

"The conclusion is reminiscent of the acclamation of the emperor: 'One God, one Logos, one emperor,'" writes historian Hermann Dorries. "The perversions implicit in this formulation became
manifest in the words of Louis XIV, '*Un roi, une loi, une foi*'"—"One
king, one law, one faith"—"and in the vastly more sinister slogan of
the Nazis, '*Ein Volk, ein Reich, ein Führer*'"—"One people, one nation, one leader."[38]

The New Age

Perhaps the single most illuminating (and oft-quoted) description of
the battleground on which the war of God against the gods was
fought is provided by Franz Cumont, the early-twentieth-century
Belgian historian. He invites his readers in the Western world—
Catholics, Protestants and perhaps a few Jews—to imagine themselves in a time and place of religious and cultural diversity so
extravagant and so unlikely that he means them to experience it as a
dream, if not a nightmare.

> Let us suppose that in modern Europe the faithful had deserted
> the Christian churches to worship Allah or Brahma, to follow the
> precepts of Confucius or Buddha, or to adopt the maxims of the
> Shinto; let us imagine a great confusion of all the races of the world
> in which Arabian mullahs, Chinese scholars, Japanese bonzes, Ti-
> betan lamas and Hindu pundits would be preaching fatalism and
> predestination, ancestor-worship and devotion to a deified sover-
> eign, pessimism and deliverance through annihilation—a confu-
> sion in which all those priests would erect temples of exotic
> architecture in our cities and celebrate their disparate rites
> therein.[39]

Cumont's whole point in offering up such a phantasmagoria is to allow us a glimpse of the world into which Constantine and Julian were born. "Such a dream," he remarks, "would offer a pretty accurate picture of the religious chaos in which the ancient world was struggling before the reign of Constantine." But Cumont remarks in passing that it is a dream "which the modern world may perhaps realize."[40] And, of course, the scene that he conjures up *has* been fully realized—Cumont could have been describing New York or Los Angeles, London or Paris, in the twenty-first century. What we sometimes call "the New Age"—an age of religious liberty and diversity in which each of us is permitted to mix and match our religious beliefs and practices according to our own taste and inspiration—is really something very, very old. Indeed, it is the oldest religious tradition of all, one that predates monotheism and very nearly prevailed over it.

Of all the ironies that we have encountered so far, here is the richest and cruelest. Those of us who live in the Western world are no longer at risk of torture and death by agents of the church or the state for believing in more than one god or no god at all. And yet we find ourselves very much at risk from the latest generation of religious zealots who have preserved the oldest traditions of monotheism, including holy war and martyrdom. The new rigorists include Jews, Christians and Muslims, and the atrocities of September 11 are only the most recent examples of the violence that men and women are inspired to commit against their fellow human beings by their true belief in the Only True God.

Indeed, *all* the excesses of religious extremism in the modern world can be seen as the latest manifestation of a dangerous tradition that began in the distant past. When the Taliban dynamited the Buddhist statuary of Afghanistan, they were following the example of the idol-smashers of antiquity. When Arab suicide bombers carried out "martyr operations" in Haifa, Tel Aviv and Jerusalem, and when a Jewish physician opened fire on Muslims at prayer at the Tomb of the Patriarchs, each one was acting out a kind of zealotry that was inspired by a tragic misreading and misapplication of ancient texts.

The dark side of monotheism, of course, is not its only side. The blessings of Judaism, Christianity and Islam far outweigh—and, we must hope, will long outlast—the curse of religious fanaticism that is implicit in the very notion of the Only True God. But it also true that we make a mistake when we write off the pagan tradition as something crude and demonic. After all, the values that the Western world embraces and celebrates—cultural diversity and religious liberty—are pagan values. And so, even when we congratulate ourselves on being the beneficiaries of twenty centuries of "ethical monotheism," we might pause and ponder how the world would have turned out if the war of God against the gods had ended with an armistice rather than the victory of the Only True God.

Chronology

"Before the Common Era" (B.C.E.) is the equivalent of "Before Christ" (B.C.), and "Common Era" (C.E.) is the equivalent of *Anno Domini* (A.D.), which literally means "In the year of Our Lord." The abbreviations are used in Jewish and secular scholarship to avoid the theological implications of B.C. and A.D.

Before the Common Era (B.C.E.)

c.1364–1347 Reign of Akhenaton, the world's first recorded mono-theist.

c. 640–609 Reign of Josiah, the king of Judah and reformer of the faith of ancient Israel.

586 Destruction of the Temple of Yahweh at Jerusalem during the Babylonian Conquest.

356–323 Life of Alexander the Great.

204 Worship of the Great Mother (*Magna Mater*) comes to Rome.

164 Defeat of Antiochus IV, Syrian king and conqueror of Judea, by the Maccabees.

97 Roman Senate bans human sacrifice in pagan worship.

63 Jerusalem is conquered by the Roman general Pompey and Judea is absorbed into the Roman empire.

Common Era (C.E.)

64 First persecution of Christians at Rome under the emperor Nero.

66–70 The Jewish War against Rome, ending in the defeat of the Zealots and destruction of the Temple at Jerusalem.

72 Mass suicide by the Jewish defenders of Masada.

132–135 Jewish insurrection against Roman occupation of Palestine under Bar Kokhba.

February 27, 274 Traditional birthdate of Constantine. (The earliest of several dates proposed by various scholars is 271.)

293 Diocletian establishes the Tetrarchy, consisting of a pair of rulers (an "Augustus" and a "Caesar") in both the western and eastern portions of the Roman empire.

303 Diocletian issues an edict that criminalizes the practice of Christianity, and the Great Persecution begins.

305 Abdication of Diocletian.

306 Death of Constantius the Pale and acclamation of his son, Constantine, as Augustus.

312 Constantine embraces Christianity after a vision on the eve of the Battle of the Milvian Bridge.

313 Religious toleration extended to Christians under the Edict of Milan.

321 Excommunication and first exile of Arius by Bishop Alexander of Alexandria.

324 Defeat and execution of Licinius; Constantine becomes the sole emperor of Rome.

325 Council of Nicaea.

325–326 Constantine orders the execution of his eldest son, Crispus, offspring of his first wife, Minervina.

c. 325 Birth of Gallus, nephew of Constantine and half brother of Julian.

326 Edict of Constantine against Christian heretics.

330 Dedication of Constantinople as "New Rome."

c. 331 Birth of Julian, nephew of Constantine.

336 Death of Arius.

May 22, 337 Baptism and death of Constantine the Great.

September 9, 337   Three sons of Constantine the Great (Constantine II, Constantius II and Constans) declared Augusti (emperors).

337–338   Murder of siblings and other male relations of Constantine the Great by his son Constantius II.

340   Constantine II, eldest son of Constantine the Great, is ambushed and killed by the forces of his brother, Constans.

341   First imperial decree against the offering of pagan sacrifices.

350   Constans is assassinated by the forces of the pagan usurper Magnentius, leaving his brother Constantius II as last surviving son of Constantine the Great and sole emperor of Roman empire.

351   Gallus, half brother of Julian, is appointed Caesar by Constantius II.

354   Death of Gallus.

355   Julian is appointed Caesar by Constantius II and marries Helena, sister of Constantius II.

357   Altar of the goddess of Victory removed from the Roman Senate by order of Constantius II.

359   Death of Eusebia, second wife of Constantius II.

February 360   Julian proclaimed Augustus by his troops in Paris.

November 360   Julian issues edict of toleration in favor of paganism.

361   Death of Helena, wife of Julian.

November 3, 361   Death of Constantius II, last surviving son of Constantine the Great, en route to battle with Julian.

December 11, 361   Julian enters Constantinople as the sole Augustus of the Roman empire.

February 4, 362   Decree ordering the reopening of pagan temples published at Alexandria.

June 26, 363   Death of Julian in battle with the Persians.

379   Ascension of Theodosius I to imperial throne.

380   Theodosius I elevates Christianity to status of state religion of Rome.

381 Theodosius I condemns Arianism and other "heresies."

385 Death of Priscillian, first Christian to be tried and executed by a public court for doctrinal "error."

386 Destruction of temple of Zeus at Apamea by imperial soldiers.

390 Destruction of the library at Alexandria.

391 Destruction of Serapeum at Alexandria.

392 Absolute prohibition against offering pagan sacrifices or visiting temples.

395 Death of Theodosius I.

415 Death of Hypatia.

Major Historical Figures

Akhenaton (Amenhotep IV) (d. c. 1347 B.C.E.): Pharaoh of Egypt and founder of the first recorded monotheistic religion, a faith based on the worship of the sun god called Aton. His original throne name was Amenhotep IV, but he changed his name to Akhenaton to signify his allegiance to Aton.

Alexander (d. 328): Bishop of Alexandria and early leader of the orthodox church in its struggle against Arius and the so-called Arian heresy.

Alexander the Great (356–323 B.C.E.): Macedonian king and conqueror who spread Hellenism—the culture, religion and language of ancient Greece—throughout the ancient world.

Antiochus IV (c. 215–164 B.C.E.): King of Syria and conqueror of the land of Judea. He sought to impose Hellenism on the Jews but was defeated after a long guerrilla war with Judah and the Maccabees.

Arius (c. 250–336): Alexandrian priest whose teachings on the divinity of Jesus of Nazareth were condemned by the orthodox church and sparked the division in the early Christian church between orthodoxy and the so-called Arian heresy.

Athanasius (c. 293–373): Orthodox bishop of Alexandria and leader of the struggle against Arius and the so-called Arian heresy and other dissenting factions in the church.

Basilina (died c. 331): Mother of Julian.

Constans (c. 323–350): Youngest son of Constantine the Great and coemperor in the western Roman empire.

Constantia (d. c. 336): Half-sister of Constantine the Great and wife of his coemperor, Licinius.

Constantina (d. c. 354): Daughter of Constantine the Great and wife of Gallus, the older half brother of Julian.

Constantine the Great (c. 274–337): Roman emperor who embraced and legalized Christianity and commenced the process that ultimately raised Christianity to the status of the state religion of the Roman empire.

Constantine II (c. 316–340): Son of Constantine the Great and coemperor in the western Roman empire.

Constantius Chlorus (Constantius the Pale) (c. 250–306): Roman general and emperor, father of Constantine the Great.

Constantius II (317–361): Son of Constantine the Great who reigned as Augustus first in the eastern empire and later as the sole emperor after the death of his two brothers, Constantine II and Constans, before raising his cousin Julian to the rank of Caesar.

Crispus (d. c. 326): Son of Constantine the Great by Minervina, his first wife (or his concubine). Reigned briefly as Caesar under his father before his arrest and execution on his father's orders.

Diocletian (245–316): Roman emperor, founder of the Tetrarchy (by which four emperors shared in the rule of the Roman empire), and the last Roman emperor to persecute Christianity during the so-called Great Persecution.

Donatus (d. c. 355): Bishop of the so-called Church of the Martyrs, which broke away from the orthodox church over charges that some orthodox clergy cooperated with pagan authorities during the Great Persecution. His followers are known as Donatists and the rift between the orthodox church and the Church of the Martyrs is known as the Donatist schism.

Eusebia (d. 359): Second wife of the emperor Constantius II. She encouraged her husband to raise Julian to the rank of Caesar.

Eusebius (d. 361): The influential eunuch who served as chamberlain of the imperial palace during the reigns of Constantine the Great and his son Constantius II.

Eusebius of Caesarea (c. 265–340): Arian bishop who was a contemporary of Constantine the Great; author of *Life of Constantine* and other works on the Bible, theology and history.

Eusebius of Nicomedia (d. c. 342): Arian bishop and imperial counselor who baptized Constantine the Great on his deathbed.

Fausta (289–326): Daughter of the emperor Maximian, wife of Constantine the Great, and mother of some or all of the three sons who later reigned as Roman emperors, Constantine II, Constantius II, and Constans. Constantine "put away" his first consort, Minervina, in order to marry Fausta in 307.

Galerius (c. 250–311): Pagan coemperor under Diocletian and persecutor of Christianity. His death marked the end of the Great Persecution.

Gallus (c. 325–354): Nephew of Constantine the Great and half brother of Julian. Served as Caesar under his cousin, the Augustus Constantius II, until he was deposed and murdered on the latter's order.

Helena (c. 248–328): Consort of Constantius the Pale, possibly his concubine rather than his wife, and mother of Constantine the Great.

Helena (d. 361): Daughter of Constantine the Great and his second wife, Fausta. She was named after Constantine's mother. Sister of Constantius II and wife of Julian.

Herod ("the Great") (73–4 B.C.E.): Monarch of Arab descent who was placed on the throne of Judea by the Romans, reigned as King of the Jews and refurbished the Second Temple at Jerusalem in the Hellenistic style.

Josephus (37–100): Jewish general who defected to the Romans during the Jewish War (66–70) and then wrote memoirs and historical works under imperial patronage in Rome.

Josiah (c. 640–609 B.C.E.): King of Judah, the southern kingdom of biblical Israel. He reformed the religion of the Israelites by centralizing worship in Jerusalem and purging the faith of pagan elements.

Judah ("the Maccabee") (d. c. 160 B.C.E.): Son of the Jewish priest Mattathias and leader of the Jewish war of national liberation against the Syrian occupiers of Judea. His family name was Hasmon, and his relations ruled the independent Jewish monarchy as the Hasmonean dynasty.

Julian ("the Apostate") (c. 331–363): Nephew of Constantine the Great, and the last pagan emperor of the Roman empire.

Julius Constantius (d. c. 337): Half brother of Constantine the Great and father of Julian. He was murdered during the blood purge that followed the death of Constantine.

Licinius (c. 265–324): Coemperor and brother-in-law of Constantine the Great. His defeat allowed Constantine to rule as the sole Augustus of the Roman empire.

Magnentius (d. 353): Pagan general who tried and failed to depose Constantius II as Roman emperor and restore paganism in the Roman empire.

Mattathias: See Judah.

Maxentius (c. 278–312): Son of the emperor Maximian and rival of Constantine for the imperial throne. Constantine's defeat of Maxentius at the Battle of the Milvian Bridge in 312 was the occasion for the miraculous vision that prompted Constantine to embrace Christianity.

Maximian (c. 240–310): Roman emperor who was father-in-law of both Constantius the Pale and his son, Constantine the Great, and who was ultimately defeated by Constantine in the struggle for the imperial throne.

Minervina: First consort of Constantine the Great and mother of his firstborn son, Crispus. Constantine "put away" Minervina in order to marry Fausta, daughter of the emperor Maximian, in 307.

Nero (37–68): First emperor to persecute Christians in ancient Rome.

Paul (d. c. 64): Apostle who converted from Judaism to Christianity, encouraged the early Christian church to abandon the observance of Jewish ritual law and carried the message of Christianity throughout the Roman empire, including the city of Rome.

Theodora: Wife of Constantius the Pale, stepmother of Constantine the Great and paternal grandmother of Julian. Constantius the Pale married Theodora in 293 after "putting away" his first consort, Helena, Constantine's mother.

Theodosius I (c. 346–395): Christian emperor who established orthodox Christianity as the state religion of Rome and completed the criminalization of paganism.

Notes

I have taken the liberty of omitting words and phrases from some quoted material without using brackets and ellipses to indicate the omissions. Whenever I have done so, I use the word "adapted" in the note that identifies the source of the quotation. In all instances, the omissions do not affect the meaning of the quoted material. A key to abbreviations used in Biblical citations is provided on page 315.

PROLOGUE: The Everlasting Fire

1. Karen Armstrong, *A History of God* (New York: Alfred A. Knopf, 1993), xix.
2. David Zucchino, "The Last Days of Bamian's Buddhas," *Los Angeles Times*, February 24, 2002, A10–A11.
3. Gore Vidal, *Julian* (1962; reprint, New York: Ballantine, 1986) "A Note" (not paginated).
4. Hans Lietzmann, *From Constantine to Julian: A History of the Early Church,* trans. Bertram Lee Woolf, (New York: Charles Scribner's Sons, 1950), 3:156–57, paraphrasing Constantine.
5. F. J. Foakes-Jackson, *The History of the Christian Church from the Earliest Times to A.D. 461* (1891; reprint, Chicago: W. P. Blessing, 1927), 328.
6. Quoted in Pierre Chuvin, *A Chronicle of the Last Pagans,* trans. B. A. Archer (Cambridge, Mass.: Harvard University Press, 1990), 58.
7. J. L. Myers, quoted in Robin Lane Fox, *Pagans and Christians* (New York: Alfred A. Knopf, 1987), 204.
8. Franz Cumont, *Oriental Religions in Roman Paganism* (1911; reprint, New York: Dover, 1956), 35.
9. Ramsay MacMullen, *Christianity and Paganism in the Fourth to Eighth Centuries* (New Haven: Yale University Press, 1997), 2.

10. John Holland Smith, *The Death of Classical Paganism* (New York: Charles Scribner's Sons, 1976), 6.

11. 1 Cor. 8:5–6 (adapted).

12. Jer. 10:10.

13. John 17:3.

14. Jer. 2:11.

15. 1 Cor. 10:21.

16. Quoted in Daniel B. Clendenin, *Many Gods, Many Lords: Christianity Encounters World Religions* (Grand Rapids, Mich.: Baker Books, 1995), 71 (adapted).

17. Walter Burkert, *Homo Necans: The Anthropology of Ancient Greek Sacrificial Ritual and Myth*, trans. Peter Bing (1972; reprint, Berkeley: University of California Press, 1983), 48, 49.

18. Fox, 672.

19. Ibid., 261.

20. Martin of Braga, *On the Castigation of the Rustics*, quoted in J. N. Hillgarth, ed., *Christianity and Paganism, 350–750: The Conversation of Western Europe,* (rev. ed. (Philadelphia: University of Pennsylvania Press, 1986), 58.

21. Quoted in ibid., 12.

22. See, e.g., Lev. 18:26.

23. Rev. 17:5. Babylon is named here, but it is commonly understood as a reference to Rome.

24. Num. 25:11. The Hebrew word *ki-nah*, translated here as "zeal," is sometimes rendered as "passion" (New JPS) or "jealousy" (NEB).

25. *Random House Webster's Unabridged Dictionary.*

26. Quoted in Cumont, 41.

27. Num. 25:11.

28. *Random House Webster's Unabridged Dictionary.*

29. Edward Gibbon, *The Decline and Fall of the Roman Empire* (1776; reprint, New York: Heritage, 1946) 1: 421.

30. Quoted in ibid., 1:427.

31. Diana Bowder, *The Age of Constantine and Julian* (New York: Barnes & Noble, 1978), xii, xiii.

32. Kenneth Scott Latourette, *A History of Christianity* (New York: Harper & Row, 1975), 1:23.

33. Quoted in Cumont, 160.

34. James Carroll, *Constantine's Sword: The Church and the Jews* (New York: Houghton Mifflin, 2001), 171.

35. Julian, *To the Uneducated Cynics*, in Wilmer Cave Wright, trans., *The Works of the Emperor Julian* (1913; reprint, Cambridge: Harvard University Press 1980), 2:5 and fn. 1.

CHAPTER ONE: **Against All the Gods of Egypt**

1. According to the Bible, Abram is given a new name—"Abraham," which is said to mean "Father of Many Nations"—when God and his very first worshipper enter into a covenant with each other.
2. Gen. 12:7.
3. Ex. 5:2.
4. Ex. 12:12.
5. Various dates are proposed for the life and reign of Akhenaton. I have adopted the dates given by Egyptologist John Bright: c. 1364–1347 B.C.E. John Bright, *A History of Israel*, 2d ed. (Philadelphia: Westminster Press, 1972), 108.
6. Franz Cumont, *Oriental Religions in Roman Paganism* (1911; reprint, New York: Dover 1956), 78.
7. Bright, 108.
8. Jan Assmann, *Moses the Egyptian: The Memory of Egypt in Western Monotheism* (Cambridge: Harvard University Press, 1997), 25.
9. Ex. 3:2.
10. Acts 9:3.
11. Donald B. Redford, "Akhenaton," in *The Anchor Bible Dictionary*, ed. David Noel Freedman (Garden City, N.Y.: Doubleday, 1992), 1:135.
12. Bright, 108.
13. Quoted in Sigmund Freud, *Moses and Monotheism*, trans. Katherine Jones (1939; reprint, New York: Vintage, 1967), 24, citing James Henry Breasted.
14. Deut. 6:4.
15. Ps. 104:12 (New JPS).
16. Assmann, 24.
17. Freud, 16, 31–32 (adapted). Freud's reference to Moses as a Jew is an anachronism—"Jew" is a term derived from the tribe of Judah, but Moses is described in the Bible as a member of the tribe of Levi, one of the twelve tribes of ancient Israel.
18. Gen. 1:26.
19. E. A. Speiser, trans., intro., and notes, *Genesis: The Anchor Bible* (Garden City, N.Y.: Doubleday, 1987), 1:45.

20. The Hebrew text of Gen. 6:3 and 6:4 refers to *"B'nai ha Elohim,"* that is, the "sons of Elohim." a phrase that is rendered as "the sons of the gods" in the NEB and "the divine beings" in the New JPS.

21. Gen. 6:2, 4 (New JPS).

22. Gen: 31:19.

23. 1 Sam. 19:13.

24. Ex. 20:4.

25. Num. 21:9.

26. Ex. 15:11.

27. Ex. 20:3.

28. Quoted in J. E. Emerton, "Yahweh and His Asherah," *Vetus Testamentum,* vol. XLIX, No. 3, July 1999, 315–337, p. 320. (Leiden: E. J. Brill).

29. Deut. 12: 2–3.

30. 2 Kings 21:2.

31. 1 Kings 10:24.

32. 1 Kings 11:4 (NEB).

33. Ex. 19:5 (New JPS).

34. Ex. 32:10.

35. Ex. 32:12.

36. Ex. 32:27.

37. Jer. 2:11.

38. Ezra 9:2.

39. Prov. 11:31.

40. Isa. 58:7 (adapted from New JPS).

41. Deut. 32:17 (adapted).

42. Deut. 32: 22, 25 (adapted from JPS and New JPS).

43. Ex. 20:5.

44. Ezek. 16:7–34 (adapted from New JPS).

45. Ezek. 16:37–41 (adapted from New JPS).

46. Nah. 1:2.

CHAPTER TWO: **What Did Pagans Do?**

1. Ezek. 16:17, 19–21 (adapted from New JPS).

2. Josh. 23:13.

3. Elaine Adler Goodfriend, "Prostitution (OT)," in *The Anchor Bible Dictionary*, ed. David Noel Freedman (Garden City, N.Y.: Doubleday, 1992), 5: 505 *et seq.*, and Karel Van Der Toorn, "Prostitution (Cultic)," in ibid., 5:511 *et seq.*

4. Quoted in Eugene J. Fisher, "Cultic Prostitution in the Ancient Near

East? A Reassessment," *Biblical Theology Bulletin* 6, nos. 2–3 (June–October 1976): 226.

5. Quoted in Prudence Jones and Nigel Pennick, *A History of Pagan Europe* (London: Routledge, 1995), 63.

6. Quoted in John Holland Smith, *Constantine the Great* (New York: Charles Scribner's Sons, 1971), 287–288.

7. Quoted in John Holland Smith, *The Death of Classical Paganism* (New York: Charles Scribner's Sons, 1976), 65.

8. Dan. 11:31; Matt. 24:15.

9. Isa. 44:17 (New JPS).

10. Franz Cumont, *Oriental Religions in Roman Paganism* (1911; reprint, New York: Dover 1956), 96.

11. Quoted in Hans-Josef Klauck, *Magic and Paganism in Early Christianity: The World of the Acts of the Apostles*, trans. Brian McNeil (Edinburgh: T&T Clark, 2000), 84.

12. Quoted in Johannes Weiss, *The History of Primitive Christianity* (New York: Wilson-Erickson, 1937), 1:238, fn. 22.

13. Deut 18:10; Exod. 22:18.

14. Rev. 21:8.

15. Robin Lane Fox, *Pagans and Christians* (New York: Alfred A. Knopf, 1987), 228.

16. Robert Browning, *The Emperor Julian* (Berkeley: University of California Press, 1976), 58.

17. Quoted in Fox, 135.

18. Ibid., 136.

19. J. L. Myers, quoted in ibid., 204.

20. Smith, *Death of Classical Paganism* 31.

21. Fox, 151.

22. Ibid., 163 (adapted).

23. All of the questions are quoted in Klauck, 67, except "Will my son be born with a big nose?," which is paraphrased from Cumont, 165.

24. Ps. 106:38. Strictly speaking, the Psalmist is complaining about the conduct of the Israelites, whom he accuses of aping their Canaanite neighbors by offering human sacrifice.

25. Walter Burkert, *Homo Necans: The Anthropology of Ancient Greek Sacrificial Ritual and Myth*, trans. Peter Bing (Berkeley: University of California Press, 1983) (Orig. Pub. 1972), 2, 3.

26. Quoted in in Nigel Davies, *Human Sacrifice: In History and Today* (New York: William Morrow, 1981), 24–25.

27. Gen. 22:13.

28. Davies, 43.

29. Ibid., 47.

30. Ibid., 47.

31. Ross Shepard Kraemer, *Her Share of the Blessings: Women's Religions Among Pagans, Jews and Christians in the Greco-Roman World* (Oxford: Oxford University Press, 1992), 51.

32. Merlin Stone, *When God Was a Woman* (New York: Harcourt Brace Jovanovich, 1976), 3.

33. Franz Cumont, *Oriental Religions in Roman Paganism*, 186.

34. Pierre Chuvin, *A Chronicle of the Last Pagans*, trans. B. A. Archer (Cambridge, Mass.: Harvard University Press, 1990), 33.

35. Fox, 343.

36. Julian, *Heroic Deeds*, quoted in (and slightly adapted from) Giuseppe Ricciotti, *Julian the Apostate, Roman Emperor, 361–363*, trans. M. Joseph Costelloe (1960; reprint, Rockford, Ill.: Tan Books, 1999), 117.

37. Num 12:6 (adapted).

38. Num. 5:17, 27.

39. Exod. 29:20.

40. Julian, *Against the Galileans*, quoted in (and slightly adapted from) Ricciotti, 223.

41. Ramsay MacMullen, *Christianity and Paganism in the Fourth to Eighth Centuries* (New Haven: Yale University Press, 1997), 2.

42. Ibid., 32.

43. Quoted in Smith, *Death of Classical Paganism*, 81 (adapted).

44. Samuel Dill, *Roman Society in the Last Century of the Western Empire*, 2d rev. ed. (New York: Meridian, 1958), 132–133.

45. Edward Gibbon, *The Decline and Fall of the Roman Empire*, (1776; reprint, New York: Heritage, 1946), 1: 432.

46. Fox, 30.

47. Acts 17:23–24.

48. Klauck, 82–83.

49. Quoted in August Neander, *The Emperor Julian and His Generation*, trans. C. V. Cox (1812; reprint, Eugene, Ore.: Wipf and Stock, 2001) 58 (adapted).

50. Ezek 16:15; Rev. 17:5.

CHAPTER THREE: **Terror and True Belief**

1. Lev. 19:34 (adapted from JPS and NEB).

2. Deut. 4:34, 2:25.

3. Deut. 6:10–11.

4. Deut. 20:16–17 (adapted).

5. Deut. 2:34.

6. Exod. 34:13.

7. E.g., Jer. 2:19 (NEB).

8. Deut. 3:22.

9. Num. 25:8.

10. Num. 25:11. The Hebrew word *Ki-nah* is variously translated as "zealous" and "jealous."

11. Num. 31:15, 17–18.

12. 1 Sam. 15:3, 12.

13. 1 Sam. 15:3, 9, 23 (adapted from JPS and NEB).

14. According to the Bible, the land of Israel was united under a single monarch during the reigns of David and Solomon. On the death of Solomon, as a punishment for his acts of apostasy, a civil war ensued and the kingdom was split into two separate monarchies. The southern kingdom was called Judah and the northern kingdom Israel. Shortly after Solomon's death, the monarch of the northern kingdom, Jereboam, set up sanctuaries for the worship of Yahweh in the northern cities of Bethel and Dan as alternatives to the Temple of Solomon in Jerusalem, the royal capital of the kingdom of Judah.

15. 2 Chron. 34:3.

16. Richard Elliott Friedman, *Who Wrote the Bible?* (New York: Summit Books, 1987), 102.

17. 2 Kings 23:4 (New JPS).

18. 2 Kings 23:13 (New JPS).

19. Israel Finkelstein and Neil Asher Silberman, *The Bible Unearthed: Archaeology's New Vision of Ancient Israel and the Origin of Its Sacred Texts* (New York: Free Press, 2001), 275, 276.

20. Ibid., 122.

21. 2 Chron. 35:23.

22. Flavius Josephus, *The Works of Josephus*, trans. William Whiston (Peabody, Mass.: Hendrickson, 1987), *Antiquities of the Jews*, 324.

23. 1 Macc. 2:24, 26, 27 (NEB).

24. Steven Weitzman, "Forced Circumcision and the Shifting Role of Gentiles in Hasmonean Ideology," *Harvard Theological Review* 92, no.1 (January 1999): 59.

25. 2 Macc. 7:2, 29 (NEB).

26. Emil L. Fackenheim, *What Is Judaism? An Interpretation for the Present Age* (New York: Summit, 1987), 67, 68.

27. Caecilius, quoted in Augustus Neander, *The Emperor Julian and His Generation*, trans. C. V. Cox (1812; reprint, Eugene, Ore.: Wipf and Stock, 2001), 56.

28. Flavius Josephus, *The Jewish War*, rev. ed., trans. G. A. Williamson (New York: Dorset Press, 1981), 404.

29. Ibid., 404–5.

30. Ibid., 405.

31. Flavius Josephus, *Works, Antiquities of the Jews*, 743.

32. Deut. 12:11.

33. Quoted in Jacob Neusner, *A Life of Yohanan ben Zakkai, ca. 1–80 C.E.* (Leiden: E. J. Brill, 1962), 142. Yohanan ben Zakkai is quoting Hos. 6:6.

34. Zvi Kaplan, "Hanina Segan Ha-Kohanim," *Encyclopedia Judaica* corr. ed. (Jerusalem: Keter, n.d.), 7: 1266–67, citing Avot 3:2.

35. A. N. Wilson, *Paul: The Mind of the Apostle* (New York: W. W. Norton, 1997), 5.

CHAPTER FOUR: **Confessors and Traitors**

1. Quoted in Franz Cumont, *Oriental Religions in Roman Paganism* (1911; reprint, New York: Dover, Publications, 1956) 37.

2. Ibid., 28, 31.

3. Ibid., 24.

4. Ibid., 66.

5. Quoted in Samuel Dill, *Roman Society in the Last Century of the Western Empire*, 2d rev. ed. (New York: Meridian, 1958), 32.

6. Quoted in Patrick Tierney, *The Highest Altar: Unveiling the Mystery of Human Sacrifice* (New York: Penguin, n.d.), 441.

7. James George Frazer, *The Golden Bough: A Study in Magic and Religion*, abridged ed. (1922; reprint, New York: Macmillan, 1979) 406.

8. Ibid., 406 (adapted).

9. Ibid., 445 (adapted).

10. Adapted from Apuleius, *The Golden Ass*, trans. Jack Lindsay (1932; reprint, Bloomington: Indiana University Press, 1962) 237–238.

11. Quoted in Augustus Neander, *The Emperor Julian and His Generation*, trans. C. V. Cox (1812; reprint, Eugene, Ore.: Wipf and Stock, 2001) 58.

12. Hans-Josef Klauck, *Magic and Paganism in Early Christianity: The World of the Acts of the Apostles*, trans. Brian McNeil (Edinburgh: T&T Clark, 2000), 77 (referring specifically to the Epicureans and Stoics).

13. Pseudo-Plutarch, quoted in Abraham J. Malherbe, *Moral Exhortation: A Greco-Roman Sourcebook* (Philadelphia: Westminster Press, 1986), 30–31.

14. Dio Chrysostom, quoted in ibid. 24.

15. Acts 14:12.

16. Robin Lane Fox, *Pagans and Christians* (New York: Alfred A. Knopf, 1987), 119.

17. Quoted in John Holland Smith, *Constantine the Great* (New York: Charles Scribner's Sons, 1971), 43.

18. Quoted in (and slightly adapted from) Jan Assmann, *Moses the Egyptian: The Memory of Egypt in Western Monotheism* (Cambridge, Mass.: Harvard University Press, 1997), 53.

19. *Saturnalia* of Macrobius, quoted in Dill, 92–93.

20. Quoted in Smith, *Constantine*, 1971, 44.

21. Diana Bowder, *The Age of Constantine and Julian* (New York: Barnes & Noble, 1978), 98.

22. Dill, 98.

23. Bowder, 83.

24. Quoted in Fox, 165.

25. Quoted in A. N. Wilson, *Paul: The Mind of the Apostle* (New York: W. W. Norton, 1997), 4.

26. Gal. 3:13, 28.

27. Acts 23:11.

28. 1 Cor. 10:20.

29. Exod. 34:13–14.

30. Minucius Felix, quoted in John Holland Smith, *The Death of Classical Paganism* (New York: Charles Scribner's Sons, 1976), 5. Minucius, a Christian writer of the third century C.E., "put this scandal together in order to refute it."

31. Quoted in (and slightly adapted from) ibid.

32. Quoted in Fox, 420.

33. Ibid.

34. Edward Gibbon, *The Decline and Fall of the Roman Empire*, (1776; reprint, New York: Heritage, 1946), 1:420–21.

35. Ibid. 1: 450.

36. Fox, 434.

37. Quoted in Gibbon, 1: 427.

38. Rev. 16:6, 17:5, 6. The mention of Babylon in the Book of Revelation is understood by most scholars as a reference to Rome.

CHAPTER FIVE: "In This Sign, Conquer"

1. John Holland Smith, *Constantine the Great* (New York: Charles Scribner's Sons, 1971), 3.

2. Quoted in ibid., 16.

3. Ibid., citing Zosimus and Orosius.

4. Quoted in Prudence Jones and Nigel Pennick, *A History of Pagan Europe* (London: Routledge, 1995), 55.

5. Quoted in A. Nicholas Sherwin-White, "The Empire of Rome," in Arnold Toynbee, *The Crucible of Christianity: Judaism, Hellenism and the Historical Background to the Christian Faith* (Cleveland: World, 1969), 146.

6. Smith, *Constantine*, 7.

7. Quoted in ibid. 22–23.

8. Andrew Alfoldi, *The Conversion of Constantine and Pagan Rome*, trans. Harold Mattingly (1948; reprint, Oxford: Clarendon/Oxford University Press, 1998), 20. "Childish silliness" is a phrase used by historian P. Batiffol to argue that a certain letter attributed to Constantine was a forgery. "[S]uch primitive ideas characterize the whole of Constantine's religious writings," counter Alfoldi, "and betray thereby their imperial composition."

9. Smith, Constantine, 21.

10. Quoted in ibid. 26.

11. Quoted in Alfoldi, 22.

12. Edward Gibbon, *The Decline and Fall of the Roman Empire*, (1776; reprint New York: Heritage, 1946) 1:441–42.

13. Jones and Pennick, 64.

14. Quoted in Smith, *Constantine*, 98.

15. Quoted in Pierre Chuvin, *A Chronicle of the Last Pagans*, trans. B. A. Archer (Cambridge, Mass.: Harvard University Press, 1990), 18.

16. Smith, *Constantine*, 60.

17. Ibid.

18. Quoted in ibid. 63.

19. Lactantius, quoted in ibid., 103.

20. Historians do not agree on the origins of the *chi-rho*. "As a Christian symbol, it is definitely documented since the mid-second century," insists Carsten Peter Thiede, *The Dead Sea Scrolls and the Jewish Origins of Christianity* (New York: Palgrave, 2001), 82. Robin Lane Fox, however, insists that, "despite much debate and searching, no 'chi-rho' sign has been found in a Christian context which is datable with certainty to the years before Constantine's vision." Robin Lane Fox, *Pagans and Christians* (New York: Alfred A. Knopf, 1987), 616.

21. Fox, 616.

22. Quoted in Smith, *Constantine*, 106.

CHAPTER SIX: **The Harlot in the Bishop's Bed**

1. Quoted in Diana Bowder, *The Age of Constantine and Julian* (New York: Barnes & Noble, 1978) 28–29 (adapted).

2. Ibid.

3. Ibid.

4. Ramsay MacMullen, *Christianity and Paganism in the Fourth to Eighth Centuries* (New Haven: Yale University Press, 1997), 14.

5. Quoted in John Holland Smith, *Constantine the Great* (New York: Charles Scribner's Sons, 1971), 273.

6. A. R. Whitham, *The History of the Christian Church to the Separation of East and West* 4th ed. (London: Rivingtons, 1954), 255.

7. Robin Lane Fox, *Pagans and Christians* (New York: Alfred A. Knopf, 1987), 358.

8. Ibid., 559.

9. Smith, *Constantine*, 187, citing Epiphanius.

10. John 3:16.

11. Deut. 6:4.

12. 1 Cor. 8:6.

13. Acts 5:32 (adapted).

14. Whitham, 185.

15. Matt. 28:18–19.

16. Theodosius, quoted in Richard E. Rubenstein, *When Jesus Became God: The Struggle to Define Christianity During the Last Days of Rome* (San Diego: Harcourt, 1999), 220.

17. Augustine, *The Confessions of Saint Augustine*, trans. Edward B. Pusey (New York: Modern Library, 1949), 304, 308.

18. J. N. Hillgarth, ed., *Christianity and Paganism, 350–750: The Conversion of Western Europe*, rev. ed. (Philadelphia: University of Pennsylvania Press, 1986), 3.

19. Whitham, 186.

20. Ibid.

21. Quoted in Robert M. Grant, *Gods and the One God* (Philadelphia: Westminster Press, 1986), 160–61.

22. Edward Gibbon, *The Decline and Fall of the Roman Empire* (1776; reprint, New York: Heritage, 1946), 1:604.

23. Ibid.

24. Gregory of Nyassa, quoted in Rubenstein, 6–7 (the quotation from Gregory has been slightly adapted).

25. Smith, *Constantine*, 162.

26. Prudence Jones and Nigel Pennick, *A History of Pagan Europe* (London: Routledge, 1995), 67.

27. Quoted in Hermann Dorries, *Constantine the Great*, trans. Roland H. Bainton (New York: Harper & Row, 1972), 57.

28. Quoted in Smith, *Constantine*, 130.

29. Dorries, 61.

30. Jerome's *Chronicle*, quoted in John Holland Smith, *The Death of Classical Paganism* (New York: Charles Scribner's Sons, 1976), 61.

CHAPTER SEVEN: **The Ruler of the Whole World**

1. Quoted in Herman Dorries, *Constantine the Great*, trans. Roland H. Bainton (New York: Harper & Row, 1972), 143.

2. Andrew Alfoldi, *The Conversion of Constantine and Pagan Rome*, trans. Harold Mattingly (Oxford: Clarendon/Oxford University Press, 1998), 11.

3. Eusebius, "The Oration of Eusebius Pamphilus in Praise of the Emperor Constantine" in Philip Schaff and Henry Wace, eds., *A Select Library of Nicene and Post-Nicene Fathers of the Christian Church* (2d. Series), Vol. 1, *Eusebius* (1890; Reprint, Grand Rapids, Mich.: Wm. B. Eerdmans, 1997), 584.

4. Alfoldi, 13 (adapted).

5. Quoted in Ramsay MacMullen, *Christianity and Paganism in the Fourth to Eighth Centuries* (New Haven: Yale University Press, 1997), 130.

6. A. N. Wilson, *Paul: The Mind of the Apostle* (New York: W. W. Norton, 1997), 9.

7. Quoted in John Holland Smith, *Constantine the Great* (New York: Charles Scribner's Sons, 1971), 183.

8. Quoted in James Carroll, *Constantine's Sword: The Church and the Jews* (New York: Houghton Mifflin, 2001), 187.

9. Quoted in Smith, *Constantine*, 201.

10. Quoted in Dorries, 136.

11. Quoted in Diana Bowder, *The Age of Constantine and Julian* (New York: Barnes & Noble, 1978), 71.

12. Quoted in ibid., 67.

13. Quoted in Smith, *Constantine*, 202.

14. Ibid., 113.

15. Edward Gibbon, *The Decline and Fall of the Roman Empire* (1776; reprint, New York: Heritage, 1946), 1:608.

16. Pierre Chuvin, *A Chronicle of the Last Pagans*, trans. B.A. Archer (Cambridge, Mass.: Harvard University Press, 1990), 22.

17. Prudence Jones and Nigel Pennick, *A History of Pagan Europe* (London: Routledge, 1995), 68.

18. Robin Lane Fox, *Pagans and Christians* (New York: Alfred A. Knopf, 1987), 667.

19. Quoted in Jacob Neusner, *Judaism and Christianity in the Age of Constantine: History, Messiah, Israel and the Initial Confrontation* (Chicago: University of Chicago Press, 1987), 14–15.

20. Quoted in Chuvin, 22.

21. Gibbon, 1:499.

22. Quoted in Smith, *Constantine*, 220.

23. Quoted in (and adapted from) Jacob Burckhardt, *The Age of Constantine* (1852; reprint, Garden City, N.Y.: Doubleday/Anchor, 1949), 337.

24. Jones and Pennick, 68.

25. Bowder, 35.

26. Burckhardt, 294.

27. Jones and Pennick, 68.

28. Burckhardt, 340.

29. Gibbon, 1:303.

30. Quoted in Samuel N.C. Lieu and Dominic Montserrat, eds., *From Constantine to Julian: Pagan and Byzantine Views, A Source History* (London: Routledge, 1996), 5.

31. Ibid.

32. Quoted in Smith, *Constantine*, 289.

33. Gibbon, 1:495.

34. Smith, *Constantine*, 40.

35. Alfoldi, 6 (adapted).

36. John Holland Smith, *The Death of Classical Paganism* (New York: Charles Scribner's Sons, 1976), 37.

37. Bowder, xii.

38. J. Bidez, quoted in Alfoldi, 30.

39. Eusebius of Caesarea, *Life of Constantine*, quoted in ibid., 33.

40. Ammianus, quoted in ibid., 31.

41. Jones and Pennick, 66, 69.

42. Bowder, 80.

43. Strictly speaking, the baptism of Constantine II is not confirmed in the historical record, and some historians question whether he was in fact baptized.

44. Quoted in Fox, 339.
45. Bowder, 33, citing Zosimus and Julian.
46. Ibid., 34.
47. Chuvin, 32.
48. Ibid., 29.
49. Fox, 619–20.
50. Constantine's year of birth is the subject of much scholarly debate. Eusebius proposes a date of birth between 273 and 275 (Smith, *Constantine*, 1); Gibbon adopts the earlier date, which puts his age at death at sixty-four. (Gibbon, 1:508.) According to the earliest year of birth proposed by modern scholars, 271, he would have been sixty-six years old on the day of his death.

CHAPTER EIGHT: **The Orphans of Macellum**

1. Gerald Henry Rendall, *The Emperor Julian: Paganism and Christianity* (Cambridge: Deighton, Bell and Co., and London: George Bell and Sons, 1879), 35.
2. Julian, *Letter to the Athenians*, in Wilmer Cave Wright, trans., *The Works of the Emperor Julian*, (1913; reprint, Cambridge, Mass.: Harvard University Press, 1980), 2:249. Gerald Henry Rendall argues that the death toll of seven cousins and uncles of Constantine II results from an erroneous translation of Julian's account in *Letter to the Athenians*, and puts the total number at six. "[T]here were not seven *cousins* left to murder," he insists. Rendall, 35–36, fn. 1.
3. Constantine II, one of the three surviving sons of Constantine, may have a different mother, but they were all regarded as legitimate offspring and legal heirs of their father. John Holland Smith, *The Death of Classical Paganism* (New York: Charles Scribner's Sons, 1976), 67.
4. The birthdates for Gallus and Julian are subject to debate but are generally given as 325 or 326 for Gallus and 331 or 332 for Julian.
5. Quoted in ibid. 79.
6. Quoted in Rendall, 32.
7. Quoted in Richard E. Rubenstein, *When Jesus Became God: The Struggle to Define Christianity During the Last Days of Rome* (San Diego: Harcourt, 1999), 196.
8. Edward Gibbon, *The Decline and Fall of the Roman Empire*, 1776; reprint, (New York: Heritage, 1946), 1:517.
9. Rendall, 32.
10. Quoted in Pierre Chuvin, *A Chronicle of the Last Pagans*, trans. B. A. Archer (Cambridge, Mass.: Harvard University Press, 1990), 36.

11. Quoted in Gibbon, 1:636.
12. Quoted in (and slightly adapted from) Diana Bowder, *The Age of Constantine and Julian* (New York: Barnes & Noble, 1978), 82.
13. Gibbon, 1:636.
14. Quoted in Chuvin, 37.
15. Quoted in Gibbon, 1:636.
16. Bowder, 96.
17. Smith, *Death of Classical Paganism*, 77.
18. Quoted in ibid., 82.
19. Gibbon, 1:518.
20. Rendall, 35.
21. Julian, *Letter to the Athenians*, in Wright, 2:251 (adapted).
22. Julian, *Letter to the Athenians*, in ibid., 2:255 (adapted).
23. Julian, *Letter to the Athenians*, in ibid., 2:249–251.
24. Julian, *Letter to the Athenians*, in ibid., 2:251.
25. Augustus Neander, *The Emperor Julian and His Generation*, trans. C. V. Cox (1812; reprint, Eugene, Ore.: Wipf and Stock, 2001), 74.
26. Giuseppe Ricciotti, *Julian the Apostate, Roman Emperor, 361–363*, trans. M. Joseph Costelloe, (S. J. 1960; reprint, Rockford, Ill.: Tan Books, 1999), 51.
27. Quoted in "Gallus Caesar," Thomas M. Bancich, De Imperatoribus Romanis (www.roman-emperors.org/gallus.htm).
28. Julian, *Letter to the Athenians*, in Wright, 2:253 (adapted).
29. Rendall, 53 (adapted).
30. Ibid., 33–34.
31. Quoted in Hermann Dorries, *Constantine the Great*, trans. Roland H. Bainton (New York: Harper & Row, 1972), 152.
32. Quoted in Chuvin, 39.
33. Quoted in Bowder, 84.
34. Quoted in Gibbon, 1:603.
35. Ibid., 1:622 (adapted).
36. Ibid., 1:628 (adapted).
37. Ibid., 1:630 (adapted).
38. Rendall, 32 (adapted).
39. Quoted in Bowder, 108 (adapted).

CHAPTER NINE: The Secret Pagan

1. Julian, *To a Priest*, in Wilmer Cave Wright, trans., *The Works of the Emperor Julian*, 1913; reprint, (Cambridge, Mass.: Harvard University Press, 1980), 3:51.

2. Julian, *To a Priest*, quoted in Giuseppe Ricciotti, *Julian the Apostate, Roman Emperor, 361–363*, trans. M. Joseph Costelloe, S. J. (1960; reprint, Rockford, Ill.: Tan Books, 1999), 54.

3. Julian, *To a Priest*, in Wright, 3:53.

4. Gerald Henry Rendall, *The Emperor Julian: Paganism and Christianity* (Cambridge: Deighton, Bell and Co., and London: George Bell and Sons, 1879), 37.

5. Quoted in "Gallus Caesar" Thomas M. Bancich, De Imperatoribus Romanis (www.roman-emperors.org/gallus.htm).

6. Rendall, 37 (adapted).

7. Ibid., 45 (adapted).

8. Julian, *Mispogon*, in Wright, 2:463.

9. Ricciotti, 12.

10. Julian, *Mispogon*, quoted in ibid., 11.

11. Julian, *Mispogon*, in Wright, 2:459.

12. Ricciotti, 11.

13. Rendall, 38.

14. Julian, *Mispogon*, in Wright, 2:458–59.

15. Ibid., 2:459.

16. Quoted in John Holland Smith, *The Death of Classical Paganism* (New York: Charles Scribner's Sons, 1976), 105.

17. Julian, *Mispogon*, in Wright, 2:465 (adapted).

18. Julian, *Hymn to the Mother of the Gods*, in Wright, 1:487 (adapted).

19. Julian, *Letter to the Athenians*, in Wright, 2:251.

20. Julian, *Hymn to King Helios*, in Wright, 1:353.

21. Ibid. 1:353.

22. Ricciotti, 19, referring to accounts in Sozomen, Theodoret and Gregory of Nazianzus.

23. Augustus Neander, *The Emperor Julian and His Generation*, trans. C. V. Cox (1812; reprint, Eugene, Ore.: Wipf and Stock, 2001), 74.

24. Rendall, 39 (adapted).

25. Julian, *To the Cynic Heracleios*, in Wright, 2:151 (adapted).

26. Ricciotti, 16.

27. Robert Browning, *The Emperor Julian* (Berkeley: University of California Press, 1976), 44–45.

28. Smith, *Death of Classical Paganism*, 56 (adapted).

29. Quoted in Diana Bowder, *The Age of Constantine and Julian* (New York: Barnes & Noble, 1978), 85.

30. Quoted in Browning, 55.

31. Bowder, 98, and Browning, 56.

32. Browning, 56.

33. Ibid., 58.

34. Walter Burkert, *Ancient Mystery Cults* (Cambridge, Mass.: Harvard University Press, 1987), 91.

35. Edward J. Martin, *The Emperor Julian: An Essay on His Relations with the Christian Religion* New York: Macmillan, 1919), 28, citing Sozomen and Gregory of Nazianzus.

36. Edward Gibbon, *The Decline and Fall of the Roman Empire* (1776; reprint, New York: Heritage, 1946), 1:669, fn. 11.

37. Ricciotti, 207.

38. Neander, 79.

39. A letter preserved from antiquity suggests that Gallus, while still reigning as Caesar, had already received reports that his younger half brother, "goaded by some evil kind of madness," had turned to paganism, and that Gallus had then urged Julian remain faithful to the Christian deity. W. C. Wright insists, however, that "[n]early all the critics reject this letter as a Christian forgery." *Gallus Caesar to His Brother Julian*, in Wright, 3:288, fn. 1, 289.

40. Julian, *Panegyric in Honour of Eusebia*, in ibid., 1:315.

41. Julian, *Panegyric in Honour of Eusebia*, in ibid., 1:311 (". . . zealous on my behalf . . ."); Julian, *Letter to the Athenians*, in ibid., 2:255 ("I could not have . . .").

42. Julian, *Letter to the Athenians*, quoted in Ricciotti, 67.

43. Ricciotti, 35, paraphrasing Ammianus.

44. Julian, *Mispogon*, in Wright, 2:425.

45. Ricciotti, 35.

46. Julian, *Misopogon*, in Wright, 2:423, 427 (adapted).

47. Quoted in Browning, 65.

48. Quoted in Smith, *Death of Classical Paganism*, 98.

49. Julian, *To the Athenians*, quoted in Ricciotti, 103–04 (adapted).

50. Julian, *Misopogon*, in Wright, 2:429 (adapted).

51. Quoted in Smith, *Death of Classical Paganism*, 98.

52. Ammianus, quoted in Browning, 71.

53. Ammianus, quoted in ibid., 72.

54. Quoted in Ricciotti, 69. The verse that Julian recites is found in the *Iliad* (5.83).

55. Julian, *Letter to the Athenians*, in Wright, 2:265 (adapted).

56. Ibid.

57. Quoted in Bowder, 50.

58. Julian, *Letter to the Athenians*, in Wright, 2:267.

59. Ricciotti, 82–83.

60. Ibid., 110.

61. Julian, *Letter to the Athenians*, in Wright, 2:271.

62. Browning, 86–87.

63. Ibid., 92.

64. Julian, *Heroic Deeds*, quoted in Ricciotti, 117 (adapted).

65. Julian, *To the Athenians*, quoted in ibid., 67.

66. Quoted in Browning, 95.

67. Julian, *Panegyric in Honour of Eusebia*, in Wright, 1:329.

68. Quoted in Ricciotti, 58.

69. Julian, *Panegyric in Honour of Eusebia*, in Wright, 1:327.

70. Ricciotti, 59.

71. Gibbon, 1:655 (adapted).

72. Quoted in Ricciotti, 126.

73. Quoted in Smith, *Death of Classical Paganism*, 107 (adapted).

74. Ricciotti, 59–60.

75. Browning, 102.

76. Julian, *Letter to the Athenians*, in Wright. 2:283 (adapted).

77. Quoted in Browning, 103.

78. Quoted in ibid. (adapted). The complete formula Browning gives is: "*Imperator Caesar dominus noster Flavius Claudius Iulianus pius felix victor ac triumphator semper Augustus.*"

CHAPTER TEN: "Behold, the Rivers Are Running Backwards"

1. Quoted in (and adapted from) Robert Browning, *The Emperor Julian* (Berkeley: University of California Press, 1976), 107, and Edward Gibbon, *The Decline and Fall of the Roman Empire*, (New York: Heritage, 1946), 1: 647.

2. "It was probably on this occasion that he issued his first edict of toleration. Its precise terms are unknown, but it seems to have accorded freedom of public worship to adherents of pagan cults. . . ." Browning, 108–9.

3. Julian, *Letter to the Athenians*, in Wilmer Cave Wright, Mass. trans., *The Works of the Emperor Julian*, (1913; reprint Cambridge Mass.: Harvard University Press, 1980) 2: 249 (adapted). We do not know the name of the "eldest brother" whom Julian includes in the list of victims of Constantius II's purge.

4. Julian, *Letter to the Athenians*, in ibid. 2: 251, 253.

5. Julian, *Letter to the Athenians*, in ibid. 2: 261.

6. Ibid.

7. Quoted in Samuel N. C. Lieu, ed., *The Emperor Julian: Panegyric and Polemic*, 2d ed. (Liverpool: Liverpool University Press, 1989), 3 (adapted).

8. Quoted in Browning, 135.

9. Quoted in Giuseppe Ricciotti, *Julian the Apostate, Roman Emperor, 361–363*, trans. M. Joseph Costelloe, S. J. (1960; reprint, Rockford, Ill.: Tan Books, 1999), 179.

10. Quoted in Lieu, 59.

11. Julian, *To the Uneducated Cynics*, in Wright, 2: 5 (adapted) and fn. 1.

12. Quoted in Browning, 134.

13. Gibbon, 1:636.

14. Julian, *The Caesars*, quoted in Ricciotti, 170.

15. Quoted in Lieu, 60 (adapted).

16. Quoted in Gibbon, 1:656.

17. Ibid., 1:655.

18. Julian, *Misopogon*, in Wright, 2:429.

19. Gibbon, 1:655 (adapted).

20. Gibbon, 1:660.

21. Ibid., 1:661.

22. Julian, *To Artabius*, quoted in Ricciotti, 202.

23. Quoted in Augustus Neander, *The Emperor Julian and His Generation* trans. C. V. Cox, (1812; reprint, Eugene, Ore.: Wipf and Stock, 2001), xiii.

24. Quoted in John Holland Smith, *The Death of Classical Paganism* (New York: Charles Scribner's Sons, 1976), 106 (adapted).

25. Ps. 97:7.

26. The *Artemio Passio*, quoted in Samuel N. C. Lieu and Dominic Montserrat, eds., *From Constantine to Julian: Pagan and Byzantine Views, A Source History* (London: Routledge, 1996), 249, 250, 251 (adapted from various passages).

27. Quoted in Smith, *Death of Classical Paganism*, 117.

28. Quoted in Pierre Chuvin, *A Chronicle of the Last Pagans* trans. B. A. Archer, (Cambridge, Mass.: Harvard University Press, 1990), 47.

29. Julian, *Mispogon,* quoted in Smith, 1976, 108.

30. Quoted in Chuvin, 46.

31. Quoted in Ricciotti, 199 (adapted).

32. Quoted in Edward J. Martin, *The Emperor Julian: An Essay on His Relations with the Christian Religion.* (New York: Macmillan, 1919), 46 (adapted).

33. Julian, *Against the Galileans*, quoted in Smith, *Death of Classical Paganism*, 109.

34. Julian, *Against the Galileans*, quoted in Martin, 31.

35. Julian, *The Caesars*, in Wright, 2:411, 413 (adapted.)

36. Quoted in Diana Bowder, *The Age of Constantine and Julian* (New York: Barnes & Noble, 1978), 120.

37. Ibid. (adapted).

38. Quoted in Ricciotti, 188.

39. Browning, 175–76.

40. Quoted in Ricciotti, 189.

41. Ricciotti, 190, paraphrasing Gregory of Nazianzus and John Chrysostom.

42. Julian, *Hymn to King Helios*, in Wright, 1:357 (adapted).

43. Julian, *Hymn to the Mother of the Gods*, in ibid., 1:449 (adapted).

44. Quoted in Robin Lane Fox, *Pagans and Christians* (New York: Alfred A. Knopf, 1987), 149.

45. Browning, 139.

46. The pagan emperor Maximinus Daia (c. 270–313) had tried but failed to establish a unified pagan church about a half century earlier.

47. Browning, 139.

48. Julian, *Against the Galileans*, in Wright, 3:323.

49. Ricciotti, 184.

50. Quoted in Chuvin, 43.

51. Julian, *To Ecdicius*, quoted in (and adapted from) Ricciotti, 17.

52. Julian, *To the People of Alexandria*, in Wright, 3:63, 67 (adapted).

53. Ricciotti, 184.

54. Ibid., 185.

55. Julian, *To the Community of the Jews*, in Wright, 3:179.

56. Julian, *Against the Galileans*, quoted in (and slightly adapted from) Ricciotti, 223.

57. Matt. 24: 1–2 (adapted).

58. John 2:21.

59. Ricciotti, 224.

60. Hershel Shanks, *Jerusalem: An Archaeological Biography* (New York: Random House, 1995). The inscription, which is only partially quoted here, is from Isa. 66:14.

61. Quoted in Ricciotti, 225.

62. S. Safrai, "The Era of the Mishnah and Talmud (70–640)," in H. H. Ben-Sasson, ed. *A History of the Jewish People* (Cambridge, Mass.: Harvard University Press, 1976), 353–54.

63. Julian, *To the Community of the Jews*, in Wright, 3:181.

64. Julian, *Misopogon*, in ibid., 2:423.

65. Quoted in Browning, 198.

66. Ricciotti, 245, paraphrasing Ammianus.
67. Browning, 207.
68. Quoted in Smith, 1976, 119, fn. 28.
69. Chuvin, 48.
70. Quoted in Ricciotti, 254, citing Theodoret and Sozomen.

EPILOGUE: **The Handless Scribe**

1. Ramsay MacMullen, *Christianity and Paganism in the Fourth to Eighth Centuries* (New Haven: Yale University Press, 1997), 128.
2. Quoted in John Holland Smith, *The Death of Classical Paganism* (New York: Charles Scribner's Sons, 1976), 95, 96.
3. Edward Gibbon, *The Decline and Fall of the Roman Empire* (1776; reprint, New York: Heritage, 1946), 1:655.
4. Edward J. Martin, *The Emperor Julian: An Essay on His Relations with the Christian Religion.* (New York: Macmillan, 1919), 7.
5. Paraphrased in Robert Browning, *The Emperor Julian* (Berkeley: University of California Press, 1976), 219.
6. Quoted in Gerald Henry Rendall, *The Emperor Julian: Paganism and Christianity* (Cambridge: Deighton, Bell and Co., and London: George Bell and Sons, 1879), 274.
7. Quoted in Browning, 217.
8. Quoted in Prudence Jones and Nigel Pennick, *A History of Pagan Europe* (London: Routledge, 1995), 72.
9. Quoted in Pierre Chuvin, trans. *A Chronicle of the Last Pagans* B. A. Archer, (Cambridge, Mass.: Harvard University Press, 1990), 76.
10. J. N. Hillgarth, ed., *Christianity and Paganism, 350–750: The Conversion of Western Europe*, rev. ed. (Philadelphia: University of Pennsylvania Press, 1986), 5, quoting Gilbert Murray.
11. Jacob Burckhardt, *The Age of Constantine the Great*, trans. Moses Hadas (1852; reprint Garden City, N.Y.: Doubleday Anchor, 1949), quoting Jacques Callot (adapted).
12. Quoted in Smith, *Death of Classical Paganism*, 166.
13. Ibid., 162.
14. Samuel Dill, *Roman Society in the Last Century of the Western Empire*, 2d rev. ed. (New York: Meridian, 1958) 26.
15. Jacob Neusner, *Judaism and Christianity in the Age of Constantine: History, Messiah, Israel and the Initial Confrontation* (Chicago: University of Chicago Press, 1987), 16 (adapted).
16. Quoted in James Carroll, *Constantine's Sword: The Church and the Jews* (New York: Houghton Mifflin, 2001), 206.

17. Quoted in Hillgarth, 47 (adapted).

18. Quoted in A. R. Whitham, *The History of the Christian Church to the Separation of East and West*, 4th ed. (London: Rivingtons, 1954), 256.

19. Quoted in Dill, 28.

20. Richard E. Rubenstein, *When Jesus Became God: The Struggle to Define Christianity During the Last Days of Rome* (San Diego: Harcourt, 1999), 224.

21. Edward Alexander Parsons, *The Alexandrian Library: Glory of the Hellenic World* (London: Cleaver-Hume, 1952), 344 (adapted).

22. Chuvin, 67.

23. Quoted in Parsons, 354.

24. Chuvin, 66.

25. Quoted in Smith, *Death of Classical Paganism*, 169–70.

26. Quoted in Chuvin, 86.

27. Quoted in Parsons, 356.

28. E. M. Forster, *Alexandria: A History and a Guide* (Alexandria: Whitehead Morris, 1938), 46.

29. Hillgarth, 2.

30. Ibid., 4 (adapted).

31. MacMullen, 4.

32. Browning, 175.

33. James George Frazer, *The Golden Bough: A Study in Magic and Religion*, abridged ed. (1922; reprint, New York: Macmillan, 1979), 445.

34. Quoted in MacMullen, 124.

35. Jones and Pennick, 2.

36. Quoted in Caesar E. Farah, *Islam: Beliefs and Observances* (Woodbury, N.Y.: Barron's, 1970).

37. Karen Armstrong, *Holy War: The Crusades and Their Impact on Today's World* (New York: Anchor, 2001).

38. Hermann Dorries, *Constantine the Great*, trans. Roland H. Bainton (New York: Harper & Row, 1972), 199.

39. Franz Cumont, *Oriental Religions in Roman Paganism* (1911; reprint, New York: Dover, 1956), 197.

40. Ibid.

Bibliography

Note on Adaptation and Bible Usage:

Where I have altered punctuation and capitalization or omitted words and phrases from quoted material without changing the meaning of the text, I have taken the liberty of generally omitting brackets and ellipses to indicate the alterations and omissions. Whenever I have done so, the note identifies the quotation as "adapted."

As one example, I have not followed the tradition of capitalizing the personal pronouns that refer to God. As a more substantive matter, I have sometimes used "Yahweh," the personal name of God, in place of "Lord," its customary English translation.

Where no specific source is given in the text or the endnotes, quotations from the Hebrew Bible are taken (and, in some cases, adapted) from the 1961 edition of the Jewish Publication Society's *The Holy Scriptures According to the Masoretic Text* (JPS), and quotations from the Christian Bible are taken from the 1909 Oxford University Press edition of the *King James Version* (KJV). All other quotations from various English translations of the Bible are cited in the text or the notes using the following abbreviations to identify the source:

NEB *The New English Bible with the Apocrypha.* 2d ed. New York: Oxford University Press, 1970.

New JPS *Tanakh, The Holy Scriptures: The New JPS Translation According to the Traditional Hebrew Text.* Philadelphia: Jewish Publication Society, 1985.

Another Bible that I have consulted is:

Speiser, E. A., trans., intro., and notes. *Genesis. The Anchor Bible.* Vol. 1. Garden City, N.Y.: Doubleday, 1987.

Reference Works

Freedman, David Noel, ed. *The Anchor Bible Dictionary.* 6 vols. Garden City, N.Y.: Doubleday, 1992.
Encyclopedia Judaica. Corrected ed. 17 vols. Jerusalem: Keter, n.d.

BOOKS

Alfoldi, Andrew. *The Conversion of Constantine and Pagan Rome.* Translated by Harold Mattingly. 1948. Reprint, Oxford: Clarendon/Oxford University Press, 1998.

Apuleius. *The Golden Ass.* Translated by Jack Lindsay. 1932. Reprint, Bloomington: Indiana University Press, 1962).

Armstrong, Karen. *A History of God: The 4,000-Year Quest of Judaism, Christianity and Islam.* New York: Alfred A. Knopf, 1993.

————. *Holy War: The Crusades and Their Impact on Today's World.* New York: Anchor, 2001.

Assmann, Jan. *Moses the Egyptian: The Memory of Egypt in Western Monotheism.* Cambridge, Mass.: Harvard University Press, 1997.

Augustine, Edward B. Pusey. *The Confessions of Saint Augustine.* Translated by New York: Modern Library, 1949.

Aurelius, Marcus, et al. *Marcus Aurelius and His Times: The Transition from Paganism to Christianity.* New York: Walter J. Black for the Classics Club, 1945.

Ben-Sasson, H. H., ed. *A History of the Jewish People.* Cambridge, Mass.: Harvard University Press, 1976.

Bowder, Diana. *The Age of Constantine and Julian.* New York: Barnes & Noble, 1978.

Bright, John. *A History of Israel.* 2d ed. Philadelphia: Westminster Press, 1972.

Browning, Robert. *The Emperor Julian.* Berkeley: University of California Press, 1976.

Bulfinch, Thomas. *Bulfinch's Mythology.* 1855–1863. Reprint, New York: Modern Library, n.d.

Burckhardt, Jacob. *The Age of Constantine the Great.* Translated by Moses Hadas. 1852. Reprint, Garden City, N.Y.: Doubleday/Anchor, 1949.

Burkert, Walter. *Ancient Mystery Cults*. Cambridge, Mass.: Harvard University Press, 1987.

———. *Homo Necans: The Anthropology of Ancient Greek Sacrificial Ritual and Myth*. Translated by Peter Bing. Berkeley: University of California Press, 1983.

Carroll, James. *Constantine's Sword: The Church and the Jews*. New York: Houghton Mifflin, 2001.

Chadwick, Henry. *Heresy and Orthodoxy in the Early Church*. Hampshire, U.K.: Variorum, 1991.

Chuvin, Pierre. *A Chronicle of the Last Pagans*. Translated by B. A. Archer. Cambridge, Mass.: Harvard University Press, 1990.

Clark, Gillian. *Women in Late Antiquity: Pagan and Christian Life-styles*. Oxford: Clarendon Press, 1993.

Clendenin, Daniel B. *Many Gods, Many Lords: Christianity Encounters World Religions*. Grand Rapids, Mich.: Baker Books, 1995.

Cotterell, Arthur, ed. *The Penguin Encyclopedia of Classical Civilizations*. New York: Penguin, 1995.

Cumont, Franz. *Oriental Religions in Roman Paganism*. 1911. Reprint, New York: Dover 1956.

Davies, Nigel. *Human Sacrifice: In History and Today*. New York: William Morrow, 1981.

De Chair, Somerset. *Bring Back the Gods: The Epic Career of the Emperor Julian, the Great*. London: George G. Harrap, 1962.

De Vaux, Roland. *The Early History of Israel*. Translated by David Smith. Philadelphia: Westminster Press, 1978.

Dill, Samuel. *Roman Society in the Last Century of the Western Empire*. 2d rev. ed. New York: Meridian, 1958.

Dorries, Hermann. *Constantine the Great*. Translated by Roland H. Bainton. New York: Harper & Row, 1972.

Durant, Will. *The Story of Civilization*. Vol. 3, *Caesar and Christ*. Vol. 4, *The Age of Faith*. New York: Simon and Schuster, 1944, 1950.

Fackenheim, Emil L. *What Is Judaism? An Interpretation for the Present Age*. New York: Summit, 1987.

Farah, Caesar E. *Islam: Beliefs and Observances*. Woodbury, N.Y.: Barron's, 1970.

Ferguson, John. *Gods Many and Lords Many: A Study in Primal Religions*. Guildford, Eng.: Lutterworth, 1982.

Finkelstein, Israel, and Neil Asher Silberman. *The Bible Unearthed: Archaeology's New Vision of Ancient Israel and the Origin of Its Sacred Texts*. New York: Free Press, 2001.

Fleming, Fergus, and Alan Lothian. *Myth and Mankind: The Way to Eternity, Egyptian Myth*. London: Duncan Baird, 1997.

Fletcher, Richard. *The Barbarian Conversion: From Paganism to Christianity*. New York: Henry Holt, 1997.

Foakes-Jackson, F. J. *The History of the Christian Church from the Earliest Times to A.D. 461*. 1891. Reprint, Chicago: W. P. Blessing, 1927.

Forster, E. M. *Alexandria: A History and a Guide*. Alexandria: Whitehead Morris 1938.

Fox, Robin Lane. *Pagans and Christians*. New York: Alfred A. Knopf, 1987.

Frazer, James George. *The Golden Bough: A Study in Magic and Religion*. Abridged ed. 1922. Reprint, New York: Macmillan, 1979.

Freud, Sigmund. *Moses and Monotheism*. Translated by Katherine Jones. 1939. Reprint, New York: Vintage, 1967.

Friedman, Richard Elliott. *Who Wrote the Bible?* New York: Summit, 1987.

Gibbon, Edward. *The Decline and Fall of the Roman Empire*. 3 vols. 1776. Reprint, New York: Heritage, 1946.

Grant, Robert M. *Gods and the One God*. Philadelphia: Westminster Press, 1986.

Graves, Robert. *King Jesus*. New York: Farrar Straus Giroux, 1946.

———. *The White Goddess: A Historical Grammar of Poetic Myth*. Amended and enlarged ed. New York: Farrar, Straus Giroux, 1966.

Grayzel, Solomon. *A History of the Jews*. Philadelphia: Jewish Publication Society of America, 1952.

Greenslade, S. L. *Schism in the Early Church*. New York: Harper & Brothers, n.d.

Guitton, Jean. *Great Heresies & Church Councils*. Translated by F. D. Wieck. New York: Harper & Row, 1965.

Hawass, Zahi. *Valley of the Golden Mummies*. New York: Harry N. Abrams, 2000.

Hillgarth, J. N., ed. *Christianity and Paganism, 350–750: The Conversion of Western Europe*. Rev. ed. Philadelphia: University of Pennsylvania Press, 1986.

Jones, Prudence, and Nigel Pennick. *A History of Pagan Europe*. London: Routledge, 1995.

Josephus, Flavius. *The Jewish War*. Rev. ed. Translated by G. A. Williamson. New York: Dorset Press, 1981.

———. *The Works of Josephus*. Translated by William Whiston. Peabody, Mass.: Hendrickson, 1987.

Klauck, Hans-Josef. *Magic and Paganism in Early Christianity: The World of the Acts of the Apostles*. Translated by Brian McNeil. Edinburgh: T&T Clark, 2000.

Kraemer, Ross Shepard. *Her Share of the Blessings: Women's Religions Among Pagans, Jews and Christians in the Greco-Roman World.* Oxford: Oxford University Press, 1992.

Latourette, Kenneth Scott. *A History of Christianity.* Vol. 1. New York: Harper & Row, 1975.

Lebreton, Jules, S.J., and Jacques Zeiller. *Heresy and Orthodoxy.* Vol. 3. of *A History of the Early Church.* Translated by Ernest C. Messenger. 1946. Reprint, New York: Collier, 1962.

Lietzmann, Hans. *From Constantine to Julian: A History of the Early Church.* Vol. 3. Translated by Bertram Lee Woolf. New York: Charles Scribner's Sons, 1950.

Lieu, Samuel N. C., ed. *The Emperor Julian: Panegyric and Polemic.* 2d ed. Liverpool: Liverpool University Press, 1989.

Lieu, Samuel N. C., and Dominic Montserrat eds. *From Constantine to Julian: Pagan and Byzantine Views, A Source History.* London: Routledge, 1996.

Maccoby, Hyam. *The Sacred Executioner: Human Sacrifice and the Legacy of Guilt.* New York: Thames and Hudson, 1982.

MacMullen, Ramsay. *Christianity and Paganism in the Fourth to Eighth Centuries.* New Haven, Conn.: Yale University Press, 1997.

Malherbe, Abraham J. *Moral Exhortation: A Greco-Roman Sourcebook.* Philadelphia: Westminster Press, 1986.

Martin, Edward J. *The Emperor Julian: An Essay on His Relations with the Christian Religion.* New York: Macmillan, 1919.

Miles, Jack. *Christ: A Crisis in the Life of God.* New York: Alfred A. Knopf, 2001.
———. *God: A Biography.* New York: Alfred A. Knopf, 1995.

Neander, Augustus. *The Emperor Julian and His Generation.* Translated by C. V. Cox. 1812. Reprint, Eugene, Ore.: Wipf and Stock, 2001.

Neusner, Jacob. *Judaism and Christianity in the Age of Constantine: History, Messiah, Israel and the Initial Confrontation.* Chicago: University of Chicago Press, 1987.
———. *A Life of Yohanan ben Zakkai, ca. 1–80 C.E.* Leiden: E. J. Brill, 1962.

Parsons, Edward Alexander. *The Alexandrian Library: Glory of the Hellenic World.* London: Cleaver-Hume, 1952.

Patai, Raphael. *The Jewish Mind.* New York: Charles Scribner's Sons, 1977.

Rendall, Gerald Henry. *The Emperor Julian: Paganism and Christianity.* Cambridge: Deighton, Bell and Co, and London: George Bell and Sons, 1879.

Ricciotti, Giuseppe. *Julian the Apostate, Roman Emperor, 361–363.* Translated by M. Joseph Costelloe, S. J. 1960. Reprint, Rockford, Ill.: Tan Books, 1999.

Roth, Cecil. *A Short History of the Jewish People.* London: East and West Library, 1959.

Rubenstein, Richard E. *When Jesus Became God: The Struggle to Define Christianity During the Last Days of Rome.* San Diego and Harcourt, 1999.

Schaff, Philip and Wace, Henry, eds. *A Select Library of Nicene and Post-Nicene Fathers of the Christian Church* (2d series). Vol. 1, *Eusebius.* 1890. Reprint, Grand Rapids, Mich.: Wm. B. Eerdmans, 1997.

Shanks, Hershel. *Jerusalem: An Archaeological Biography.* New York: Random House, 1995.

Shlain, Leonard. *The Alphabet Versus the Goddess.* New York: Penguin/Arkana, 1988.

Smith, John Holland. *Constantine the Great.* New York: Charles Scribner's Sons, 1971.

———. *The Death of Classical Paganism.* New York: Charles Scribner's Sons, 1976.

Stone, Merlin. *When God Was a Woman.* New York: Harcourt Brace Jovanovich, 1976.

Thiede, Carsten Peter. *The Dead Sea Scrolls and the Jewish Origins of Christianity.* New York: Palgrave, 2001.

Thompson, Thomas L. *The Mythic Past: Biblical Archaeology and the Myth of Israel.* New York: Basic Books, 1999.

Tierney, Patrick. *The Highest Altar: Unveiling the Mystery of Human Sacrifice.* New York: Penguin, n.d.

Toynbee, Arnold. *The Crucible of Christianity: Judaism, Hellenism and the Historical Background to the Christian Faith.* Cleveland: World, 1969.

Vidal, Gore. *Julian.* 1962. Reprint, New York: Ballantine, 1986.

Weiss, Johannes. *The History of Primitive Christianity.* 2 vols. New York: Wilson-Erickson, 1937.

Whitham, A. R. *The History of the Christian Church to the Separation of East and West.* 4th ed. London: Rivingtons, 1954.

Wilson, A. N. *Paul: The Mind of the Apostle.* New York: W. W. Norton, 1997.

Wright, Wilmer Cave, trans. *The Works of the Emperor Julian.* 3 vols. 1913. Reprint, Cambridge, Mass.: Harvard University Press, 1980.

JOURNALS AND PERIODICALS

Emerton, J. E. "Yahweh and His Asherah. *Vetus Testamentum*, Vol. XLIX, no. 3, July 1999, 315–337 (Leiden: E. J. Brill).

Fisher, Eugene J. "Cultic Prostitution in the Ancient Near East? A Reassessment." *Biblical Theology Bulletin* 6, nos. 2–3 (June–October 1976): 225–36.

"Papal Letters Excerpt." *Los Angeles Times*, March 22, 2002, A18.

Weitzman, Steven. "Forced Circumcision and the Shifting Role of Gentiles in

Hasmonean Ideology." *Harvard Theological Review* 92, no. 1 (January 1999): 37–59.

Zucchino, David. "The Last Days of Bamian's Buddhas." *Los Angeles Times*, February 24, 2002, A10–A11.

ON-LINE AND DIGITAL RESOURCES

BibleWorks 5 (Hermeneutika Bible Research Software)

Britannica.com (www.britannica.com)

De Imperatoribus Romanis: An Online Encyclopedia of Roman Emperors (www.roman-emperors.org)

Index

**For more of Jonathan Kirsch's dramatic
and eye-opening accounts of religion,
faith, and tradition,
look for the**

*The Woman Who Laughed at God:
The Untold History of the Jewish People*

"A grand story, grandly told."   —*Chicago Tribune*

"An entertaining tour of Jewish history."
                              —*The Washington Post*

Who is a Jew? In this colorful, eye-opening work, best-selling author and lecturer Jonathan Kirsch reveals that Judaism has *never* been a religion of strict and narrow orthodoxy. For every accepted tradition in Jewish faith there are countertraditions rooted in biblical antiquity: the Maccabee freedom fighters who closed the Bible and picked up swords; dervishlike ecstatics who claimed to enjoy direct communication with God even after they had been excommunicated by a distrustful rabbinate; and courageous men and women who were the forgotten heroes of the Holocaust. With drama and narrative verve, Kirsch explores these and many other "Judaisms" that make up the rich tapestry of Jewish identity.

ISBN 0-14-219611-8

FOR THE BEST IN PAPERBACKS, LOOK FOR THE Ⓟ

In every corner of the world, on every subject under the sun, Penguin represents quality and variety—the very best in publishing today.

For complete information about books available from Penguin—including Penguin Classics, Penguin Compass, and Puffins—and how to order them, write to us at the appropriate address below. Please note that for copyright reasons the selection of books varies from country to country.

In the United States: Please write to *Penguin Group (USA), P.O. Box 12289 Dept. B, Newark, New Jersey 07101-5289* or call 1-800-788-6262.

In the United Kingdom: Please write to *Dept. EP, Penguin Books Ltd, Bath Road, Harmondsworth, West Drayton, Middlesex UB7 0DA.*

In Canada: Please write to *Penguin Books Canada Ltd, 10 Alcorn Avenue, Suite 300, Toronto, Ontario M4V 3B2.*

In Australia: Please write to *Penguin Books Australia Ltd, P.O. Box 257, Ringwood, Victoria 3134.*

In New Zealand: Please write to *Penguin Books (NZ) Ltd, Private Bag 102902, North Shore Mail Centre, Auckland 10.*

In India: Please write to *Penguin Books India Pvt Ltd, 11 Panchsheel Shopping Centre, Panchsheel Park, New Delhi 110 017.*

In the Netherlands: Please write to *Penguin Books Netherlands bv, Postbus 3507, NL-1001 AH Amsterdam.*

In Germany: Please write to *Penguin Books Deutschland GmbH, Metzlerstrasse 26, 60594 Frankfurt am Main.*

In Spain: Please write to *Penguin Books S. A., Bravo Murillo 19, 1° B, 28015 Madrid.*

In Italy: Please write to *Penguin Italia s.r.l., Via Benedetto Croce 2, 20094 Corsico, Milano.*

In France: Please write to *Penguin France, Le Carré Wilson, 62 rue Benjamin Baillaud, 31500 Toulouse.*

In Japan: Please write to *Penguin Books Japan Ltd, Kaneko Building, 2-3-25 Koraku, Bunkyo-Ku, Tokyo 112.*

In South Africa: Please write to *Penguin Books South Africa (Pty) Ltd, Private Bag X14, Parkview, 2122 Johannesburg.*